AMERICAN RULE

AMERICAN RULE

★ ★ ★

HOW A NATION CONQUERED THE WORLD
BUT FAILED ITS PEOPLE

JARED YATES SEXTON

DUTTON

DUTTON

An imprint of Penguin Random House LLC

penguinrandomhouse.com

Copyright © 2020 by Jared Yates Sexton

Penguin supports copyright. Copyright fuels creativity, encourages diverse voices, promotes free speech, and creates a vibrant culture. Thank you for buying an authorized edition of this book and for complying with copyright laws by not reproducing, scanning, or distributing any part of it in any form without permission. You are supporting writers and allowing Penguin to continue to publish books for every reader.

DUTTON and the D colophon are registered trademarks of Penguin Random House LLC.

LIBRARY OF CONGRESS CATALOGING-IN-PUBLICATION DATA

Names: Sexton, Jared, author.
Title: American rule: how a nation conquered the world but failed its people / Jared Yates Sexton.
Description: New York: Dutton, An imprint of Penguin Random House LLC, [2020] | Includes bibliographical references and index. |
Identifiers: LCCN 2020005155 (print) | LCCN 2020005156 (ebook) | ISBN 9781524745714 (hardcover) | ISBN 9781524745721 (ebook)
Subjects: LCSH: United States—Politics and government.
Classification: LCC JK275 .S49 2020 (print) | LCC JK275 (ebook) | DDC 973—dc23
LC record available at https://lccn.loc.gov/2020005155
LC ebook record available at https://lccn.loc.gov/2020005156

Printed in the United States of America
1   3   5   7   9   10   8   6   4   2

BOOK DESIGN BY ELKE SIGAL

While the author has made every effort to provide accurate telephone numbers, internet addresses, and other contact information at the time of publication, neither the publisher nor the author assumes any responsibility for errors or for changes that occur after publication. Further, the publisher does not have any control over and does not assume any responsibility for author or third-party websites or their content.

This book is for Norman Rexford Burk

CONTENTS

It is well that we keep in mind the fact that not all of American history is recorded. And in some ways we are fortunate that it isn't, for if it were, we might become so chagrined by the discrepancies which exist between our democratic ideals and our social reality that we'd soon lose heart. Perhaps this is why we possess two basic versions of American history: one which is written and as neatly stylized as ancient myth, and the other unwritten and as chaotic and full of contradictions, changes of pace, and surprises as life itself.

—RALPH ELLISON, *Going to the Territory*, 1986

AMERICAN RULE

* * *

Prologue

On the first anniversary of the disastrous election of 2016, I drove a few hours to a discussion about my recent book chronicling the rise of Donald Trump's movement, *The People Are Going to Rise Like the Waters Upon Your Shore: A Story of American Rage*. It was a cold and rainy night, and the audience came dressed for warmth and armed with questions about the sorry state of political affairs. Like most Americans, they were starving for hope. Already they were dismayed by Trump's cruel presidency and questioning whether the America they had known and loved would ever return. I did my best to give cogent, interesting answers, grabbed a coffee for the road, and braved the drizzle to find my car.

As I was about to step into the shimmering street, a hand landed on my shoulder. I jumped. I'd been getting death threats for months. People had shown up at my house in the middle of the night, and hardly a day passed where I didn't receive an odd, fascist message detailing murderous fantasies. When I spun around, I half expected to find a jackbooted neo-Nazi thug looking to make good on those threats. Instead, it was a kind-faced middle-aged woman I recognized from the crowd.

"I'm sorry to bother you," she said, "but I had a question. Something I didn't want to ask in front of anyone else."

"Sure," I said, gripping my to-go coffee for the heat.

"I have to ask . . . is this the end of America?"

Since lighting off on the campaign trail in 2015 and watching Trump form a movement girded by white identity politics and despotic rhetoric, a movement unburdened by shame or the onus of truth, I'd been wondering the same thing. It was an anxiety I never wanted to give voice to lest I gift it weight. A man like Donald Trump winning the presidency meant that something was very, very wrong with the United States of America.

Before I could answer, the woman asked another question: "How did we get here?"

This one I had covered. I'd been answering it at every book tour stop and in every interview. I rattled off something about the radicalization of the Republican Party, the effects of polarization, the media's insatiable desire to turn politics into entertainment, the corrosive influence of new technologies, and the betrayal of the American people by a government bought and sold. It all came out in a practiced stream that sounded rehearsed and performed.

The stranger winced. "Yeah," she reluctantly agreed, "that makes sense, but how did all that happen? How did we get *here*?"

★

I wrestled with that on my long drive home. For the most part, I could trace the explanation through Richard Nixon, the civil rights movement and social revolutions of the 1960s and 1970s, and the struggle of the Cold War. But as I continued to think about it, that story devolved into simplistic parody. Over the course of those hours on the road, I realized that while I had a working understanding of

American history that I'd gleaned through the years, I lacked a deeper grasp. The history I understood was the history featured in television shows, popular movies, textbooks that meant to guide students with as few bumps along the way as possible.

The past year had proven that this history didn't work anymore. When Trump's victory was added at the end as yet another twist, the narrative I'd subscribed to lost all sense and meaning. The arc of time that I'd heard spoken about so eloquently fractured under the weight. I could explain Trump's victory politically, demographically, and socially, but historically, I was at a loss.

By the time I pulled into my driveway in Georgia the next day, I had resolved to overcome my ignorance and relearn history from the very beginning. I had learned dates and surface-level details about the most important events, amassed an extensive repertoire of facts about wars and leading figures, but was lacking in a coherent and comprehensive understanding. What I knew was a privileged version of history that had been crafted to showcase America as the moral protagonist of a larger narrative—and now that narrative had all but collapsed.

I knew American history but needed to learn the history of America.

★

I grew up in a rural Indiana community in a poor family of factory workers and laborers. Coming of age in the 1980s, I was surrounded by all the pageantry of idyllic America. Every Fourth of July a giant parade flowed through the center of my sleepy town. My neighbors waved bright American flags as bands played "The Stars and Stripes Forever" and "God Bless America." In school I was taught that an exceptional country founded by revolutionary fathers conquered a continent, overcame its vices in a terrible civil war, and then healed to spread its message of freedom and liberty to every corner of the globe. My family was impoverished, dysfunctional, abusive, but at least I'd been lucky enough to be born in the United States of America, a divine blessing repeated by my elders and teachers and stressed by my preacher every Sunday morning as he pounded his pulpit.

Reality is an odd thing. We see the world through the prism imposed upon us. When I talk about my childhood, both in the church and in abusive households, people often react in horror. They can't believe I didn't suspect something was wrong, that I didn't intuitively understand reality was different from the world I languished in. But without the necessary context and without needed exposure to the outside world, I was trapped. I didn't know there was a way out because I didn't know there was somewhere to escape to.

Despite our indoctrination, my family still understood that not everything was perfect. Our financial and personal struggles nodded toward some underlying problem. The way the world worked around us didn't make sense. If America was a faultless country operating based on God's will, then how were we, his chosen people, still suffering? Why were our jobs disappearing? Why was our town deteriorating?

To my family, the answer was a conspiracy theory that appeared across the country, a supernatural narrative that cemented America as God's chosen nation and pitted it against an evil other responsible for our ills. The story was both organic and manufactured by political messaging, popular culture, and rhetorical appeals by evangelical leaders. It was the kind of myth that races through populations like a runaway virus.

In our evangelical church, sermons painted America as beset on all sides by sinister forces. In my church, Satan wasn't merely a metaphor but a literal evil being who could appear at any moment and was actively gathering an army of the wicked to wage an unholy war. That army was nebulous and constantly changing. Our preacher referred to an ill-defined "they" we were warned to avoid. In hushed, closed-door conversations, however, the people around me were more specific. Satan's army was everyone outside of our church, outside of our sleepy town, outside of the United States of America, and even some within who had fallen under the spell of the devilish trickster. They were people who didn't look like us. Who didn't think like us. People we needed to be ready to fight and kill when the Second Coming arrived and the battle for the end of the world commenced.

A firm believer in this myth, my grandmother bought cabinets full of books dedicated to understanding the evil conspiracy, a plot by an international cabal obsessed with destroying America and its Christians, a plot that mirrored the Book of Revelation, which our preachers turned to more than any other volume in the Bible. In these worn and well-parsed paperbacks, ordered from catalogs and picked up secondhand at yard sales, our evangelical faith merged with the occult and American history, creating a mystical reality where spiritual and civic warfare raged every single day.

I had no way of knowing I was a member of a cult. As in other cults, our leaders demanded we ignore dissenting voices and alternate sources of information. We were told to scorn culture and remain ideologically pure. We were under attack, after all, and even listening to a song on the radio or catching the wrong movie at the theater downtown could give Satan his opportunity to pounce. To exist in God's good graces, we had to rely on our leaders, remain obedient, and never, ever question the gospel of American history.

It wasn't until years later that I was able to escape that world and understand its true nature. I'd been a member of what I now call the Cult of the Shining City: a white identity evangelicalism rooted in the myth of American exceptionalism, a myth that has co-opted the United States of America and, by proxy, the rest of the world. That nationalistic, white identity evangelicalism has corrupted American religion and all but broken our politics.

In 2016, as I watched the people from my past throw themselves into the thrall of Donald Trump, an embarrassing reality television star, I knew something bizarre was happening. Conversations with supporters at Trump's rallies reminded me of the stories that had defined my childhood; now they had evolved into something larger and more sinister. A year later, that long drive home sent me down the path to a deeper understanding.

★

The moment we find ourselves in today is the result of a long line of decisions to advantage the wealthy and powerful—primarily the white and wealthy—and position the United States as the dominant influence in world affairs through one strategic manipulation after another. The narrative of American exceptionalism, beginning with the founding of the United States, has provided cover for aristocracy at home and imperialism abroad. Over time, it has grown more complicated and contradictory, distorting reality and tearing our understanding of the world to pieces. Now, trapped in a cycle of self-mythology and atrocity, Americans feel immobilized and confused, incapable of change and troubled by a moment inundated with inconsistencies, contradictions, and outright nonsense.

That discomfort is natural, as recent years have made it all but impossible to take comfort in convenient stories of inherent righteousness. In the two centuries since its founding, America has grown from a confederacy to a republic, and from a republic to an empire. Now, as we peer back into our history, we can recognize the story of our rise as one of disenchantment and redemption, of horrors and glories, of principles and glaring inconsistencies, of an oppressive state and its people who have achieved amazing things in spite of that oppression.

With these twists and turns, the story with which America has conquered the world makes little sense anymore. There have been too many discrepancies, too many contradictions. The myths and metaphors have lost their sheen and meaning as new perspectives and histories challenge the dominance of a perspective solely dedicated to Western civilization. Deluges of horrifying headlines stand in total contrast to the defining myth of an America founded on freedom and the advancement of life, liberty, and the pursuit of happiness.

This seems to be a new phenomenon, but the ailment has always afflicted America. What feels like reality disintegrating is really truth manifesting, as some Americans' perception of the United States was never true to begin with. The reality the Cult of the Shining City and devotees of American exceptionalism clung to was a fiction to begin with, a subjective reality serving the interests of white patriarchal supremacy at the expense of everyone else. The story we relied on as the gravity for our world never existed beyond our imaginations and our ability to force the disadvantaged to act within its definitions.

American Rule is the story of how a myth constructed an empire and led to its downfall. It is the story of an ideology that changed the course of history and the men who have used it as a means to gain power, wealth, and dominion. It is the story of a philosophy rooted in the empowerment of the people that was perverted and harnessed to establish systems that failed the very people it purported to free.

It is a chronicle of oppression, of how the supposed transfer of power from kings to the people was interrupted and co-opted by a new ruling class that recognized the moment of change as an effective and potent means of hiding control behind the auspices of freedom. It is a purposeful rejection of nationalism and exceptionalism that provides a more objective view of the rise and fall of the American empire. Though wars figure into that narrative, it rejects the traditional means of defining America by its triumphs on the battlefield and crediting those victories as proof of divine purpose. Though it touches on historical figures and movements that have troubled the oppressive state, it is not meant to be a definitive history of them. Readers interested in and inspired by persons and movements that have fought against oppressive control should absolutely seek out those stories. Those lives and those histories, so often extinguished and eclipsed by the myth of exceptionalism, are vital to understanding the nuanced and complicated history of the United States of America.

While this exploration constitutes a destruction of the American Myth, it is my hope it might help in some way to replace it with something better, something sounder, something genuine. America is certainly in danger, but what we have now, as the façade has begun to crumble, is an opportunity to reconsider the traditions and narratives that have held us captive and caused untold suffering for generations. In doing so, we might just avert crisis and begin the necessary healing. We can establish a new reality encompassing a broader spectrum of perspectives instead of one that dictates the will of a vested minority.

A familiar refrain has emerged in the past few years for Americans horrified by scenes of blatant cruelty and prejudice. Confronted with immigrant children in cages, with unarmed African Americans slain by law enforcement in the streets, with white supremacists marching through cities brandishing Nazi and Confederate flags, they shake their heads and say, "This is not who we are."

Unfortunately, that isn't true.

These horrors are not aberrations. They are a continuance of a disease that has afflicted us since the moment of our founding. The United States of America, armed with its myth of American exceptionalism, has perpetrated some of the worst crimes in the history of humanity. It has subjugated the people of the world, inflicted a possibly mortal blow to the concepts of truth and human dignity, and manufactured an alternate reality that now threatens everyone and everything we purport to hold dear.

Sadly, this is who we are.

But it is not who we have to be.

CHAPTER 1

★　　★　　★

A Revolution and a Coup

On the frigid morning of January 30, 1649, Charles I, the king of England, was led out onto a scaffold erected outside the Palace of Whitehall in Westminster. Below him, a swarming crowd of his subjects waited with bated breath to witness the murder of their king. Charles declared himself a martyr, restated his right to the crown, and placed his head upon the waiting chopping block. After the king signaled his preparedness to die, a masked executioner beheaded him with a swift blow of the axe and lifted the bloody head of the deposed monarch for all the crowd to see.

Charles had been convicted of treason following the English Civil War, in which his loyalists had battled with forces aligned with Parliament, then an advisory body with limited influence. Following the execution, general and protofascist Oliver Cromwell seized power and ruled the empire as a protectorate, asserting for himself a right to govern through military force in what the British have come to call the Interregnum. The monarchy was restored in 1660, but more instability followed in 1688 when King James II was ensnared in the Glorious Revolution, which shifted power to Parliament.

As the supposed embodiment of God's will on Earth, England's monarchy had long been held as unquestionable. This perception of the divine right of kings was forged in the centuries following the fall of Rome as civilization in Western Europe languished in apocalyptic ruin and struggled through the so-called Dark Ages. In this time, the one uniting tether of humanity was religion; from that unification came the concept of God's will as manifest in the chosen race of kings and queens, who, through their very existence and judgment, had determined the future of the world, guided by an all-knowing deity.

By the mid-seventeenth century, the philosophical foundations of the monarchial system were being questioned by developing philosophical thought and an emphasis on reasoning. This skepticism prompted Robert Filmer, an English philosopher, to author his 1680 work *Patriarcha; or The Natural Power of Kings*, a full-throated defense of unimpeded monarchy that maintained God had given kings authority over Earth beginning with Adam, the first man. Similarly, Thomas Hobbes's seminal work *Leviathan*, a treatise prepared in the midst of the chaos of the English Civil War, championed the necessity of the monarchy by offering a pessimistic portrait of humanity as a greedy, fearful, and vain species that has "no pleasure, but on the contrary a great deal of grief in keeping company where there is no power able to overawe them all."[1] According to Hobbes, who proved highly influential in matters of government and governing, humans were self-interested creatures who could only prosper if they were to give absolute sovereignty to a force larger and better suited for it than themselves.

In response, English philosopher John Locke published his *Two Treatises of Government* in 1690 and summarily dismantled the case for unfettered monarchy, making the argument that when a king is in "breach of trust" with his subjects, he is in a state of war and no longer king, thus requiring his removal.[2] Locke's belief in individual rights and views on the nature of just government not only inspired succeeding philosophers and challenged monarchial rule but exerted a heavy influence nearly a century later on America's Founding Fathers, including Thomas Jefferson.

Perhaps no one encompasses the contradictions of American principles and actions more than Jefferson, a Virginia-born plantation owner who championed "inalienable rights" while enslaving more than six hundred human beings and preached that all men were created equal while his writings dripped with shocking bigotry. As a self-styled man of reason, Jefferson blended the thought of several philosophers, including Locke's view on revolution, Jean-Jacques Rousseau's idea of the social contract, and Richard Price's faith in the goodness of mankind and its ability to self-govern.

Jefferson made an effective figure in the eighteenth century as philosophers and budding scientists were coalescing and questioning the orders of the day. Called the Enlightenment, this time period was marked with rampant curiosity and ever-present challenging of existing institutions, with the notable exceptions of racism and patriarchal power, and men like Jefferson were central to the push to overthrow those institutions and improve upon them to progress past tired and flawed traditions.

The era was ripe for change as the colonizing countries' expansion left them vulnerable to uprisings. The difficulties with the English monarchy reflected that vulnerability, and it isn't surprising that colonialists in America saw an opportunity to challenge the authority of a king when hardly a century had passed since one had been executed in full view of his subjects.

In 1774, Jefferson penned *A Summary View of the Rights of British America*, a forebearer to the Declaration of Independence that shared its structure and philosophy. That tract laid forth a set of indictments against British rule and continually appealed to the idea of the colonies' holding indisputable rights. Much to his dismay, the Continental

Congress did not act upon Jefferson's suggestions or adopt the philosophy, instead choosing to stay the course while much of the country called for revolution.

In two years' time, however, the colonies were ready for independence. Traditional narratives tend to paint the inspiration as one of great patriotism, a moment of unrestrained pride that changed history. People writing those idealized histories have tended to downplay any other motivations for the Revolutionary War, instead choosing to focus on the patriots and Founding Fathers as figures who inspired an entire country to rise up and realize its destiny, including nineteenth-century historian George Bancroft, who wrote, "The people of the continent with irresistible energy obeyed one general impulse, as the earth in spring listens to the command of nature," leading to a revolution "which Divine wisdom ordained."[3]

Despite Bancroft's romantic assertion, the entire continent did not rise up as one in favor of divinely inspired freedom. Some were inspired by the philosophy of and vision for a new society based on liberty and freedom, while others saw it as a decision predicated on economic and political grounds, creating a complicated coalition that has been largely ignored in favor of constructing a myth of divine inspiration and purpose.

In reality, the American Revolution wasn't exclusively tied to Jefferson's personal convictions but instead relied on a collection of colonialists with differing motivations for severing ties with England. Some, like Jefferson and Thomas Paine, who authored the pamphlet *Common Sense* and attacked the British as an "aristocratical tyranny," supported the war as a means of liberation of the individual from oppression, while others, particularly the wealthy, resented British taxes. There were myriad reasons for Americans to rebel: For some it was unrestrained patriotism and for others a purely economic desire to be free of British control. In fact, upwards of at least a third of the population opposed independence altogether.

As the Second Continental Congress debated severing ties with

Britain, Jefferson began drafting the Declaration of Independence, an indictment of British rule that simultaneously espoused the new nation's belief in "inalienable rights" and dedication to "life, liberty, and the pursuit of happiness," institutionalized the concept of a government receiving its sovereignty from the people, and argued that when authority becomes "destructive" it is "the Right of the People to alter or to abolish it."

In every sense of the word it is a revolutionary document. Jefferson's argument is the enactment of Enlightenment principles, a nod to Locke's assertion of the right of the governed to overthrow despots. In a world that functioned by the logic of the Declaration of Independence, governments would operate with the explicit purpose of serving their citizens while understanding that any violation of that trust might result in revolution. The new world that Jefferson hoped to create would fundamentally serve as a clean slate that prioritized liberty and fostered continuous improvement and progress. In his drafting he laid out these principles while intending to concurrently indict the British for their offenses and shape the nature of the future United States.

Jefferson himself believed in perpetual revolution and saw a need for succeeding generations to overthrow their rulers and continually improve government. A decade later, in a 1787 letter to William Smith, Jefferson addressed concerns over Shays's Rebellion, an uprising in Massachusetts that frightened the framers of the Constitution into devising a covert system of control, saying, "God forbid we should ever be 20 years without such a rebellion . . . What country can preserve its liberties if their rulers are not warned from time to time that their people preserve the spirit of resistance . . . the tree of liberty must be refreshed from time to time with the blood of patriots & tyrants."[4]

When Jefferson delivered his initial draft of the Declaration to Congress on June 28, 1776, the document read fairly similarly to the iconic manuscript with which Americans have become so familiar, but with one notable exception. In that first draft, in the section of indictments against England's King George III, Jefferson had crafted a long and passionate condemnation of slavery:

> he has waged cruel war against human nature itself, violating it's [*sic*] most sacred rights of life & liberty in the persons of a distant people who never offended him, captivating & carrying them into slavery in another hemisphere, or to incur miserable death in their transportation thither. this piratical warfare, the opprobrium of *infidel* powers, is the warfare of the CHRISTIAN king of Great Britain. determined to keep open a market where MEN should be bought & sold, he has prostituted his negative for suppressing every legislative attempt to prohibit or to restrain this execrable commerce: and that this assemblage of horrors might want no fact of distinguished die, he is now exciting those very people to rise in arms among us, and to purchase that liberty of which *he* has deprived them, by murdering the people upon whom *he* also obtruded them; thus paying off former crimes committed against the *liberties* of one people, with crimes which he urges them to commit against the *lives* of another.[5]

The importance with which Jefferson viewed this condemnation is undeniable, as he reserved it as the final indictment of the king and it is decidedly longer than any of the accompanying text, comprising nearly a quarter of the entire section.

Before adopting the Declaration, Congress struck the slavery section of the indictment and with it any trace of Jefferson's proposal for an America free of the scourge of human bondage. From that moment, it was immediately clear the revolution would be limited in terms of its scope and influence. Exiting the British Empire meant a new sovereignty, but it wouldn't mean an entirely new society, as past hierarchies predicated on race and wealth remained firmly in place, and the country that would be birthed from the Revolutionary War entrenched those hierarchies in its laws and foundations.

The disconnect between the rhetoric of the American Revolution and the operation of the United States is a glaring inconsistency that critics have cited since the founding, and though America boasted of its dedication to the rights and liberty of its people, its construction begs to differ. At the moment of America's independence, slaves accounted for roughly 20 percent of the country's population, and the rights and the liberties that the country was dedicated to remained those of wealthy white men served by the subsequent constitutions of the states of the Union and the eventual Constitution, at the expense of slaves, women, and other minorities.

For the American Myth to survive it is necessary for this inconsistency to be both excused and overlooked, for Jefferson's rhetoric of liberty to serve as the basis for America's moral authority while conveniently circumventing the innate contradictions of a band of liberty-loving patriots' intentionally perpetuating the enslavement, exploitation, and systematic torture, rape, and murder of a people for the purposes of economic profit.

That paradox is made possible by an intrinsic American belief in white supremacy with roots in the legacy of Western civilization and its empires, a narrative that positions the United States of America as the paragon of that tradition and the definitive arbiter of right and wrong. This belief has engendered the great majority of America's mistakes but has also allowed the country to consolidate power through manipulation, conquest, and oppression of supposed "lesser peoples." This mindset justified slavery as a means of economic necessity, the displacement and genocide of the Native American as a catalyst to realized destiny, the subjugation of foreign peoples and the exploitation of the Third World, and ultimately a worldview in which the white race has been minted as superior by the universe, a worldview inherited from the overthrown monarchial system.

The revolution succeeded in the sense that Americans earned

their independence by means of war and bloodshed. England's dominion over the colonies was refuted once and for all and colonialists, particularly the white property-owning males, were free to chart their own course. In a sense, though, the revolution as defined by its espoused principles would fail. Just as it had been in the past, one king had been overthrown only for another to take his place.

★

In January of 1787 an article penned by Benjamin Rush appeared in the magazine *American Museum*, a publication read by the Founding Fathers. A signer of the Declaration of Independence who served as a doctor in the Revolutionary War while concurrently a member of the Continental Congress, Rush titled the piece "Address to the People of the United States" and cautioned, "There is nothing more common than to confound the terms of the American Revolution with those of the late American war. The American war is over: but this is far from being the case with the American revolution."[6]

Rush advised that there was still much work to be done to fortify the country and solidify its democratic principles, including an address of the deficiencies found within the Articles of Confederation, the original binding document of the United States of America, and the establishment of an educational system necessary to illuminate the citizenry. Rush lamented a loss of energy and drive in the decade since he'd lent his name to the Declaration of Independence, saying, "I am extremely sorry to find a passion for retirement so universal among the patriots and heroes of the war," before comparing them to sailors who had survived a turbulent storm only to retire "in the middle of the ocean" and leave the rest of the voyage to lesser men. Their country was calling to those patriots, "proclaiming, in sighs and groans, in her governments, in her finances, in her trade, in her manufactures, in her morals, and in her manners, 'THE REVOLUTION IS NOT OVER!'"

Likewise, Thomas Jefferson had seen America's revolution not as the fulfillment of a plan but as the beginning of a movement, a means of unraveling a past system of oppression. The very definition of a revolution is to continue and change, to move like a fire until the entire world is engulfed, and a revolution could only end once the flames die out. For Jefferson, eternal and unimpeded change was necessary to continue the revolution's blaze. Jefferson's belief led him to France, where he played an integral role in defining their coming revolution, a role that precluded him from participating in the framing of the American Constitution.

As the Philadelphia Convention debated the means of selecting presidents, Jefferson wrote to James Madison from revolutionary France with his treatise on that need for change; he believed that no government should be erected in perpetuity but reconstructed and changed with every generation, writing, "The earth belongs in usufruct to the living," and "the dead have neither powers nor rights over it."[7]

In the United States, the prospect of such volatility was daunting. Though America had won its independence, the future was most tentative. The original binding document, the Articles of Confederation, had been poorly crafted and hobbled the nation's ability to conduct business. The economy was suffering, disputes between the states went unmitigated, and the country had no means with which to protect its shipping and trade, and, perhaps most troubling, no means of controlling its people.

Following the Revolutionary War, many Americans, particularly those of less wealth and devoid of property, found that their lives had not necessarily improved. They saw in the new United States of America that the rule of a king had been intentionally replaced by the rule of an aristocracy. Most of the states required voters and office-holders to hold property, and some even required a certain level of property or wealth to participate. Citizens were finding that this new country, supposedly founded on fairness and representation, was not living up to its professed principles.

As tensions rose, the people formed pockets of resistance and actively challenged the authority of their states. The most famous instance of this was called Shays's Rebellion, after Daniel Shays, a Revolutionary War veteran who participated in radical actions throughout Massachusetts in 1786 and 1787. In the war Shays had been an honored soldier and had "received an ornamental sword from General Lafayette as a mark of personal esteem" before falling into debt and selling the token "for a few measly dollars," but now Shays used his military acumen as a leader of a burgeoning populist resistance.[8]

Shays's Rebellion confronted the state and effectively ground it to a halt as its members demanded fairer government. Because the Articles of Confederation didn't allow for a federal army or facilitate assistance between the states, Massachusetts was largely incapable of addressing the resistance before the state's wealthy merchants pooled their resources to pay for a private militia to crush the rebellion and restore an uneasy order.

Despite the fact that the insurrection was rooted in the same ideals we now associate with the American Revolution, the ruling class saw the disruption as a dangerous development and a possible omen of chaos to come. George Washington, in writing to Secretary of War Henry Knox, admitted the incident had filled him with "great & anxious uneasiness" and saw it as a threat to "not only the hemisphere of Massachusetts but by spreading its baneful influence, the tranquility of the Union."[9] Many of Washington's contemporaries shared his unease, and the possibility of further uprisings played a prominent role in their writings, their discussions, and eventually their decision to seek a centralized government.

With the Articles of Confederation proving economically insufficient and incapable of protecting the Union from challenges, the ruling class recognized the necessity of a new course of action. If their investments, financial futures, and institutional advantage were to survive, it would be crucial to forge some new path that supported the principles of self-governance and the people's right to revolt while also solidifying their power. If they were to avoid the fate of deposed and executed kings, they would have to craft a hearth with which to contain Jefferson's flame of revolution and reduce it to a manageable flicker.

★

As James Madison of Virginia waited for his colleagues to arrive for the Philadelphia Convention in May of 1787, he began sketching out a plan. A child of privilege surrounded by slaves throughout his life, Madison was well educated and a firm believer in the necessity of systems of control.

The Philadelphia Convention was never intended to draft a new constitution. Its meeting had been called as a means to address serious flaws in the Articles of Confederation, and its participants had been given the charge of improving the document as a means of answering the challenges of the day. Instead, as he bided his time, Madison weaved together an entirely new charter that fundamentally altered the nature of American government. He had no right to do so, was given no authority to undertake such a task, and yet, by the time the other states arrived, it was too late to change the course of history.

Before quorum could be reached, the Virginian and Pennsylvanian delegations had coalesced behind the plan, forming a coalition that framed the convention from the very beginning as a body with the intention of replacing the Articles of Confederation with a new constitution despite their lack of authority. When delegates from the other colonies arrived with their charge to revise the Articles, they were met with the proposal and a debate that was focused on totally transforming the government according to what has since been dubbed the Virginia Plan. Their deliberations were held in secret, the doors locked and even the windows nailed shut.

As John W. Burgess, one of the founders of political science and a constitutional law professor at Columbia in the late nineteenth and early twentieth centuries, explained: "What they actually did, stripped of all fiction and verbiage, was to assume constituent powers, ordain a constitution of government and of liberty, and demand the *plébiscite* thereon . . . Had Julius or Napoleon committed these acts, they would have been pronounced *coup d'état*."[10]

The men who carried out the coup in Philadelphia that summer were representatives of the wealthy landowning class, the majority of them lawyers or plantation owners, others successful merchants or affluent speculators. Nearly half owned slaves. They held economic incentives not only to preserve the Union but to frame the law to benefit themselves and their peers, the constituency of the wealthy.

From May to mid-September, delegates from every colony but Rhode Island, none of them authorized by their states or their constituencies to do anything more than revise the Articles of Confederation, took it upon themselves to seize the moment and radically transform the nation. The American Myth paints the process as divinely inspired and the result of a work of distinctly American genius, the Constitution itself an impeccable guide in all things and a means by which freedom and liberty might be bestowed upon every citizen. The convention's secrecy, both in its work and in the embargoing of the members' notes until all participants had died, lent itself to this mythmaking, but the eventual release of Madison's notes of the proceedings revealed a disorganized, fractious debate. In that room, the only unifying ideologies were a distrust and fear of the American people; a belief in the superiority of the wealthy, white elite; and a need for a government to prevent the people from carrying out further revolution.

Naturally, from the very beginning, the tone was decidedly elitist; one Founding Father, Roger Sherman of Connecticut, declared, "The people immediately should have as little to do as may be about the government. They want information and are constantly liable to be misled."[11] In agreement, Elbridge Gerry of Massachusetts concurred that the problem was the "excess of democracy" and alluded to Shays's Rebellion, which had taught him "the danger of the leveling spirit."[12]

To combat that leveling spirit, Madison took his inspiration from French philosopher Montesquieu and his concept of the *trias politica*, a government engineered to be divided between the separate interests of the monarchy, the aristocracy, and the common people, enshrining in the government of the United States of America a permanent recognition of the wealthy over the poor. To quell the people and their illogical passions, Madison posited the House of Representatives, a body elected by the people that presented the illusion of representation while placing it safely within the confines of a system designed to undermine its power. Countering the populist nature of the House, Madison envisioned that the Senate would be populated by the most fit members of society; they were to be appointed by the state legislatures, which were, as dictated by their states' voting rights and the expectations of officeholders, made up of the most wealthy and powerful landowners in the country. In this way, the Senate would proceed "with more coolness, with more system, and with more wisdom than the popular branch."[13]

In Madison's vision of the country, as in all "civilized societies," he saw a nation divided into "different sects, factions, and interests" consisting of the "rich and poor, debtors and creditors, the landed, the manufacturing, the commercial interests." This system worked to "divide the community into so great a number of interests and parties" that the majority of the population would never threaten the minority.[14]

To be clear, Madison's argument for the protection of the minority had little to do with the term as we have come to understand it as meaning vulnerable populations. He sought to protect the wealthy landowning class—a minority group set apart for its privilege—from another revolution like Shays's, focused on replacing the newly formed aristocracy with something more closely resembling democracy. Of course, these planned institutional divides over wealth and property also manifested socially; the people themselves, in a reflection of the divided government, effectively served as checks and balances on any possibility of uniting in a new revolution.

In electing the president, the convention also agreed that direct vote by the people was a mistake. Madison believed that property owners made "the safest depositories of Republican liberty" and worried that in a future where everyone enjoyed the right to vote, the people would be manipulated and "become the tools of opulence and ambition."[15] Echoing these sentiments was George Mason, who maintained it was "unnatural" for voters to choose the executive and that to trust them in doing so would be like referring "a trial of colors to a blind man."

Eighty-one years old and frail, Benjamin Franklin attended the convention in a ceremonial capacity, but he did attempt to serve as the conscience of the proceedings. As they discussed the superiority of the wealthy ruling class and the dangers of trusting the people, he urged them to remember "the common people" and the "virtue and public spirit" they had displayed during the Revolutionary War and how their participation had helped win independence. Immediately, John Mercer contradicted the legendary Franklin, saying, "The people cannot know and judge of the characters of candidates. The worst possible choice will be made."[16]

In the end, the Electoral College was designed to safeguard the election of the executive from the people's ignorance and to give the more capable and intelligent ruling class power over the process. The system preserved the illusion of democracy and representation while ensuring the wealthy ruling class held the Senate and the presidency and could overrule any damage the House might inflict.

Outside of this general agreement on the need to prevent the masses from threatening their property or the fundamental hierarchy of class and wealth, the framers battled continuously and fractiously. Alexander Hamilton saw the convention's lack of progress as resulting from "a contest for power, not for liberty."[17] Of the wrangling, Madison noticed the states weren't divided by size "but by other circumstances, the most material of which resulted partly from climate but principally from the effects of their having or not having slaves." [18]

Desperate to find a solution that ensured a working government, Madison briefly proposed a new ordering of his republican plan that would rearrange the House and the Senate, constituting them as being dedicated respectively to represent free states and those dedicated to slavery. "By this arrangement," Madison surmised, "the southern scale would have the advantage in one house and the northern in the other." [19]

Nearing the eleventh anniversary of the Declaration of Independence and an adjournment to celebrate the Fourth of July holiday, the Philadelphia Convention seemed deadlocked, disgruntled, at odds, and fearful that their plan might not take shape. Before they adjourned, the last voice was Elbridge Gerry of Massachusetts, reminding the delegates of the consequences of failure to compromise. Likely with an eye toward the suppressed revolution in his home state, Gerry asked for "consideration of the state we should be thrown into by the failure of the Union." He urged them, "We must make concessions on both sides."

The Southern representatives, particularly those from South Carolina, were prepared to capitalize on the desperation of their Northern colleagues by threatening the deliberations. Heeding Gerry's call for compromise, and fearful of a new revolution, this one aimed at their lives and their property, representatives of the Northern states ceded ground. Desperate to leave the convention with a consensus-driven plan, they gifted the South assurances that the slave trade would be protected for a period of twenty years, allowing the barbaric practice to grow and take root, and accepted the abominable Three-Fifths Compromise, which allowed slave owners in the South to wield unequal power over the government. John Ellsworth of Connecticut's justification for the compromise proved eerily prescient: "If we do not agree on this middle and moderate ground . . . we should lose two states with such others as may be disposed to stand aloof; should fly into a variety of shapes and directions; and most probably into several confederations, and not without bloodshed."[20]

As the convention neared its dreary end, the drafted Constitution having enshrined and institutionalized slavery and racial inequality into the foundation of the United States of America, prominent delegates voiced their hesitations. George Mason objected strongly to proceeding, announcing he would "rather chop off his right hand than put it to the Constitution as it now stands." He later warned the government would "end either in monarchy or a tyrannical aristocracy—which, he was in doubt, but one or other, he was sure."[21] The Constitution, he warned, "had been formed without the knowledge or idea of the people . . . It was improper to say to the people, Take this or nothing."

In a final address, Benjamin Franklin stood in front of the convention and admitted there were "several parts of this Constitution" which he did not approve of, but he acknowledged the need for unity.[22] He agreed to "sacrifice to the public good" his disagreements and urged the holdouts to do the same.

As the delegates signed the document that would shape the world's future and ensure the political and economic exploitation of all the people not represented in that single cramped room, Franklin noticed the chair from which George Washington, the nation's most powerful and wealthiest citizen, had overlooked the actions as the convention's president general. The seat was decorated with a painting of the sun, and Franklin mentioned that in paintings it was often hard to tell a sunrise from a sunset. But now, with the tumultuous convention at an end, he had no doubt it was the beginning of a new day.

★

The period of debate over the Constitution is largely obfuscated in American history in favor of presenting the Declaration of Independence and the Constitution as twin documents linked in divinity and universal support, but ratification of the framers' government was never a certainty. The process itself was fraught with manipulation, dishonesty, a rigging of the eventual vote, and the development of the American Myth as a means of selling the new political order.

What is generally known about the process is confined to the publication of *The Federalist Papers*, a series of treatises written by James Madison, John Jay, and Alexander Hamilton under the pen name "Publius" that appeared in Northern publications and argued for the ratification of the Constitution. The debate over ratification largely took place in the nation's newspapers, which had more than doubled in number since the Revolutionary War.[23]

Scholars and citizens alike hold these essays as proof of the noble intentions of the framers, but further examination reveals a divide between the ideologies of the framers and the perception of the framing. This rift was intentional, as Madison, Jay, and Hamilton mischaracterized the framing and obscured the process by which it was created.

The debate over the proposed government quickly settled into two distinct camps: the Federalists, who supported ratification outright, and the Antifederalists, many of whom weren't particularly anti–federal government and simply voiced their criticisms to improve the plan but were nonetheless framed as opponents. This narrowing of the political debate, made possible by newspapers owned by wealthy and partisan publishers, dictated that the debate be fought, as George Mason had worried, on a central subject: whether there would be the Constitution in its existing form or nothing. In a sign of the partisanship and violent rhetoric that constituted America's political discourse for centuries to come, the first public criticism of the proposed Constitution, published in Philadelphia's *Freeman's Journal*, was met with a vicious response in which the author was labeled an "Antifederalist" by publishers who proposed he should be "honored" with a tar-and-feathering.[24]

The so-called Antifederalists, who have been largely lost to history, published under pseudonyms and called into question the ₚₒsed Constitution and the rhetoric used by its proponents. One calling himself "John Dewitt" argued that the delegates clearly worked in favor of the wealthy. He warned that the country would "degenerate to a complete aristocracy" and predicted it was "nothing less than a hasty stride to Universal Empire in this Western World, flattering, very flattering to young ambitious minds, but fatal to the liberties of the people."[25]

Those young ambitious minds did not take the criticism lightly. Madison, Jay, and Hamilton blitzed the opposition with an overwhelming number of publications and provided a more palatable narrative to the populace. The effort employed a rhetoric of fear, unvarnished ambition, and the tried-and-true dogma of the American Revolution. All three of the authors cited warnings of foreign influence, war, invasion by other countries, future insurrections larger and more unified than Shays's Rebellion, and even the danger of the Native Americans at their borders. Failure to immediately ratify the Constitution as it was written, they repeatedly claimed, would lead to unthinkable disaster.

Hamilton, a fervent capitalist, based his arguments in the realm of the market. Instead of focusing on the benefits of Locke's self-government or Rousseau's concept of the social contract, he seemed to draw from the work of Scottish economist Adam Smith. Smith's 1776 book *The Wealth of Nations* posited that the self-interest of the individual could be harnessed to create a system where countries grew large and powerful by means of capitalism and eventually became interlocking circuits of wealth, the entire process overseen by the "invisible hand" of capitalism, or, arguably, the will of God himself working through the economy. In his essays, Hamilton appealed to his readers to move beyond sectionalism—decrying what he called an "infinity of little, jealous, clashing, tumultuous commonwealths"—so the United States could jump-start its economic and territorial ambitions.[26]

All three authors made the case that America's Constitution was meant as a means to consolidate the influence of the states, improving upon the Greek, Roman, and British systems. They suggested that the United States, with the correct engineering, would become the heir to these empires and grow more powerful than any empire that had come before, but that mission required the cessation of the perpetual revolution as envisioned by Jefferson in favor of a system that protected the wealthy. This approach blended the rigidity of control in past and existing empires with Enlightenment thinking, instituting a new reality where people were to be controlled but believe themselves to be free.

The Founders' plan for perpetual control of the people also required a narrative to protect it from scrutiny, and in *The Federalist Papers*, Madison, Jay, and Hamilton found an opportunity to establish that narrative. Their essays coupled the Constitution with the appeal of divine inspiration and the tenets of the revolution, with an emphasis on unity against outsiders. They argued that God had given "one connected country to one united people—a people descended from the same ancestors, speaking the same language, professing the same religion, attached to the same principles of government, very similar in their manners and customs."[27]

Through this framing, the Founders planted the concept of American identity and American exceptionalism, particularly white American exceptionalism: a worldview in which the creator of the universe had touched a people and made them superior to carry out his plans. It was a remnant of ideology from the age of kings, disguised as progress toward something utterly free and new.

The chosen people the Federalists truly elevate are the people who were given full citizenship, namely those white and wealthy few. To stabilize the country and ensure future growth, though, it was crucial to expand the story to include the entire population. The narrative is rooted in the Greek philosopher Plato's "Noble Lie," the concept that myths or pious untruths are necessary to stabilize society and promote progress, an idea he elucidated in his work *The*

Republic. Plato supposed that in order for society to flourish, there must be a story of unification that yokes citizens to one another while managing their discontent.

He wonders: "Could we somehow contrive one of those lies that come into being in case of need . . . some one noble lie to persuade, in the best case, even the rulers, but if not them, the rest of the city?"[28]

That lie, as Plato continues, is a tale of a society in which the people are citizens of a country watched over by a moral God who oversees a system of inequality that still manages to reward hard work and talent, inspiring a faith in a moral and fair hierarchy. In this society, some citizens are mixed with gold and, like kings, are rightful rulers. The lower classes serve these rulers, work hard, and are occasionally raised up to a higher class and positions of power, thus affirming their faith in the Noble Lie.

America's original Noble Lie is the mischaracterization of its founding. The facts of its conception, its independence, and the process by which its Constitution was penned and then sold to the world have been twisted to fit a larger story of universal morality, white supremacy, and social Darwinism, and it has been used since its beginning as a means of manipulation and control.

The lie was crafted and sold by *The Federalist Papers*, which whitewashed the framing and its accompanying debates; while the scene in Independence Hall was one of wealthy elites designing a hierarchical order to their own political and economic advantage, it is described to the public as an endeavor the Founders undertook "without . . . having been influenced by any passions except love for their country."[29] To seal the deal, *The Federalist Papers* crafted a national identity to paper over divisions and promote an overarching federal government.

James Madison was especially effective at manipulating history in his and the Constitution's favor. In a shameful defense of the institutionalization of slavery into the laws of the country, Madison considered it a "great point gained in favor of humanity" that the practice might be abolished after twenty years.[30] In response to criticism that the Philadelphia Convention wasn't authorized to draft a new government, Madison offered, behind a pen name, that if the delegates had "exceeded their powers, they were not only warranted, but required as the confidential servants of their country" and that even if they had "violated both their powers and obligations," the new system "ought nevertheless to be embraced."[31]

This stunning rationalization of an admitted coup d'état provided a blueprint for the United States of America moving forward. Because the American Myth was founded on the concept of exceptionalism as denoted by divinity, its "confidential servants," as vessels for God's will, would be justified in doing anything they thought necessary to promote America's interests.

That justification meant the conquering and subjugation of peoples, the genocide of Native Americans, the enslavement of African Americans, the dehumanizing of women and vulnerable populations, and sacrificing the good of citizens for the good of the market. It also established the domination of the narrative of history as a means of perpetuating an all-powerful, all-uniting, all-fabricated lie that the United States of America was founded upon, and dedicated to, the liberty and freedom of the people of the world, all while it continued to consolidate power and empire under the invisible flag of white supremacy.

The machine Madison had designed was unlike anything the world had ever seen. Harnessing the spirit of revolution and dedicated to presenting the illusion of democracy and self-governance, he had given to the country and the world an invention solely devoted to the amassment and protection of wealth, a permanent hierarchy clothed in meritocratic robes, and an ever-shifting reality as useful and as dangerous as any weapon.

CHAPTER 2

*   *   *

Of Gods and Men

James Madison's vaunted system lasted all of eleven years before suffering a major constitutional and electoral crisis. The election of 1800 was a vicious contest between Thomas Jefferson and John Adams that saw Jefferson prevail, only for the Electoral College to trouble his victory. Jefferson's running mate, Aaron Burr, also received seventy-three electoral votes, throwing the quagmire to the House of Representatives, where backroom dealing and partisan squabbles threatened to undermine the will of the electorate in only the fourth presidential election.

The electoral crisis stemmed from a major design flaw in Madison's machine. His government was meant to function as a tool wielded by a unified class of elites, and disagreement was intended to hinge on predictable struggles between competitive branches. As he'd sketched the concept, the possibility of political parties never figured into the equation. By the election of 1800, however, the United States had toddled toward disaster as rival factions—consisting of the same patriots who had supposedly been inspired by selflessness and divine calling only years before—warred for power.

The antipathy between these fledgling parties—the Federalists and the Democratic-Republicans—rose from the inherent divisions between Madison's and Jefferson's visions of how the new country should operate and whom it should serve. Federalists were wealthy elites concerned with continued enrichment and perpetual control, their plans patterned after those of Great Britain. Democratic-Republicans, like Jefferson, championed populism and favored revolutionary France. These polarized interests clashed in 1800 and tested the system like it had never been tested before as factional tribalism and the thirst for power inspired individuals to put their own interests above the good of the country.

Federalist John Adams, the second president of the United States, was notorious for his unpredictable temperament and ceaseless paranoia. His self-doubt, coupled with his oft-expressed distrust of the common people, made for an erratic and combative presidency that saw Adams endanger the young Constitution. With the passage of the Alien and Sedition Acts of 1798, Adams's administration upended the right to free speech to jail his critics, deported immigrants he thought might support the opponents of his political party, and changed immigration policies specifically to hurt his rival Jefferson's chances of wresting away the presidency.

Of the difference between Jefferson's new Democratic-Republican Party and Adams's Federalists, who had maintained control of the country since its founding, Jefferson wrote that the Federalists were defined by their "fear and distrust" of the people and a philosophy that was closer to "genuine monarchism" than the democracy Jefferson championed.[1] In the so-called Revolution of 1800, Jefferson's message for his presidency was directly opposed to the Federalists, calling them "aristocrats," "stock counters," and "the plunderers of the people."[2]

Despite Adams's attempt at disenfranchising his way to re-election, Jefferson won easily with the help of a growing electorate that reflected the blossoming country. His appeal to populism and the concerns of those who felt the Federalists had ruled without much concern for their well-being fundamentally altered the course of America's history and the operation of American politics. Again, Jefferson's ideals centered on the concepts of perpetual revolution and the power of the individual, and now, at the turn of the nineteenth century, Jefferson's radical ideas moved from the theoretical realm to determining the future of a young nation.

Jefferson was correct in assessing the Federalists' fear of the people as they immediately prepared for the worst and considered intervention. The design flaw in the Electoral College and the tie between Jefferson and Burr presented the Federalists with an opportunity to possibly undermine the will of the people and give the presidency to Burr over Jefferson, but Alexander Hamilton's influence ended that idea while not doing much to assuage the terror of a Jefferson presidency. John Rutledge Jr., whose father and uncle had both been delegates to the Philadelphia Convention, wrote to Hamilton of his fear that Jefferson would subvert the Constitution by "throwing everything" into the hands of the people but suggested the Federalists could use their waning power to try to stave off that possibility.[3]

To achieve this goal, Adams reduced the number of Supreme Court justices, so that Jefferson couldn't name a successor if one of the existing justices passed, while also flooding the judiciary with judges specifically opposing Jefferson and his policies. These "Midnight Judges," named for their appointments at the midnight hour of Adams's presidency, led to a showdown between Jefferson and his hated cousin John Marshall, the chief justice of the Supreme Court, who created with no precedent, in the case *Marbury v. Madison*, the court's ability to judge laws as to their constitutionality and strike them down, establishing a new power that was not ordained in the Constitution for the specific purpose of checking political opposition.

In theory, Jefferson's populism was a radical concept that rippled through the soul of the country and inspired not only the events of the nineteenth century but those to come for generations. It attempted to change the focus of representative politics from the machine Madison had created to control the masses to something more human and democratic, but Jefferson's poisonous personal contradictions and sins would plague mankind.

The Revolution of 1800 was a defining moment in American history and inspired a new era of individualism that set into motion a chain of events Jefferson couldn't have imagined. After winning the contingent election and securing the presidency on the thirty-sixth ballot, Jefferson and his theories, which had inspired the American Revolution and given the necessary fuel to the oppressive Constitution, were now set to remake the face of religion and the nature of intellectual American thought, and inspire a movement that would eventually conquer the world but result in the genocide of a people and the economic domination of billions.

★

If Jefferson's democratic principles and ideology of populist revolution were the fire in Madison's machine, the turn of the nineteenth century saw that fire escape and rage across the land. It awakened in the growing American populace the need for a fairer and more humane world, a nation with a loftier purpose and grander design. With their power plays and manipulation, beginning with *The Federalist Papers*, the Federalists had all but snuffed out that flame by the turn of the century, but Jefferson's ascension was a rebirth of sorts, a messianic return that portended the dawning of a new age.

The religious nature of this resurrection was both informed by and inspired by the Second Great Awakening, a revival of American Christianity that followed years of declining church attendance and membership. The First Great Awakening had preceded the revolution and had served to unite the thirteen colonies and partly inspire the rebellion. America's founding, however, had meant to sever the tie between the secular government and religion and shift the unifying focus from faith to public identity. For some, this shift was successful, resulting in declining church membership and a general malaise settling over the religious community, but soon many Americans reignited their faith and focused their fervor on bettering the world. Whereas religion had been in decline since the founding, by the mid-nineteenth century, one-third of the population identified as religious, twice as many as in 1776.[4]

The Second Great Awakening was decidedly populist, a change compelled by the forces that had originally led religion to decline. The First Great Awakening had been characterized by fear of an angry God who had chosen peoples and who smote sinners; the Second was oriented toward saving people from damnation and offering personal redemption. This new focus inspired the pursuit of a "Benevolent Empire" to lead the world by example and convert followers by demonstrations of goodness; vigorous reform in the spirit of equality for all races and peoples; an opposition to greed, slavery, and discrimination; and the spreading of the new message by way of missionaries and evangelism. This idealism that mirrored the founding of the country, however, would fall short of its espoused principles.

Jefferson's emphasis on the individual helped inspire a new philosophy and spirituality called transcendentalism. This line of thought, most famously espoused by Ralph Waldo Emerson and Henry David Thoreau, also focused on the individual, in this case sharing Jefferson's view of people as being "perfectible" and championing the concept that "God is in every man."[5] Emerson lamented that "men ha[d] come to speak of the revelation as somewhat long ago given and done, as if God were dead," an echo of the Second Great Awakening's message that the divine was not yet finished with the world. For Emerson, who wasn't "interested in secondhand revelations, secondhand gospels," the true nature of the world, reflected in transcendentalist thought, "put every person directly in touch with the divine, without any need for tradition, a written scripture, or an institutional church." Individuals could reason for themselves what was truth, and that ability to reason meant they were capable of discerning the course of human events.

Like Jefferson, the transcendentalists were enamored with the natural world and fearful of government overreach. Likewise, they distrusted the advancements of technology, particularly the creeping automation of the Industrial Revolution, and advocated a life dedicated to pastoral and intellectual pursuits. To that end, transcendentalists often formed their own communities intentionally constructed around their principles. Thoreau famously removed himself to Walden Pond, built his own cabin, harvested his own food, and lived a life of solitude and personal sovereignty, an experience that informed his burgeoning theory of civil disobedience, in which the individual, as the sole vessel of truth, could challenge the sovereignty of government and its laws.

Jefferson's assertion of inalienable rights, the sovereignty of the people, and the limitation of government in favor of democratic principles was being used to create a new world in which each individual was like their own nation. The principle of divine inspiration, the Noble Lie that had powered the United States from its founding and upheld its aristocratic order, was at risk of being overtaken.

In typical fashion, Jefferson both believed these principles and acted against them. Hamilton had reassured his colleagues in preparation for the incoming president that Jefferson, though predisposed to radicalism, would ultimately maintain the Federalists' established order. He noted that Jefferson was ensnared by the financial system he had personally engineered, writing, "[Jefferson] is as likely as any man I know to temporize—to calculate what will be likely to promote his own reputation and advantage; and the probable result of such a temper is the preservation of systems."[6]

A year into his administration, Jefferson conceded that Hamilton was right, writing to Samuel du Pont de Nemours that Hamilton's "English, half-lettered ideas" had so deeply rooted a capitalist system in the United States that Jefferson had no hopes of being able to dislodge it.[7] So, confronted with a well-established system, Jefferson did what many powerful men would do in his position: He laid aside his quibbles with large government and used the office of the presidency to perform a massive power grab the likes of which would be emulated by nearly every successive president of note.

Jefferson wasted no time in reimagining the scope and authority at his disposal, including the literal scope of United States territory. His presidency is notable for the Louisiana Purchase, in which Jefferson radically increased the size of the country by purchasing from France over eight hundred thousand square miles of territory, that expanse constituting the totality or portions of fourteen future states. This play by a president has absolutely no correlation with the office as it was designed, and Jefferson's purchase was a gamble. Without a formal rule or constituency in place to stop him, however, he was successful. By exposing the arbitrary and malleable nature of reality, Jefferson's venture expanded the scope of presidential power and recalibrated the operation of government.

The acquisition of territory to the west was essential for Jefferson's vision for the future United States. Acting upon his principles of individualistic determination, Jefferson sought to establish in America a republic of independent farmers, an agrarian utopia where citizens would exist self-sufficiently and enjoy the type of liberty he had preached. This vision was informed not only by Jefferson's own livelihood as a farmer and his continued allegiance to the Southern agrarian existence, but also his distaste and antipathy for the mechanization of the Industrial Revolution.

Jefferson's utopian America, predicated upon the labor of enslaved peoples and a forebear of the eventual Confederate States of America, would position the nation as the supplier of the world's crops, particularly cotton, the demand for which was growing exponentially, by harvesting the expanse of the continent and then sending the crops to Europe. The industrialized nations across the Atlantic would handle the hard and dirty work of manufacturing, leaving America clean of the blight of industry while maintaining its financial footing. Jefferson had first envisioned such an arrangement in his 1787 work *Notes on the State of Virginia,* reasoning that "those who labor in the earth are the chosen people of God" and stating, "While we have land to labor then, let us never wish to see our citizens occupied at a work bench."[8]

This reconstitution of American society would, in theory and application, constitute at least as much governmental control as the Federalists had once held, if not more. But in this new era of democratic priorities, Jefferson saw himself as the receptacle of the will of the people, an individual through whom the divine might guide the moral arc of the universe. Moral relativism, then, dictated that Jefferson, being the diviner of right and wrong, was afforded the privilege of determining what actions were necessary, even if they were unethical or immoral in the moment, to produce his desired outcome.

Following Jefferson's example, the presidency of the United States of America transformed into a position limited only by the imagination of the individual and their ability to sway the electorate. The people lent their collected consent to a singular ruler as opposed to the shared aristocratic ruling class, as designed by Madison, and that individual, divinely inspired, was to be tasked with guiding the country by their own intuition and sense of morality, especially if the will of the leader furthered the myth of American exceptionalism.

As the executor of this myth, Jefferson dispatched Captain Meriwether Lewis, Second Lieutenant William Clark, and the Corps of Discovery into the western expanse of the continent in May 1804. Their mission was to make their way across the territories to develop trading routes that would support Jefferson's agrarian plan and prepare the continent for its eventual conquering. To do so, they charted the geography of the land while conditioning the Native American tribes for an American future in which the indigenous people could be conquered to make way for expansion and economic growth.

To aid this venture, Lewis and Clark were armed with a story and a powerful weapon. In their visitations with the various tribes, they spoke of Jefferson as a "Great Father," a deity meant to fit snugly into the tribes' established religions and enable the United States government to serve as an overruling power, a divine entity that must be obeyed. Past colonialists had pioneered this manipulation, but Lewis and Clark told the tribes they must return the flags and gifts of their previous gods because they now belonged to the "Great Father." To prove this divine transfer, they carried with them more than eighty medals bearing Jefferson's likeness with the words "TH. JEFFERSON President of the U.S. A.D. 1801" printed on the front, and a crossed tomahawk and pipe over a pair of clasped hands on the back.

When Lewis and Clark gave these medals to the chiefs of the tribes, they sought to make them "sensible of their dependence on the will of our government for every species of merchandize [*sic*] as well [as] for their defense & comfort; and apprized them of the strength of our government."[9] Jefferson had asked them to "inform the tribes that the new father intended to embrace them into a commercial system that would benefit all involved"[10] and deliver a message that centered Jefferson as a new god and the Native American people as his obedient children:

> *Children*—Know that the great chief who has thus offered you the hand of unalterable friendship, is the Great Chief of the Seventeen great Nations of America, whose cities are as numerous as the stars in the heavens, and whose people like the grass of your plains, cover with their cultivated fields and wigwams, the wide Extended country, reaching from the western borders of the Mississippi to the great lakes of the East, where the land ends and the Sun rises from the face of the great waters—
>
> *Children*—Know that this great chief, as powerfull [*sic*] as he is just, and as beneficent as he is wise, always entertain-

ing a Sincere and friendly disposition towards the red people of America, has commanded us his war chiefs to undertake this long journey, which we have so far accomplished with great labour & much expence [*sic*], in order to council with yourselves and his other red-children on the troubled waters, to give you his good advice; to point out to you the road in which you must walk to obtain happiness[.] He has further commanded us to tell you that when you accept his flag and medal, you accept therewith his hand of friendship, which will never be withdrawn from your nation as long as you continue to follow the councils which he may command his chiefs to give you.[11]

Lewis and Clark had a warning for anyone who might upset this new and benevolent god: "By one false step you should bring upon your nation the displeasure of your great father, the great chief of the Seventeen great nations of America, who would consume you as the fire consumes the grass of the plains."[12]

The expedition successfully carried out its mission as the Corps of Discovery charted the path of future American territorial and economic expansion and established relationships with the tribes they encountered, planting within them the seeds of a new reality in which the sitting American president held not only earthly sway over them but divine right. On July 26, 1806, however, as Lewis led his division on the return trip, he and his men encountered members of the Blackfoot tribe in the Marias River country in what would become Montana. What happened there shattered the false sense of peace they had worked to create and portended the eventual and tragic destruction of the Native people.

On that day, Lewis and his men made contact with a Blackfoot scouting party who made camp with the expedition. They smoked with Lewis, who gifted them the ceremonial flag and Jefferson medal. In their discussion, Lewis relayed to them the Great Father story and urged them to make peace with their fellow tribes and accept American dominance. Lewis made a miscalculation, however, as he told the Blackfeet he had already negotiated with the tribe's enemies, a piece of information that sounded like a threat.

The next morning, Lewis woke with a start. His party's watchman was fighting over his gun with one of the Blackfoot men and all hell was breaking loose. Eventually the watchman wrestled back his weapon and "stabed [*sic*] the indian to the heart with his knife."[13] In the pandemonium, Lewis spotted some Blackfeet taking off with horses, and though there were plenty remaining even if they got away, he gave chase, eventually cornering one of the men and shooting him.

Before they left, Lewis and his men stole the Blackfoot horses, and Lewis found that one of the murdered men held the flag and medal that had been gifted the night before. The flag, which the expedition had told the tribes protected them as friends of the seventeen great nations of America, was repossessed by Lewis. But the medal bearing the image of Jefferson, the Great Father, Lewis left "about the neck of the dead man that they might be informed who we were."[14]

Fearful of retaliation, Lewis and his party raced from the scene of the murders and hurried through the terrain. Satisfied they were a safe distance from the massacre, they made camp and Lewis jotted down his thoughts, noting, "My indian horse carried very well in short much better than my own would have done and leaves me with but little reason to complain of the robbery."[15]

Setting an awful precedent for the future, Lewis had found what so many Americans would come to realize in the very near future: The murder and plunder of people across the land proved most beneficial to the aims of the United States of America.

★

The conquering of the North American continent began not long after, in the presidency of James Monroe, an Antifederalist who had opposed ratification of the Constitution but, like Jefferson before him, took full advantage of the centralized power of the United States government. Monroe's most significant contribution was the Monroe Doctrine, a foreign policy he coauthored with his secretary of state and eventual successor John Quincy Adams that warned other countries the interests of the North American continent belonged to the United States alone, and any attempt to interfere would be considered an aggressive act.

Monroe and Adams reasoned that to compete with European nations, the United States needed to operate like one. This position stood contrary to the espoused principles of the founding: Rather than focusing on liberty for its people, America began expansionist efforts and interfered in the sovereignty of other nations and peoples.

Having fought a war of independence mere decades before to loose itself from the affairs of colonialists, America was now determined to emulate them. In doing so, the focus of the country, or at least the stated focus of the country, overtly shifted from the betterment and service of the citizens to the welfare and progress of the state. This was a radical realignment of principles that, when coupled with the era's emphasis on the president as the arbiter of right and wrong and the executor of divine will, would lead to staggering consequences.

Possession of the Noble Lie of the American religion was everything in this new age. Jefferson and Monroe had captured the presidency by appealing to the masses and, having done so, wielded the power of the office in expansive ways with the help of a divine mandate. In the West, with the Lewis and Clark expedition, Jefferson employed fabricated religious myth to transform himself into a god.

With this alchemy, the medals carried by Lewis and Clark were transformed from manufactured silver coins into manifestations of the favor of an almighty god, and in this way Andrew Jackson, a despot and genocidal madman, was transformed into a giant among men and the voice of the people.

Few understood better the influence of myth and narrative than

Jackson and John Eaton, an aide who carried out his transformation. The pair recognized America as a country ruled by myth, and elections as rewarding those most capable of mythmaking and wielding the Noble Lie. At the time, those myths were relegated to the past, in particular the Founding Fathers, whom the people of the nineteenth century were already granting a mythological air, but Jackson and Eaton saw an opportunity to harness myth in the present.

At the turn of the century, writer Parson Weems penned *A History of the Life and Death, Virtues and Exploits of General George Washington,* a highly embellished account of the first president's life. The book supplied the nation apocryphal tales casting Washington as a mythical figure, calling him a "golden phoenix" and portraying a Christlike deity who gave everything to his country.[16] Its most enduring story depicts young George cutting down a cherry tree and admitting the crime to his father, a story that American schoolchildren would recite for generations to come. It established for them, as a base for their learning, the concept of a just and honorable country ruled by just and honorable men.

Jackson and Eaton recognized the power of this myth, but the approach they took in harnessing it was novel. Instead of allowing the future to take the past and shape it to fit the mythological needs of the country, Jackson and Eaton saw that myth itself could be marshaled to create mythology in the present, establishing cults of personality that harnessed democratic populism and imbued godlike power in the leader.

Before he was president and the supposed voice of the people, Jackson was a general who relished the bloodshed of battle and the domination of his enemies. His defining moment was the Battle of New Orleans during the War of 1812, where Jackson overcame British forces in a largely inconsequential battle that coincided with the peace treaty that ended the war, but nevertheless positioned Jackson in the public imagination as the hero of the war. Seeking to capitalize on the moment and boost his political future, Jackson desired a biography to be written about his life that framed him in a similar light to Washington, a tome that would eventually be finished by Eaton and repeatedly revised as events and campaigns demanded.

Though Eaton's transformation of Jackson into a mythical embodiment of strength and democracy succeeded, he first had to answer criticisms relating to Jackson's questionable past—most specifically his decision during the Battle of New Orleans to institute martial law over the people and suppress their rights, even after the war had ceased. In his time lording over New Orleans, Jackson jailed dissenters, including a judge and state senator; censored critics and newspapers; and oversaw the execution of his own men who dared to undermine his unjust orders.

Of Jackson's continued martial law, Eaton wrote that Jackson had been justified as the peace treaty might have been a "devise [*sic*] to induce a relaxation in his system of operation and defence." The suppression of journalists and their constitutional rights was equally vindicated because if the freedom of the press resulted in questioning a leader during wartime it would be "a circumstance much to be regretted."[17]

That suspension of integral and guaranteed freedoms, Eaton argued, was valid and moral because Jackson, as a general, was heir to the Roman concept of *inter arma silent leges,* or the ancient belief that in times of conflict the law gives way to the instincts of warriors. As he put it, "In all governments, there are moments of danger and distress, when, no matter how cautiously protected be the rights of citizens, those rights must be disregarded, not for the purpose of being destroyed, but that they may be more permanently secured."[18]

And who was the ultimate arbiter of the necessity of the Constitution and all of its rights?

The general, through whom flowed divine knowledge.

This story of the general's need to protect liberty by subverting it would set a dangerous precedent for presidential and American power, a development that troubled the concept of guaranteed rights and lent the presidency the air of a militant dictatorship. To bolster this dangerous idea, Eaton would again and again tie Jackson's actions in New Orleans to George Washington, writing anonymous letters to Democratic newspapers in the lead-up to Jackson's presidential campaign and claiming that Jackson had "a soul that tower[ed] above intrigue" and that "no one ha[d] done more for his country since the days of Washington."[19] In this way, Washington was transformed into a malleable symbol of America who could be wielded by individuals dedicated to even the most un-American of ideals.

When Jackson ran for president in 1828, the Democratic Party perpetuated Eaton's myth and mobilized one of the first active campaigns for the office, pioneering the practices of messaging and spin. As their system of newspapers and magazines worked to transform Jackson into a historical leader, his campaign managers were "haunted by a fear that he would make some careless pronouncement that might nullify all their efforts." Eaton, who was later appointed Jackson's secretary of war, maintained it was "unnecessary for the General to state his position on any issue."[20] Jackson's relative ambiguity and silence, coupled with the machine's influence, enabled a cult of personality to be constructed around Jackson, a cult that gifted him a mandate and, following in Jefferson's footsteps, the mantle of the voice of the people and possessor of America's religion.

For a president, the American electorate had chosen a fictional character, and the man who assumed office was far from the democratic champion that had been sold to them. Though he was portrayed as a man of the people, Jackson was a wealthy plantation owner who'd made his fortune in land speculation, more specifically the speculation of Native American land. At the time of his inauguration in 1829, lust for Native American territory was growing, especially among the Southern slave-owning states, and Jackson reflected those interests.

Jackson's cruel treatment of the Native American people defined his military and political career. As a general, Jackson had slaughtered countless Native Americans in his unlawful conquest of Florida, including an ugly incident when Jackson ordered his men to execute two tribal religious leaders in cold blood, his orders demanding that the tribe "be made to know that their prophets are imposters."[21] In one battle, he snatched a Native infant boy from the arms of his dead mother and sent him back home to Tennessee to be raised by Jackson's wife. Of the slaughters, he wrote that he had seen "the raven & the vultures preying upon the carcases [*sic*] of the slain."[22]

Removal of the Native people from the southeastern United States was one of Jackson's top priorities as president, a priority based on the economic interests of Southern land speculators and wealthy plantation owners. In his first State of the Union address in 1829, Jackson wrote that his mission to relocate the Native Americans was based in kindness and empathy, continuing the United States' mission to introduce the Native American people to "the arts of civilization."[23] Perverting the principles of Christian charity, he claimed that letting them remain east of the Mississippi would be a cruelty unto itself and he didn't want to be "indifferent to their fate," as being "surrounded by the whites with their arts of civilization" would "doom them." Moving them west, the process being "voluntary" lest it be "cruel" and "unjust," would allow them to have their own space, and there "the benevolent [might] endeavor to teach them the arts of civilization, and by promoting union and harmony among them . . . attest the humanity and justice of this government."

Though he preached empathy and voluntary relocation, Jackson privately told a Georgia congressman, "Build a fire under them . . . When it gets hot enough, they'll move."[24]

A year later Jackson stopped worrying about the Native people's volunteering to leave as the tribes living east of the Mississippi made a case for their sovereignty and calls for their land increased. Spurred by Jackson, Congress narrowly passed the Indian Removal Act in May of 1830, a law that demanded the forceful removal of Native Americans to settlements in the West. In his State of the Union, Jackson called the removal "benevolent policy" that would "free them" and "enable them to pursue happiness in their own way and under their own rude institutions."[25] Perhaps, he reasoned, they might "cast off their savage habits and become an interesting, civilized, and Christian community." This policy, which led to untold deaths and unimaginable suffering, Jackson called "not only liberal, but generous."[26]

The Cherokee tribe argued their case for sovereignty and in 1832 the Supreme Court ruled that the Cherokees were their own sovereign nation, a ruling Jackson simply disregarded. In his 1833 State of the Union, he wrote that Native American tribes could no longer exist in the presence of their white conquerors, that they had "neither the intelligence, the industry, the moral habits, nor the desire of improvements which are essential to any favorable change in their condition."[27] They were, he argued, "in the midst of another and a superior race, and without appreciating the causes of their inferiority or seeking to control them, they must necessarily yield to the force of circumstances and ere long disappear."

Carrying out Jackson's decree constituted one of the most glaring national shames. Tens of thousands of Native Americans were marched across the continent, thousands dying from disease, exhaustion, or slaughter, the Cherokee alone losing "at least 4,000, or perhaps as many as 8,000," an astonishing number amounting to a reduction of their total population by 20 to 40 percent.[28] Of the atrocity, a volunteer in the removal process remarked, "I fought through civil war and have seen men shot to pieces and slaughtered by the thousands, but the Cherokee removal was the cruelest work I ever knew."

The president of the United States of America, vested with all the power and glory of the people and in representation of the interests of the white race and the wealthy, slave-owning population, had carried out a ruthless campaign of ethnic cleansing, a genocide of the

Native American people. Like an angry god of old, he had wiped them from the face of the American earth. The prophecy delivered to the tribes by Meriwether Lewis and William Clark at the command of the Great Father had been fulfilled.

A fire had consumed them like the one that consumed the grass of their prairies.

★

Even as the nation's top executive discarded the rule of law and basic decency, a potent relationship developed between the president and the American people. A feedback loop materialized as the president would offer his vision or mission through the media to the citizenry, who would take the vision, internalize it, and then reflect their manufactured will back onto the president. In this way, the executive grew beyond its narrowly defined role and came to define the very reality of the country.

Ever aware of this dynamic, Jackson amplified the relationship to the point of zealotry. His mythological placement as Champion of the People created a state in which his battles and quests were imprinted upon American citizens and reflected in their day-to-day lives. Jackson's presidency changed the destiny of America by creating a faux populism in which politicians had to mythologize themselves to capture the public's imagination, but he also stirred within them a religious fervor of white, Christian nationalism that inspired the conquering of the North American continent.

In the American Myth, this crusade would come to be called manifest destiny and be portrayed as an adventure across the map by brave men and women who staked their claim to the beautiful western frontier and came to define America by their courage, determination, and rugged individualism. It is most often recalled as a bloodless and noble pursuit, a point of pride and the very definition of American exceptionalism, and the romantic and fictionalized stories are still the foundation of folklore and pop culture to this very day.

But manifest destiny, as concept and practice, was deeply steeped in the tenets of white supremacy, particularly as it came on the heels of the Romantic movement in Britain and Germany. The Romantic movement was characterized by lush imagery in its literature and art, an emphasis on natural spaces like the plains, and a fascination with the past, particularly the Middle Ages. This interest in the Middle Ages cultivated pride in and glorification of the different ethnic tribes that settled Europe and established the major powers. In Germany, it would lead to mythmaking that eventually inspired the National Socialist Party and its cult of Aryanism. In the United States, it elevated the American people to the guardians of Western civilization, the pinnacle of the Anglo-Saxon race, and, by their ethnic superiority, the inheritors of the world.

To bolster this belief, America became obsessed with pseudo-science that proved its theory of racial superiority, including the quack science of phrenology and a rogue form of history and archaeology that claimed the white race had originally settled the continent of America. This bizarre story had its roots in the myth of the "Mound Builders," a so-called lost people who left behind strange mounds and structures in parts of the country. The discovery of these works so impressed Americans in the nineteenth century that they refused to believe Native Americans capable of such feats and reasoned that obviously an Aryan people had first settled the continent, only to be overthrown by the "savage" race of Native Americans.

Among the first critics of this baseless, ignorant theory was Thomas Jefferson, who had excavated one of the mounds himself in 1784 and declared it of Native American origin, but the myth of Aryan Mound Builders continued as it was "comforting to conquerors" who wished to see Native Americans as "intruders who had brutally shattered the glorious old . . . civilization."[29]

In Andrew Jackson's 1830 State of the Union, as he argued for the forcible removal of Native American tribes, he bizarrely cited "the monuments and fortresses of an unknown people, spread over the extensive regions of the West," who had been "exterminated or had disappeared to make room for the existing savage tribes."[30] In this alternate reality, the Native American genocide might be excused as repayment for a previous, imagined eradication, this one having been perpetrated against a mythic Caucasian race.

Jackson's story cast the United States as the executors of redemption, a nation of great people who, like the mythical Jackson, had risen from nothing, armed with only their superior sense of intellect, morality, and historical drive, to create an awe-inspiring society—people tasked to go forth and conquer the West as a means of redeeming their ancestors who had been so obscenely interrupted.

This myth found its way into the art and literature of the day, perhaps most notably in William Cullen Bryant's famous poem "The Prairies," a work of Romanticism documenting the seductive call of the West and the need for Americans to reclaim their destiny after a band of Natives decimated the true Mound Builders.[31] From this ruin, however, Bryant dreamed he could hear the approach of Western civilization to redeem the land, a call echoed by his contemporaries in their poems and works.

Powering the literature and zeitgeist of the time was the same idealization of the individual that had inspired the transcendentalists to see God in every person. The works lionized the American as a noble hero of the ages who would, through his ingenuity, pluck, and determination, tame the wild frontier and spread across the world their example of rugged individualism.

That literature helped to define the age of manifest destiny in the annals of history that served the American Myth, but the racial motivations and reasoning are largely cast aside. A glimpse at the conversations of the time reveals disturbing white supremacy fueling the movement. In the pages of *The New York Herald* it was said that "all other races . . . must bow and fade" before "the great work of subjugation and conquest to be achieved by the Anglo-Saxon race."[32] George Bancroft, the historian who created so much of the American

Myth, "maintained that through the United States the Anglo-Saxons had a special Providential destiny to fulfill" and wrote from Europe that England was "beginning to see 'the inevitable necessity which appropriates all North America to the Anglo-Saxon Race.'"

Thomas Hart Benton, who authored the first Homestead Act, which granted land to western settlers, and served as one of the architects of expansion, reasoned the march west was the destiny of "the children of Adam" who had always shown a disposition "to follow the sun."[33] Ever the proponent of expansion westward, Benton spoke to the National Railroad Convention in 1849 and advocated what he called "the Iron Road," or a massive project of interconnected railroads that tamed the country to the whims of the Caucasian race. To commemorate that conquering, Benton proposed a towering statue of Christopher Columbus hewn from the peak of the Rocky Mountains that would "point with outstretched arm to the western horizon."[34]

Also gesturing to the west was the Democratic Party, which had capitalized on Andrew Jackson's popularity and myth and established itself as the dominant political force inside the United States. As one of their main organs of communication and propaganda, and one of their intellectual havens, *The United States Magazine and Democratic Review* published essays, art, and poetry forwarding the concept of Jacksonian Democracy, many penned by founder John O'Sullivan, a man who, in the very near future, would "lecture on the value of negro slavery" and eventually support the Confederate States of America.[35]

Before O'Sullivan betrayed his country, however, in 1839 he penned his essay "The Great Nation of Futurity," which laid the groundwork for the concept of manifest destiny. Using the language and style of Romanticism, O'Sullivan claimed America's "national birth was the beginning of a new history" and the American people were "destined to manifest to mankind the excellence of divine principles." Again, the Democratic Party had taken the ideology of white supremacy and cast it in the light of divine right and inspiration. For the purposes of the party and the country, the conquering of the West meant the carrying out of the prophecy of a racist God's will.

Camouflaging the white supremacist thought at the heart of that drive could only do so much. O'Sullivan also pontificated over the issue of slavery and attempted to rationalize the *Democratic Review's* indefinite stance on the subject. He framed slavery as "unquestionably one of the most difficult of the various social problems" but wondered if it wasn't better for slaves to continue in bondage, where at least they might be protected by a superior race of masters.[36]

Though O'Sullivan and the Democratic Party could not say for certain whether the slaves should be freed or whether it was in their best interest to remain in bondage, they were certain of the destiny of the white race. Of Mexico, he wrote, "The Anglo-Saxon foot is already on its borders. Already the advance guard of the irresistible army of Anglo-Saxon emigration has begun to pour down upon it, armed with the plough and the rifle."[37]

That "irresistible army" of Anglo-Saxons was on the march, and O'Sullivan was correct that Mexico would soon feel its wrath. He was also eerily correct in another prediction that, within one hundred years, the American empire would expand and dominate the world, a prediction that bizarrely coincided with the exact end of World War II and America's growing sphere of influence.[38]

In order to conquer the world, however, America first had to subdue its continent. In 1846, the *Democratic Review* explained it was America's destiny to conquer its southern neighbor Mexico as well as its people, writing, "*Race* is the key to much that seems obscure in the history of nations. Throughout the world, the spectacle is everywhere the same, of the white race ruling the less, through all graduations of color, from the fairest European to the darkest African."[39]

Ready to lead that charge was James K. Polk, a president who had been relatively unknown when he'd received the Democratic Party's nomination two years earlier in 1844. Polk was Andrew Jackson's man, and Jackson still retained control over the party. Like Jackson, Polk was a wealthy slave owner who wasn't "averse to the use of corporal punishment with his slaves" and believed "the domination of white over black was part of God's plan." Also like Jackson, Polk wasn't afraid of being "underhanded and devious," because he too believed "that the president, as the only federal office-holder elected by all the people, was their true representative."[40]

Determined to carry out his agenda in just one term, Polk told George Bancroft, the historian who would serve as his secretary of the navy, that his priorities heading into office were largely based on expansion of territory: the settling of the "joint occupation of Oregon with Britain" and the acquisition of California and a "large district on the coast."[41] To accomplish these goals in just four years, Polk chose to accelerate matters artificially, a hastening he carried out by flexing his military might.

In Oregon, he more or less challenged England to wage war, a conflict that escalated as scores of American settlers poured into the territory. At one point, a British naval force collected off the Oregonian coast and battle seemed inevitable. Cooler heads prevailed, though, and a treaty was reached in the summer of 1846.

Avoidance of war proved impossible in the case of Polk's second priority, as Polk "tried bribery, purchase, and intrigue" to acquire territory from Mexico "before reluctantly deciding the stubborn Mexicans could be convinced only by force."[42]

To facilitate the acquirement of that territory, Polk instructed General Zachary Taylor, his eventual successor, to "approach as near the boundary line, the Rio Grande, as prudence will dictate" and told him if he "deemed it advisable he was to attack first and not wait to be attacked."[43] The message to Polk's ministers and agents was to support uprisings in Mexican territory and to prepare to plunder their land in case of the outbreak of war. Polk even negotiated with deposed Mexican general Santa Anna, who agreed, in exchange for passage back to his country and the opportunity to rule, to sell land at a favorable price—though Santa Anna reneged on his agreement upon returning to power and led the Mexican war effort.

In these acts, Polk foreshadowed nearly every American war and international interference moving forward. He created an environment in which the United States might provoke an attack to justify war, and in this case create the illusion of an attack. He instigated unrest in a sovereign nation to strategically benefit US interests. And, in the strange case of Santa Anna, the United States aided a despotic strongman whose policies and actions would hurt his people and suppress democracy and freedom, and, as would be the case time and again, it would see that strongman betray its confidence.

Of the provocation of war, Colonel Ethan Allen Hitchcock, serving under General Taylor, wrote in his diary, "We have not one particle of right to be here . . . It looks as if the government sent a small force on purpose to bring on a war, so as to have pretext for taking California and as much of this country as it chooses."[44] Colonel Hitchcock's suspicion proved correct as Polk grew tired of waiting on Mexico to take his bait and planned on declaring war regardless, telling his cabinet he didn't need an attack to declare. Bancroft cautioned Polk, telling him to wait until Mexico "committed an act of aggression," advice that Polk dismissed as he prepared to immediately announce war.[45]

Ironically enough, Polk was granted his wish as he received word that very day that Mexico had fired upon his forces. It didn't matter that the location of the incident was in dispute or that Mexico didn't recognize the land as belonging to the United States; it was the opening Polk needed. "After reiterated menaces," he declared, "Mexico has passed the boundary of the United States, has invaded our territory and shed American blood upon American soil. She has proclaimed that hostilities have commenced and that the two nations are now at war."[46]

To further his agenda, Polk relied on loyal Democratic presses, including the *Democratic Review* and *The Washington Union,* a publication Polk maintained favor with by leaking exclusives regarding his speeches and news from the war front, an exchange that ensured the papers granted Polk room to formally rebuff his opponents and promote his policies.[47] He called other papers, published in the favor and at the expense of opposing political parties, "traitors to their country."[48]

Though newspapers had largely been party affiliated and financed, the nineteenth century saw the rise of the so-called penny press as the 1830 invention of the steam printing press decreased publishing costs. These publications were written with the working-class American in mind, and their revenue originated from advertisements, so their stories were more salacious.

They found, with the outbreak of hostilities with Mexico, that the public had an insatiable hunger for coverage of war, the spectacles of which the people had "an almost irresistible fascination" for.[49] The penny press covered the Mexican–American War with a breathless style that painted the day-to-day triumphs as passion plays. This lust for information prompted the expansion of the telegraph system and the eventual founding of the Associated Press, which pooled efforts to better feed the public's addiction.

In this conflict, as it was mythologized by the coverage of the day, the American people now had a crusade behind which they could throw their weight, a testament to their might and, in their dominance, proof of the existence of a god who had chosen them to be its divine people. Their populist fervor, born of Jefferson's message of the individual and the romanticism of white supremacy, was playing out on the world stage before their very eyes.

That play existed in the black and white of their newspapers, but also in traveling shows profiting off the popularity of the war. There were circuses that re-created battles, massive productions that attempted to bring the hostilities to the people, mass-produced novels glamorizing war, and the panorama, an early precursor of what would become motion pictures. Panoramas were compelling and innovative, using flipping pictures to create the illusion of movement, including a spectacular program in St. Louis called "The Sacred Panorama, Dissolving Scenes and the Bombardment of Vera Cruz." It featured depictions of the Garden of Eden, the Biblical Flood, and a "Midnight Mass in Rome," all of it building to the apocalyptic climax of the siege of Veracruz, a Mexican beachhead captured by the United States in 1847.[50]

The Siege of Veracruz might have looked like a glorious victory for those audiences, but the story on the ground was another matter. For forty-eight hours straight, American forces shelled the city, "smashing homes, churches, and schools indiscriminately."[51] Despite repeated calls to evacuate, the barrage continued unabated, killing, in Mexico's estimate, upwards of five hundred civilians. When American forces eventually gained entry, they rioted, set fire to a settlement, looted, and raped.[52]

All the same, the public ate up the easy good-vs.-evil narrative around the conquering of the North American continent. The American people could see themselves as the manifestation of the moral direction of the universe, their wars and actions justified at all times by their inherent and inalienable rights to everything they might covet.

Following the Mexican–American War, the debate over whether to annex parts of Mexican territory or the entirety of the country revealed deep and toxic motivations. Politicians spoke openly and derisively about the Mexican people, as well as which races were capable of self-governance and which were destined to be owned and lorded over. Though Christian charity and the concept of benevolent empire continued to tinge the conversations, the nation had already strayed from its benign principles. Its politicians and citizens, however, excited by military victories and apparent dominance, cheered on the craven expansion.

The remaining debate centered around race and white supremacy as James Buchanan, then President James K. Polk's secretary of state, prized the racial purity of the United States over the potential for maximal expansion. He advocated only annexing portions of the territory already settled by Americans, asking of Mexico proper, "How should we govern the mongrel race which inhabits it? Could we admit them to seats in our Senate & House of Representatives? Are they capable of Self-Government as States of this Confederacy?"[53]

Representative Jacob Collamer of Vermont warned that by bringing Mexicans into the Union "we should destroy our own nationality . . . We shall cease to be the people that we were; we cease to be the Saxon Americanized." His colleague Edward Cabell of Florida shared his skepticism and asked, "Shall we . . . by an act of Congress, convert the black, white, red, mongrel, miserable population of Mexico . . . into free and enlightened American citizens, entitled to all the privileges which we enjoy?"

Perhaps the most boisterous and memorable opposition to Mexican annexation came from John C. Calhoun of South Carolina, a two-time vice president who had served under both John Quincy Adams and Andrew Jackson and was one of the most powerful senators at the time. An avowed white supremacist, Calhoun took the floor on January 4, 1848, and declared, "Ours, sir, is a Government of the white race. The greatest misfortunes of Spanish America are to be traced to the fatal error of placing these colored races on an equality with the white race."[54] Calhoun warned it was a "great mistake . . . when we suppose that all people are capable of self-government," maintaining that America's form of government and freedom were dependent on the rarefied intelligence and capability of its white citizens.

Calhoun's diatribe presaged even more coming horrors. America's manifest destiny had been propelled by delusions of grandeur and the worship of white supremacy, but the expansion itself continued to lay bare the divisions that would undermine the Union and Constitution. Each new territory and conquest brought to the forefront the contradictions of America's principles and actions, as well as the interminable debates over race and slavery. The endurance of the country, which Calhoun sought by maintaining white supremacy, would be seriously threatened by that very philosophy in just a few short years.

CHAPTER 3

* * *

A Nation Washed in Blood

To mark the seventy-eighth anniversary of the signing of the Declaration of Independence, ten thousand abolitionists flooded into Framingham, Massachusetts, on July 4, 1854. Their rally came on the heels of the removal of escaped slave Anthony Burns, who had been returned the month before to his Virginian master under the Fugitive Slave Act of 1850. The event had been the focus of much debate and protest, and as Burns had been led to a ship destined to return him to bondage, the scene was like a funeral for the United States, with "buildings draped in black with the American flag hanging upside down and church bells tolling a dirge to liberty."[1]

At the rally, speakers orated to a sweating, frustrated crowd about a country that had lost its moral authority. Behind them were more flags, some swathed in funereal black and others condemning villainous Virginia and urging the redemption of Massachusetts. William Lloyd Garrison, publisher of the influential antislavery paper *The Liberator*, took the stage and spoke passionately about the need for abolition. To the delight of the crowd, he brandished a copy of the Fugitive Slave Act and lit it on fire. After it had been reduced to ash, Garrison presented the Constitution of the United States of America, calling it the "parent of all atrocities" and a "covenant with death. An agreement with hell."[2] Garrison set the Constitution aflame, and as it burned he proclaimed, "So perish all compromises with tyranny! And let the people say Amen."

It had been that covenant with death that had troubled the nation since its authoring in 1787. Whether it was the disgusting Missouri Compromise or the disastrous Kansas–Nebraska Act of 1854, ill-fated workarounds that irresponsibly kicked the question of slavery down the road, the country had frantically tried one haphazard measure after another to avoid confronting America's original sin. Nearly a century earlier, James Madison and his Northern colleagues had been so desperate to avoid economic revolution they had indeed forged an agreement with hell. It was destined to fail, but in the meantime it had damned millions of men, women, and children to brutal slavery and had ensured an instability in their republic that would always end in apocalyptic violence.

The American Myth of manifest destiny is told as a triumphant race to the west but was instead a fevered run from the inevitable disaster of that original compromise, the consequences constantly nipping at the nation's heels. With every new state, there came fresh debate as to whether it would be admitted to the Union as free or slave, the precarious balance of power established by the Founders always near collapse. Determined to maintain the control over the federal government it had won by holding up the Philadelphia Convention, the South battled to spread slavery into the new territories. The North, less concerned with African-American freedom than promoting industrial labor and keeping their states devoid of freed black people, sought to keep slavery confined to east of the Mississippi.

Under this system, the American government became entirely obsessed with the battle between the regions, so much so that Northerners and Southerners began seeing themselves as separate peoples, a splitting of the Noble Lie that all Americans were united by their shared identity. There grew to be two competing Noble Lies, both founded on fraudulent narratives and both reliant on regional and economic identities.

Perhaps nowhere was this divide more evident in the middle of the nineteenth century than in the halls of Congress, where the business of the day became ideological warfare, transforming "political action from a process of accommodation to a mode of combat."[3] The South had long dominated the legislative process, particularly via the Democratic Party's formidable majority, and to aid their agenda they relied on outright intimidation and violence. They brandished knives, pulled guns on their rivals, fought fatal duels, flipped tables, and in one case took up a spittoon as a means to brain someone, all of it to terrorize any Northern representatives who dared speak against slavery.

For the most part, the North capitulated to this bullying until the rise of the Republicans in the 1850s produced a new type of Northern politician who was more than ready to fight if necessary. Picking up the pieces of past failed parties, this iteration of the Republican Party built a national base on their willingness to challenge the old order, branding themselves as an avowedly regional party concerned chiefly with furthering Northern interests.

The violence of this era is staggering and its history littered with fistfights, coercion, insults, and menaces, including Representative John Dawson of Louisiana's threat to cut an opponent "from ear to ear."[4] In 1838, Representative William J. Graves of Kentucky shot and killed Representative Jonathan Cilley in a duel outside of Washington, DC. In 1856, Representative Preston Brooks of South Carolina infamously beat Senator Charles Sumner of Massachusetts bloody on the floor of the Senate and only stopped when his cane shattered. Representative Laurence Keitt of South Carolina, who had previously aided in Graves's assault, led "battalions" of Southern representatives against his Northern colleagues in 1858 after Representative Galusha Grow of Pennsylvania delivered a passionate speech against slavery.[5] The resulting riot on the floor seemed destined to turn fatal until Representative William Barksdale of Mississippi was hit with an errant punch and his hairpiece fell off, the battle ending as the feuding men erupted in laughter.

This violent sectionalism was fueled by the economic battles of the time but was also the result of the growing influence of media. Newspapers flooded the country, and the dramas of the nation's capital were just as popular with readers as stories from the front of the Mexican–American War had been. The nineteenth century was a "great age of speechifying" where "oratory was a popular form of entertainment," and members of Congress and aspiring politicians won popularity and renown based on their ability to give long and rousing speeches that excited the electorate.[6] Politicians searched the pages of the newspapers to see if their latest speech or grandstanding had received any ink, and certainly factored their press coverage into their political movements and resulting rhetoric. In this way, newspaper publishers became a constituency all their own, a class of economically motivated peoples from whom representatives sought favor.

In this environment, America's politicians began to act like fictional characters that competed over the attention of the nation. The fights in Congress were the stuff of popular entertainment, a means by which a politician could establish himself as a warrior in the mold of Andrew Jackson, ready to fight for his state, his purpose, and his people. The Noble Lie uniting Americans lost its luster. They saw themselves as Republicans and Democrats, Northerners and Southerners, their newspapers and magazines furthering those differences by relying on sensational stories of violence and intrigue, selling the people's suspicions and worst instincts back to them.

In the South, distrust and paranoia grew that this new breed of Northern politician meant to overtake their dominance and eventually abolish slavery altogether, a worry largely unfounded, as the majority of the Republican Party meant only to oppose the expansion of slavery into the West. Though the narrative at the time, and that survives to this day, was that the Republicans meant to bring down the institution, the truth is that the divide between North and South wasn't a difference of opinion regarding African-American equality. Still, changing demographics and population disparity showed the upending of the Democratic majority and Southern power as an inevitability, and from this fact sprung a constant stream of conspiracy theories as to machinations against the South and the institution of slavery, most of them flowing through the Southern press.

These conspiracy theories emerged from the discord in Congress, but also from the growing abolitionist fervor in the North. While abolitionists waited for their politicians to fight the good battle, they also took matters into their own hands. They published their own newspapers that railed against not only expansion but the institution of slavery itself. People like Harriet Tubman and Elizabeth Rous Comstock risked their lives and safety in forming subversive networks like the Underground Railroad that rejected unjust laws and assisted African Americans in escaping the South. And, in the instance of John Brown, they attempted to purge the country of the sin of slavery by means of violence.

Much as the transcendentalists had held that the will of God flowed through the individual, John Brown believed himself touched by the divine and tasked with eradicating human bondage. One night, after reading his Bible, he rose from his study and told his wife and children "he knew it to be his duty . . . to make war on slavery."[7] Brown took this charge seriously and led a small army of men into Kansas during the border crisis of 1856, a limited civil war in its own right over the institution of slavery. They brutally hacked five slave owners to death in the middle of the night, setting off a bloody conflict foreshadowing the coming Civil War.

Three years later, still believing himself to be an instrument in the hands of God, Brown and his men moved into Virginia with a plan to bring slavery to an end. They intended to capture a federal arsenal in Harpers Ferry as a signal to the nation's slaves to rise up and fight a new American revolution. Brown successfully captured the arsenal, but the revolution never materialized. A battalion helmed by Robert E. Lee overtook Brown and he was found guilty of treason, a verdict Brown met by stating that he would have been lauded had his efforts benefited the powerful and the wealthy but maintaining should he have to give his life "for the furtherance of the ends of justice," he was more than willing to do so.[8]

After Brown was hanged, abolitionists mourned him as a martyr. "Church bells tolled, black bunting was hung out, minute guns were fired, prayer meetings assembled, and memorial resolutions were adopted," and in the days to come "lithographs of Brown circulated in vast numbers, subscriptions were organized . . . immense memorial meetings took place in New York, Boston, and Philadelphia."[9] His death galvanized the abolitionists as prominent figures eulogized him and stoked his legacy.

Ralph Waldo Emerson described Brown as "the Saint, whose fate yet hangs in suspense, but whose martyrdom, if it shall be perfected, will make the gallows as glorious as the cross."[10] Henry David Thoreau invoked the idealized memory of the American Revolution to eulogize Brown, saying, "He was like the best of those who stood at Concord Bridge once, on Lexington Common, and on Bunker Hill, only he was firmer and higher principled than any that I have chanced to hear of as there."[11] Clergyman George B. Cheever championed Brown's claim of divine inspiration, declaring, "Manifestly, God was with him."

William Lloyd Garrison, who burned the Constitution in 1854, saw Brown as a martyr and compared him to George Washington, even insisting that the general and first president had never presented "such exalted traits of character as John Brown."[12] On the night of Brown's death, Garrison answered critics who warned any attempt to free the slaves would trouble the Union by asking, "As for the Union—where is it and what is it? . . . I tell you our work is the dissolution of this slavery-cursed Union . . . There can be no union between us."[13] For Garrison, the dissolution would break slavery's back and then, in its place, "God [would] make it possible for us to form a true, vital, enduring, all-embracing Union."[14]

In this rhetoric the South saw damning validation of their paranoia, a paranoia that had grown worse when, following Brown's arrest, he was found to be in possession of letters and resources from the so-called Secret Six, a collection of affluent and influential Northerners who sought to abolish slavery and assisted Brown's quest to incite an uprising of slaves across the region. Rumors ran rampant that there were more John Browns to come and that the slave population was hoarding weapons and poison as they "plotted murder and mayhem."[15] Radical Southerners called Fire-Eaters busied themselves fanning the flames of secessionist thought by peddling conspiracy theories and implanting in the public imagination the idea of an independent country where Southerners could rule themselves and their society of agrarian oppression would continue in perpetuity.

As regionalist tensions rose, the 1860 Democratic Convention was an inevitable disaster. Following tense debate and widespread mistrust, the party split into rival factions. The Democratic Party, which had dominated American politics since Thomas Jefferson's Revolution of 1800, had splintered in what seemed to be an irrevocable divorce, and when the dust settled the Democrats fielded two separate presidential candidates and effectively split their votes. The object of their ire was Republican candidate Abraham Lincoln, and despite his absence on the ballots in Alabama, Arkansas, Florida, Georgia, Louisiana, Mississippi, North Carolina, South Carolina, Tennessee, and Texas—every future member of the Confederate States of America save for Virginia, where he received roughly 1 percent of the vote—Lincoln easily won the contest.

The South had been outpaced in terms of population and support, meaning the dominance it had enjoyed since the concessions of the Philadelphia Convention had come to an end and the government, for the foreseeable future, was likely to favor opposing interests. As has been the case throughout history, a dominant group faced with losing power combatted their new reality by embracing fascism and discarding established institutions in favor of new ones guaranteeing continued dominance.

On December 20, 1860, South Carolina, seeing their disproportionate influence waning, finally made good on generations' worth of threats and seceded from the Union. Hundreds of thousands of Americans died because of that treason, and the trajectory of the country and its story changed forever.

★

Though future biased historians and Southern apologists have insisted that secession was spurred by an interest in states' rights, the formation of the Confederate States of America was firmly and explicitly rooted in the protection of slavery and was a racist, dystopian nightmare.

In framing their own constitution, the Confederacy produced a document "identical in format and nearly so in content" to the one written in 1787, the main difference being the explicit enshrinement of slavery.[16] And if there was any doubt on the matter, Alexander Stephens, the vice president of the Confederacy, would put it to bed. He explained the new nation's purpose, as well as the intention of the Constitution, in a speech in Savannah, Georgia, in 1861, where he claimed the Confederate constitution "put at rest *forever* all the agitating questions relating to . . . the proper status of the negro in our form of civilization."[17] Stephens asserted, "Our new government . . . its foundations are laid, its cornerstone rests, upon the great truth that the negro is not equal to the white man; that slavery, subordination to the superior race, is his natural and moral condition."

The Noble Lie of the Confederate States, the new narrative that competed with the American Noble Lie, was that the South recognized an undeniable truth in the inequality of the races and that the North had violated the contract of the Constitution. Confederate president Jefferson Davis maintained that the new nation illustrated "the American idea that governments rest upon the consent of the governed, and that it is the right of the people to alter or abolish governments whenever they become destructive of the ends for which they were established" and that the Confederacy embodied Jefferson's belief in perpetual revolution and "merely asserted a right which the Declaration of Independence of 1776 had defined to be inalienable."[18]

In his second inaugural, Davis doubled down on the Confederacy's claim to the American identity when he spoke at the feet of a statue of George Washington on the first president's birthday. He cited the Founders' fear of "despotism of numbers," saying the Confederate States of America had been founded "under the favor of Divine Providence" and to "perpetuate the principles of our revolutionary fathers."[19]

These ideas, the claiming of Revolutionary heritage and that God favored slavery, were foundations for the Confederacy. The American Revolution's casting off of tyranny was emphasized as "the defining moment of their past" and it was argued that "those who will hesitate to fly to arms at such a momentous crisis cannot be the legitimate descendants of the brave and chivalrous race of '76."[20] Washington, in particular, was a hero to them, and appeared on postage stamps and their great seal.[21]

Their motto was *Deo Vindice*, or "With an avenging God," and the religious leaders of the Confederacy preached the Confederacy's righteousness. Reverend Benjamin M. Palmer spoke of a duty, to themselves, their slaves, and God, to "preserve and transmit [their] existing system of domestic servitude, with the right, unchallenged by man, to go and root itself wherever Providence and nature may carry it."[22] Robert Lewis Dabney pointed to the scripture as proof that slavery was "appointed by God as the punishment of, and remedy for . . . the peculiar moral degradation of a part of the human race."[23]

So great was the Confederate belief that God favored them and their crusade to enslave African Americans that when the rebellion was troubled, the Southern people believed Providence was testing their faith. Regularly the government and governors called on the population to observe days of atonement and confession. In January 1865, as the cause seemed all but lost, President Davis declared a day of "fasting, humiliation, and prayer" and urged the Confederate citizenry to lower themselves in an effort to implore "His divine help."[24]

In theory and practice, the Confederacy was Jefferson's agrarian vision put into action. The South, like Jefferson, despised the industrial order of the North and intended to effectively pause the progress of history and maintain an obsolete society. The Confederates wanted to continue producing cash crops, particularly cotton, and supply the world's industrial nations while preserving the antiquated plantation existence and culture of human bondage the region's economic elite had come to cherish.

Though it is often painted as a universal action, and celebrated by Confederate apologists as a regional identity, the rebellion wasn't unanimous or particularly populist. The planting elite, the center of all power in the nineteenth-century South, spurred the secession of the Southern states, but most Southerners didn't own slaves. The institution itself was a means by which enslaved labor could be used to keep in place a stark class divide while ensuring continued social harmony. The very existence of slaves meant a class of people existed for poor whites in the South to feel superior to. As Georgia governor Joseph Brown explained, "Among us the poor white laborer . . . does not belong to the menial class. The negro is in no sense his equal . . . He belongs to the only true aristocracy, the race of [white men]."[25] Or, as James P. Holcombe, a wealthy slaveholder, so plainly put it, "African slavery reconciles the antagonism of the classes that has elsewhere reduced the highest statesmanship to the verge of despair, and becomes the great Peace-maker of our society."[26]

In this way, the Confederacy in its construction echoed the

Madisonian founding of the United States of America and took on its means of hierarchical control and the American Myth for its own purposes.

For the wealthy planting elite of the South, the survival of slavery was necessary for their continued economic and political supremacy. By the time of the Civil War, they were severely outnumbered by their own slaves, and the prospect of retribution terrified them. To solve this problem, they created the myth of the Confederacy and put into action a new society that would, in theory, never result in their overthrow. To calm the working-class population that died and suffered as cannon fodder in the Civil War, they pushed Southern identity and nationalism for a nation without a past. To continue this in perpetuity, the Southern educational system focused on creating in its population ceaseless subordination, the children's books and materials studded with commands like "I must not speak evil of the rulers of my land."[27]

Though the Confederacy was founded as a means to protect the Southern elite through the protection of slavery, the South's fear of Lincoln's presidency was misplaced. Lincoln had never advocated outright abolition or made it a priority of his administration. Lincoln's opposition to the South's seceding was anchored in preserving the Union, not in a moral or philosophical crusade.

The American Myth, a story told by people looking to earnestly believe in the goodness of the country and wielded by those looking to take advantage of that belief, has managed to take this time period and construct from it an easily digestible narrative of redemption. In it, the North fights to abolish slavery and Lincoln, the Great Emancipator, benevolently frees the slaves and guides the way to a better future. But the North was arguably just as racist as the South, with an array of laws that prevented African Americans from settling in their areas and being afforded opportunities to buy homes or land or find gainful employment or education. The Northern states made sure to "discourage black emigration by law and custom," and in the

North black people suffered "daily discrimination."[28] Northerners believed "the system of slavery had stunted them" and the prospect of freeing them filled some Northerners with terror that freedom would, as historian Heather Cox Richardson elucidated, "bring swarms of bestial ex-slaves . . . to prey on white men's jobs and daughters."[29]

All efforts were made by the government to reassure the South that Republicans and Lincoln had no intention of abolishing human slavery. Republicans promised to carry out the Fugitive Slave Act and swore they would not attack the institution as they wished only to stop its expansion. Before Lincoln was inaugurated, the government raced to stave off secession by radical measures, including offers to alter the Constitution to ensure slavery's existence. Lincoln himself, two days after South Carolina's secession, wrote to Confederate vice president Alexander Stephens: "Do the people of the South really entertain fears that a Republican administration would, *directly, or indirectly*, interfere with their slaves, or with them, about their slaves? If they do, I wish to assure you . . . that there is no cause for such fears."[30]

In an address to Congress, Lincoln explicitly argued the North's cause was to preserve the Union as a means of upholding the debt accrued by the South in removing "aboriginal tribes" and the genocide of the Native Americans.[31] He said the Union's survival was a matter of fairness: "Is it just either that creditors shall go unpaid or the remaining States pay the whole? . . . If one State may secede, so may another; and when all shall have seceded, none is left to pay the debts. Is this quite just to creditors?"

If the South were to be allowed to leave the Union when membership to the Union no longer suited it, Lincoln believed, then there would be no end to secession. Predicated on agreements between the states and the federal government, the Union would unwind and the federal government would likely cease to exist. The opposition to secession was rooted in a desperate need to maintain governmental power and stave off a philosophy in which the Noble Lie could be overthrown. It wasn't the most compelling argument, and its basis was coldly pragmatic at best, but Lincoln maintained that his goal was to save the Union until a better narrative proved necessary.

Lincoln's first inaugural address in 1861, in which he appealed to the Southern states, a number of which had already seceded, by saying, "We are not enemies, but friends," and ended with an appeal to better angels, was so uninspiring and disappointing to abolitionists that many believed Lincoln to be a lost cause. Frederick Douglass lambasted the performance, writing that Lincoln had announced "his complete loyalty to slavery in the slave States" and that his insistence on failing to oppose slavery was "wholly discreditable to the head and the heart of Mr. Lincoln." In Lincoln, Douglass saw a president "prostrating himself before the foul and withering curse of slavery."[32]

The most charitable way to describe Lincoln's thoughts on race and emancipation would be "evolving." In an 1854 speech in Peoria, Illinois, Lincoln had referred to slavery as "monstrous" but admitted:

> If all earthly power were given to me, I should not know what to do, as to the existing institution. My first impulse would be to free all the slaves, and send them to Liberia,—to their own native land. But . . . free them, and make them politically and socially our equals? My own feelings will not admit of this; and if mine would, we well know that those of the great mass of white people will not.[33]

As late as 1858, in the fourth joint debate with his rival Stephen Douglas, Lincoln had attempted to ease worries that he was an abolitionist by assuring a crowd:

> I will say, then, that I am not, nor ever have been, in favor of bringing about in any way the social and political equality of the white and black races; that I am not, nor ever have been, in favor of making voters or jurors of negroes, nor of

qualifying them to hold office, nor to intermarry with white people; and I will say, in addition to this, that there is a physical difference between the white and black races which I believe will forever forbid the two races living together on terms of social and political equality. And inasmuch as they cannot so live, while they do remain together there must be the position of superior and inferior, and I as much as any other man am in favor of having the superior position assigned to the white race.[34]

When Lincoln was elected in 1860, he was possessed of "moral indifference and ignorance about emancipation" and it would not crystallize for him as an option until it was deemed as a "military necessity absolutely essential for the salvation of the Union."[35] In a well-known open letter to the *New York Tribune* on August 24, 1862, Lincoln answered the paper's editor Horace Greeley's call for emancipation:

I would save the Union. I would save it the shortest way under the Constitution. The sooner the national authority can be restored the nearer the Union will be "the Union as it was." If there be those who would not save the Union unless they could at the same time save Slavery, I do not agree with them . . . My paramount object in this struggle is to save the Union, and it is not either to save or destroy Slavery. If I could save the Union without freeing any slave, I would do it, and if I could save it by freeing all the slaves, I would do it, and if I could save it by freeing some and leaving others alone, I would also do that. What I do about Slavery and the colored race, I do because I believe it helps to save the Union.[36]

Four months later, on January 1, 1863, Lincoln issued the Emancipation Proclamation, a presidential order deemed "a fit and necessary war measure for suppressing said rebellion."[37] The proclamation was a piece of clever political imagination in which Lincoln accepted the South's definition of slaves as property, and seeing as the South was in a state of insurrection, he asserted his right to take that property from them. The act itself was rather toothless, as there was no means by which it could be instantly enforced. It only applied to the states that had seceded, making sure to leave the precious border states' slaves alone so as not to worsen the crisis. But Lincoln's action effectively changed the story of the war to one of good and evil, and ensured that the North would be cast as the conflict's protagonist.

This metamorphosis reinvigorated the cause, allowed freed African Americans to join the army, and ensured that foreign nations would stay uninvolved. The document's purpose was, as W. E. B. DuBois said, "designed to make easier the replacement of unwilling Northern white soldiers with black soldiers" and "put behind the war a new push toward Northern victory by the mighty impact of a great moral idea, both in the North and in Europe."[38]

After first reading the order to his cabinet, Lincoln was met with quiet before his attorney general Edward Bates broke the silence to sound his approval. He did have one concern, however: that the freed slaves be deported as soon as possible, as he was "fully convinced that the two races could not live and thrive in social proximity."[39] Lincoln was of a similar mind.

Throughout his presidency, Lincoln worked to resolve the dilemma he posed to his general George Butler in 1865: "But what shall we do with the Negroes after they are free? . . . I can hardly believe that the South and North can live in peace unless we get rid of the Negroes."[40] Colonization of another country seemed the only answer for Lincoln, and to aid in this mission he called on Congress to extend "diplomatic recognition to Haiti and Liberia . . . to improve prospects for black emigration."[41] In a meeting with African-American leaders he implored them to sell the idea to their people, saying, "You and we are different races," and that the best result was "for [them] both, therefore, to be separated."[42] Lincoln was so dedicated to the idea of emigrating freed African Americans and ensuring an America for the white race alone that he "actively put it into operation on an experimental basis" and sent a "shipload of Negroes to an island off the coast of Haiti in 1863."[43] This half-baked experiment, however, proved to be a tragedy as the African Americans suffered disease and starved, the ones who survived being shipped back to America.

Still, Lincoln was so dedicated to seeing out the emigration and colonization of freed slaves that he worked with his commissioner of emigration James Mitchell and a British colonization agent to set up a scheme to send newly emancipated slaves to British Honduras. They would be "provided with acreage, dwellings, and tools to begin life anew as free agricultural laborers under the supervision of the British government."[44]

Lincoln failed to understand that many of the freed slaves saw themselves as Americans and wanted nothing more than a chance to live their lives as free men and women. To Lincoln, the United States of America belonged to the white race, a sentiment that had been in place since the United States of America came to exist.

A century and a half later, it's impossible to know what would have happened to African Americans and the United States had Lincoln lived through his second term and overseen the postwar nation. Perhaps his views on race might have continued to evolve and he would have made good on the hopes ascribed to him by future generations. Perhaps there could have been a great unifying under Lincoln, a period of reconciliation in which racial and economic differences would have been soothed and resolved in the same manner as the Union had been reunited. But there's no telling, as Lincoln was shot and killed in 1865 by Confederate sympathizer John Wilkes Booth just five days after Robert E. Lee surrendered to Ulysses S. Grant.

Lincoln's death was an unspeakable trauma for a country that had been overburdened by unspeakable traumas. The Northern states fell into a deep mourning with public exhibitions of sorrow, violence between supporters and critics, and a national push to construct meaning from the tragedy. The assassination had taken place on Good Friday, and so that Easter Sunday the fallen Lincoln stood next to Jesus Christ as a fellow godly martyr. Churches contrasted their spring flowers with "black fabric to cover railings and arches, chancel and altar, pulpit and organ, and placed portraits of the late president amid the myrtle, tea roses, and heliotrope."[45]

In the popular culture Lincoln was portrayed as a martyr who had died for the sins of the American people. In some works he was shown being crowned by angels. In others the specter of George Washington, seconded by saintly choruses playing harps and preparing Lincoln's crown, welcomed him into the paradise of heaven, creating a relationship between the two that mirrored God and Christ, the father and the savior. A popular piece of art displayed the bullet that had killed him under a microscope, revealing it to be guarded by the twin angels of God and Liberty, the all-knowing eye of the Divine watching over it, all under a banner reading "DEATH IS NOT DEATH; TIS BUT THE ENNOBLEMENT OF MORTAL MAN."

Eleven years to the day after his assassination, people gathered in Lincoln Park in Washington, DC, for the unveiling of a statue commemorating Lincoln's emancipation of the slave, and to mark the moment Frederick Douglass was asked to speak. Douglass called Lincoln "the first martyr President of the United States," but reminded the crowd he was only a man, not a savior, and that any means of celebration should remember that fact lest something be lost.[46]

As a black man, Douglass told the assembled that Lincoln was "preeminently the white man's President" who was "ready and willing at any time during the first years of his administration to deny, postpone, and sacrifice the rights of humanity in the colored people to promote the welfare of the white people of this country . . .

"You are the children of Abraham Lincoln," he told the white crowd. "We are at best only his step-children; children by adoption, children by force of circumstances and necessity."[47]

Despite Douglass's reminder, Lincoln's death was especially useful for those seeking to bolster America's Noble Lie in the aftermath of the Civil War. The coincidence in timing—the Good Friday assassination, the Easter mourning—invited comparisons to Jesus. As a letter to *The New York Times* explained, "the two events have thus been providentially associated and therefore no human power can dissociate them," a relationship that gave Lincoln the title of "savior of his country."[48]

For America, Lincoln became a national messiah who piloted the ship of state through the storm of disunion and rectified the original sin of slavery, and in this new Christlike framing, Lincoln's personal failings were largely erased from memory in favor of this new myth that redeemed the American story. Slavery had been a mistake, racism a folly, but the American people, through much suffering and battle, had eradicated the practice. In doing so, they had readied the nation for the reunification of Revolutionary ideals and the practice of the Constitution; this new nation would be a place where people of every color would have equal opportunities. It was a convenient story, this fallen nation scrubbed clean of its sins by a baptism of blood.

★

During the war, in an effort to court favor among the border states and promote a unified front, Lincoln had run for reelection in 1864 under the banner of the National Union Party and chosen Andrew Johnson, a Democrat, as his running mate. Lincoln's assassination a year later meant the presidency was turned over to Johnson just as the war was ending, and the massive job of reunification and reconstruction fell under his incompetent guidance.

Johnson was among the worst people for the job. He was an avowed racist and saw Reconstruction as a moment to get past to reunite the country and ensure the growth of America's economy. He had unvarnished contempt for African Americans and eschewed the necessary work to ensure their social and political viability; instead, he focused on upending the aristocratic order of the South in favor of poor whites, whom he saw as victims of a conspiracy between the elite planters and their slaves.

In a notorious meeting in February of 1866, Johnson welcomed Frederick Douglass and a group of African-American delegates to Washington, DC, to discuss the prospect of black suffrage as a means to ensure their freedom and equality. Johnson listened to the congregation before lecturing them on what he saw as the reality of the black experience. Johnson got in Douglass's face and told him the true victims of the South were poor white laborers, accusing Douglass of playing a role in white subjugation. Johnson ended the meeting dismissing the need for black suffrage, citing the will of God: "I do not assume or pretend to be wiser than Providence or stronger than the laws of nature."

Once more, it was the opinion of the white and the powerful that God was undoubtedly on their side.

Johnson's opinion of the races and his vision for a post–Civil War America were made clear in his 1867 State of the Union. For Johnson, the problem was that while society had to reconfigure itself to allow for black freedom, to treat black Americans as equals or grant them rights as citizens would be not only imprudent but dangerous. He considered Southern whites a people who had been unnecessarily tormented by both the conflict and the prospect of equality of the races. According to Johnson, "The subjugation of the [Southern] States to negro domination would be worse than the military despotism under which they are now suffering." Measures enforcing racial equality amounted to "political privileges torn from white men."[49]

Johnson's guiding belief in Reconstruction was that "white men alone must manage the South."[50] To this end, Johnson named unabashed white supremacists as governors, including Florida governor

William Marvin, who advised African Americans to return to their plantations and "call [their] old Master[s]—'Master'" and lectured them, "You must not think because you are free as white people, that you are their equal, because you are not."[51] South Carolina's governor Benjamin Perry struck a similar tone, assuring the state: "This is a white man's government and intended for white men only."[52]

In this way, real Reconstruction was hobbled from the very beginning. The Republican Congress challenged Johnson continually, leading to extreme measures: Congress's override of his vetoes of civil rights bills, the establishment of the Freedmen's Bureau, and Johnson's impeachment in 1868. He survived conviction by a single vote, but the damage was done.

Following the 1866 midterm elections, Republicans took over Congress and set about the work of social revolution. They passed sweeping legislation intended to re-create the country and establish a just society for white and black people alike. To oversee this transformation, they reconstituted the military governorship of the South to protect African-American rights; passed the Fourteenth and Fifteenth Amendments, which guaranteed citizenship to all persons born or naturalized in the United States and voting rights regardless of "race, color, or previous condition of servitude"; and renewed the Freedmen's Bureau, an agency dedicated to assisting freed slaves that DuBois called "the most extraordinary and far-reaching institution of social uplift that America has ever attempted."[53]

With Johnson reined in and the playing field leveled, African Americans prospered in the post–Civil War era. At breathtaking speed, they built communities anchored by churches and dedicated to education and political organization. Many African Americans held seats in local, state, and national governments, including P. B. S. Pinchback of Louisiana, who served as the first black governor from 1872 to 1873. Contrary to notions that self-government was a skill belonging solely to the white race, freed African Americans showed incredible talent when given the opportunity.

Working against them, however, were the forces of traditional racism that had always plagued the South. In early Reconstruction, the process of readjustment had seen the old guard attempting to hold on to white supremacy at any cost, many of them determined to "restore slavery in substance, if not in name."[54] Racist politicians enacted "Black Codes," laws and regulations designed to manage the "savage passions of a people intoxicated with so called freedom," which closely mirrored the long-standing culture of slavery and black servitude.[55] As Edmund Rhett of South Carolina explained of his work in crafting his state's particular Black Codes, it was necessary to keep the freed slave "as near to his former condition as Law can keep him, that he should be kept as near to the condition of slavery as possible, and as far from the condition of the white man as is practicable."[56]

Under these laws, the criminal justice system became a weapon against the black population. Vagrancy laws held that an African American happened upon could be deprived of their freedom. Freed slaves could be returned to unfair servitude at a moment's notice. Black citizens were kept from voting; were forced to continually show proof of employment to the state, ensuring unfair contracts and relationships that benefited the white planting elite; and were made to marry lest they be punished or fined. And, in a particularly odious action, the children of African Americans could be possessed as "apprentices" by wealthy planters and placed in "legal" slavery.

When legislation failed to maintain white supremacy, the next alternative was violence. African Americans were murdered and beaten regularly. Agents of change and Republicans were publicly tortured and murdered by white supremacists as a warning to anyone daring to challenge the old order. To further this intimidation, the Ku Klux Klan formed in 1865 as a means of extralegal enforcement.[57] The Klan lynched black people; attacked their centers of community with political and economic terrorism, including churches and schools; and conducted an underground war meant to reestablish the white-dominated South, all the while enjoying mythical status among white Southerners.

In 1868, Ulysses S. Grant was elected president of the United States and immediately sided with Radical Republicans in Reconstruction. He used his presidency to combat prejudice in the South, including sending federal troops to battle the threat of the KKK and ensure the civil liberties of African Americans. As a former general, he liberally wielded executive power and dispatched troops at a whim, including an incident where he sent troops to New York City to combat voter fraud. This propensity for overreaching federal authority, not to mention a spate of scandals, produced a fatigue in the country. Though many citizens supported the concept of equality in theory, they drew the line at active measures like military intervention or spending to make it a reality.

By the 1870s, that fatigue and a continued undermining by Democrats and paramilitary intimidation had led to a massive sea change of public opinion and elective outcomes. Bolstered by the efforts of the KKK and disenfranchisement by means of the Black Codes, Democrats regained control of the South. Rhetorically, they attacked the spending of taxes for Reconstruction projects, whittling away at support for Reconstruction, and appealed to racist anxieties. What good the Radical Republicans and the Freedmen's Bureau had done, not to mention the awe-inspiring gains and organization by the African-American population, had been effectively all but neutralized and erased from history.

★

A contemporary of Rutherford B. Hayes once described him as "a third-rate nonentity," a dismissive label that Hayes himself seemed intent to prove accurate.[58] As governor of Ohio, Hayes was a largely indistinct figure who left little legacy in his wake when he finished his term in 1872, a decade into the Reconstruction era. Hayes enjoyed his retirement and denied attempts by supporters to persuade him to run for other positions. In his diaries, he seems content to be a private citizen spending time with his family and quite divorced from the turbulent politics of the moment.

In 1875, Hayes was drafted by the Republican Party to serve as governor once more and reluctantly accepted. A year later, the forces of the party swept Hayes into running for the presidency, a shift in momentum that seemed to surprise even Hayes himself. Out of duty, Hayes accepted this charge and squared off against Democratic contender Samuel Tilden.

Hayes's campaign was unusual in that the candidate himself was largely inconsequential; it was instead directed by party leaders and assisted by corporate and media interests. As *The Nation* lamented, "All sorts of bad characters were usefully employed in the service of a candidate of spotless reputation, under an ingenious arrangement by which he profited by their actions without incurring any responsibility for their rascality."[59] Largely checked out, Hayes remained above the fray while the party and a coalition of special interests handled the dirty work.

An important cog in this operation was the Associated Press, a coalition of newspapers that had banded together to distribute the news to the nation during the Mexican–American War. The AP was especially loyal to Republicans, who had installed a nation's worth of the telegraph wires that made the service possible, and had worked hand in hand with the Lincoln administration to shape the news to the party's favor. By 1876, the AP was a monopoly of information that wielded unprecedented influence, as newspapers that relied on the AP for national reports were kept in line for fear of being shut out completely.[60] In the election of 1876, the AP blanketed the country with positive stories about Hayes, its bias so blatant Democrats took to calling it the "Hayesociated Press."[61]

Despite this astonishing undertaking that effectively nationalized a politically expedient reality, the election itself was very close. Tilden won the popular vote, but as the returns stretched into the evening, the contest was in doubt. Most media outlets had already declared Tilden the winner, but the difference was John C. Reid, editor of the "bitterly pro-Republican paper" *The New York Times*.[62] While collecting returns for the next day's coverage, Reid was contacted by the Democratic Party seeking information, intriguing the editor and tipping him off to the fact that the election might not be lost. Reid directed coverage the next morning to paint the outcome as murky and "hurried off to Republican headquarters to inform party officials of the news and stave off any premature concession statement."[63]

Finding a drunken Zach Chandler, the Republican Party's national chairman, Reid implored him to send word to the party that they could still win and to give directions to the South, where the contest hung in the balance. The two of them rushed to the nearest Western Union office only to find that the company refused to grant the Republican Party credit to send their messages. Reid charged the cost to the *Times*.

Hayes had long since retired to get a good night's sleep, writing in his diary that the results were "not conclusive" but noting, "We must, I now think, prepare ourselves to accept the inevitable. I do it with composure and cheerfulness. To me the result is no personal calamity."[64] In his typical milquetoast fashion, Hayes seemed rather unworried by the resulting crisis. He remarked regularly that he was overjoyed by the constant visitations from his friends and family and that their presence only made him look forward to retirement once the agitation ended, but the Republican Party and its machine were just kicking into gear. Votes were bought, palms greased, and the very integrity of the electoral system was pushed to the breaking point.

This underhanded behavior was again aided by corporate special interests, again via the industry surrounding telegraphs and the distribution of information. The AP continued supporting Hayes's case by pushing a narrative that he'd actually won the election, and by continually criticizing Tilden and the Democrats' claim. In an especially odious incident, Western Union stole dispatches from the Democratic Party and forwarded them to the Republicans in an effort to expose their maneuvering and give the GOP a strategic advantage.

Seeking Hayes's election, Republicans met with Southern Democrats and struck a deal that echoed the long list of compromises that had plagued the nation since its founding. In exchange for the support of Southern Democrats, a group that had only recently carried out treason on a national scale, Republicans guaranteed that Hayes would hand the South back to white Democrats, effectively abandoning progress in Reconstruction. To give assurances, a representative promised in writing that if elected Hayes would "give to the people of the states of South Carolina and Louisiana the right to control their own affairs in their own way."[65]

With that agreement in place, Rutherford B. Hayes became the nineteenth president of the United States, an office he hadn't particularly wanted and would ultimately flounder in. He had been served by a power-hungry campaign filled with individuals of questionable intent and fueled by subterfuge and moneyed special interests. He had lost the popular vote but prevailed in the Electoral College, a resounding defeat of the idea of democratic will. By his order, federal troops left the South and Reconstruction effectively died. Black Codes became Jim Crow and African Americans were subjected to generations' worth of murder, intimidation, and unjust treatment under the law.

★

In June of 1890, just a month before the state of Louisiana passed a law segregating people by race in railroad cars, the Mohonk Conference on the Negro Question was called to order at Lake Mohonk in New York. The gathering was, according to host A. K. Smiley, called in "true Christian spirit" and in the belief that it was "exceedingly important for the Negroes to be elevated in every direction."

Smiley believed that black Americans must be educated and taught how to live properly, or else they would "become a dangerous element to the community, liable to be thrown at any moment into the hands of demagogues who may use them for bad purposes."[66]

The gathering of whites was dedicated to that purpose, the education and civilizing of the African American and the answering of the so-called Negro Question, and the unanimously elected chairman of the proceedings was none other than former president Rutherford B. Hayes. He opened the proceedings by saying, "It may be justly said, in the deepest sense of the words, that we are indeed the keepers of 'our brothers in black,'" and then telling the group, "As a man, a patriot, a Christian, I have labored for the elevation of the Negro."[67]

But Hayes admitted his pursuit hadn't been unselfish, as he believed "we are bound, hand and foot, to the lowest stratum of society. If the Negroes remain as co-occupants of the land and co-citizens of the States, and we do not lift them up, they will drag us down to industrial bankruptcy, social degradation, and political corruption."

The conference presented a bleak portrayal of the African-American experience, describing at times an incompetent race that didn't like to work, had only recently been elevated out of paganism, was having trouble buying homes and accumulating necessary property as they were incapable of understanding complicated processes like economics. As one speaker observed, "The Negro is back in the iron age [while] the white race is in its golden age."[68]

The conference proceeded with the belief that whites, as the supreme race, were responsible for the well-being of their inferior brothers and sisters. The tone had shifted since the Civil War and now they spoke openly about the crime of slavery, that crime being a past one that had been redeemed, but now, charged by God and their own moral authority, it fell upon them to benevolently lend a hand. The solutions were varied but mostly revolved around Christianizing African Americans, educating them, and helping them understand politics, ignorantly neglecting that they had already built their own churches and economic bases and prospered politically during Reconstruction.

There were dissenting opinions. Dr. Lyman Abbott contested the central premise of the convention and told those in attendance to look at themselves in the mirror and see the rampant racism and discrimination occurring in the North. He argued, "So long as Negroes are treated as they are in Boston, Brooklyn, New York, Philadelphia, we cannot wonder if they are similarly treated in Southern states and communities."[69]

Reverend R. H. Allen disputed the notion that there was a "Negro Problem" at all and reminded the audience, "They did not come to this land as our forefathers came . . . They were kidnapped, thrust into the hole of a slave-ship, and brought here against their will; and we enslaved them, the North as well as the South."[70] That business, he continued, had been done "beneath the very shadow of old Independence Hall, where liberty was proclaimed to all the land."

Despite this refutation of its convenient fictions, the conference remained convinced of its purpose. The survival and success of the African American relied on the benevolence and efforts of the white race, a carrying out of the promises of the Great Emancipator, Abraham Lincoln, in service of the moral arc of the universe. With the carnage of the Civil War and the nation's baptism of blood, it had been renewed in identity and purpose. The sins of slavery had been forgiven and expunged by the martyred death of a president and hundreds of thousands killed on the hallowed battlegrounds throughout the nation. Reconstruction had been largely glossed over as an inconvenient period with disappointing results, the incompetency of the government forgiven by the narrative that African Americans had failed because they were lesser individuals and victims of their own inferiority. The betrayal of the freed people by persons obsessed with political power and moneyed interests would be largely lost to history.

To close the proceedings, Hayes took the floor once more and remarked that the meeting had been productive and observed, "This race has much to hope for," especially if "all the good people of this country shall do their duty to them."[71]

Assured of their own generosity, cleansed of the stain of human bondage, and certainly innocent of undermining the interests and well-being of African Americans, the American people were entering a new world. With war behind them and industrialization unimpeded, their government had become an unholy partnership between ambitious politicians and wealthy businesses, its brazen goal the accumulation of influence and capital. After the Civil War, America was no longer hindered by the sectional disputes that Alexander Hamilton had warned of in *The Federalist Papers.* The nation was now free, with a clear conscience and unending faith in its own myth and divine purpose, to seek riches and empire.

CHAPTER 4

★　　★　　★

The Rise of Empires

On behalf of the Southern Pacific Railroad Company, former New York senator Roscoe Conkling stood before the Supreme Court in December 1882 and presented one of the most audacious and consequential claims in American history: that corporations were people and could appeal for "protection against invidious and discriminating state and local taxes."[1]

Considering his status as a former member of Congress and one of the more influential politicians of his day, corporations paid top dollar for Conkling's representation. Twice he had been nominated for the Supreme Court, but he had declined the position both times to continue asserting his sway over the system and raking in exorbitant fees. His standing as an attorney was above reproach, his position bolstered by sitting chief justice Morrison Waite: "No man ever came into our court who was listened to with more undivided attention." But in this instance Conkling's strategy relied on stagecraft and outright deception.[2]

During his time in Congress, Conkling had served on the committees that drafted the Fourteenth and Fifteenth Amendments, Reconstruction articles ensuring rights for "all persons born or naturalized" in the United States and prohibiting restriction of voting rights based on "race, color, or previous condition of servitude." Conkling had been a leader among Radical Republicans who fought tooth and nail for African Americans to get a fair shake in a post-Emancipation United States, but in the interest of his corporate employers, he was more than willing to sell that noble mission to the highest bidder.

As the only surviving member of the committee that drafted the Fourteenth Amendment, Conkling perjured himself in front of the court by claiming the intention in the wording of the amendment was to protect not only freed slaves but also corporations, testifying that the law was meant to "embrace artificial persons as well as natural persons."[3] To strengthen his claim, Conkling produced his never-before-seen journal and a corresponding entry that supposedly detailed the debate within the committee and the choice between using the word *citizen* and the word *person*. The latter, he argued, had been chosen to make room for corporations. Years later, examination found that Conkling had misrepresented the contents of the journal and that no such debate had ever occurred.

Though Conkling's case was settled out of court, his argument lived on. In the matter of *Santa Clara County v. Southern Pacific Railroad Company*, the Supreme Court did not decide that corporations had the same rights and privileges as private citizens under the Constitution, but court reporter Bancroft Davis, himself a former railroad executive, misleadingly reported that the court had upheld Conkling's claim.

Davis's fabrication reverberated for decades to come. Stephen Field, a Supreme Court justice so tainted by corporate money and influence that he'd personally advised businesses on which counsels to employ for cases and shared with them internal court documents, used Davis's assertion as a means to enshrine corporate personhood in law.[4] In a ruling on another case, Field dishonestly cited Davis's misrepresentation of *Santa Clara County v. Southern Pacific Railroad Company,* laying the foundation for future business-friendly justices and lawmakers to use the idea as precedent moving forward and creating corporate personhood from out of thin air.

The path to corporations' being considered constitutionally protected persons is just one of many such perversions of professed American ideals throughout the Gilded Age. During this period, a new class of the superrich sliced the country into economic kingdoms meant to serve their interests and bloated bank accounts. The rise of the corporation and the robber baron in the late nineteenth century resulted in massive upheaval at all levels of American life. Wealthy individuals and businesses wielded unprecedented, godlike influence over the economy and the government while carrying themselves like modern-day sovereigns. To maximize their profit, they subjugated the American people, forced them into dangerous and unfair labor, and exploited vulnerable immigrant populations, all the while steering the ship of state and bringing the government to heel by means of bribery and intimidation.

The success and endurance of this system owe much to the Founders, who crafted the government as a means to protect the wealthy minority and grant them outsized influence in determining the direction of the nation. For generations the laws of the land had been written in their favor and granted them more wealth and influence with every passing year. The elite were poised to assert total dominance over the United States by the end of the nineteenth century, and over the rest of the globe by the dawning of the twentieth century.

This was the fulfillment of Alexander Hamilton's vision of postsectionalist economic supremacy. The country required new and boundless infrastructure, so the government partnered with private businesses to lay telegraph wire, build transcontinental railroads, pave roads, raise towering cities, and fortify the world of tomorrow.

These public and private partnerships established massive power bases for business mavens and redistributed wealth from the state to the rich on an unprecedented scale.

Adam Smith's *The Wealth of Nations* argument that nations grew and prospered by harnessing the selfishness of individuals naturally appealed to America's Founders, themselves the wealthy elite. But it also rang true with the new generation of robber barons, including financier J. P. Morgan, steel baron Andrew Carnegie, railroad king Cornelius Vanderbilt, speculator Jay Gould, industrialist Andrew W. Mellon, and oil magnate John D. Rockefeller, who believed his "power to make money" was a "gift from God" and that therefore it was his "duty to make money and still more money," and use his money as his conscience and instincts guided him.[5]

The benefits of greed and selfishness were virtues of the age, a means by which captains of destiny could accumulate wealth at the expense of the vast majority, free from concern or guilt; according to the principles of capitalism, the suffering of the poor was natural and just. After all, if the market separated the strong from the weak, and if Charles Darwin's *On the Origin of Species*, published in 1859, was correct in stating that the march of life was one struggle after another on the road to a fitter, better species, then what else was to be done for the lowest of the low?

Social Darwinism would be one of the most prevalent philosophies moving forward. Its application served to soothe any guilt among the wealthy, as the poor amounted to what William Graham Sumner characterized in his 1883 work *What Social Classes Owe to Each Other* as little more than a burden on the country and its wealthy few.[6]

Andrew Carnegie weighed in on the subject when he penned his essay "Wealth," which argued the welfare of the citizenry was the responsibility of the wealthy but still maintained that the poor were largely undeserving. Conveniently for Carnegie, the rich made better executors of benevolent capital than charities or the government.

Carnegie also asserted that inequality was a necessary side effect of advancement because the only alternative was "universal squalor."[7] His solution was for the wealthy to distribute portions of their excess wealth via personal foundations and benevolent organizations to deserving recipients—though Carnegie maintained that "those worthy of assistance, except in rare cases, seldom require assistance"—rather than trust existing charitable groups or government oversight, as the wealthy, with their "talent for organization and management," were unparalleled.[8]

What Carnegie put forward was a new system in which the wealthiest Americans and businesses formed their own apparatus of government with little to no oversight or responsibility to the nation's people.

The Founders had intended the United States of America to serve the interests of the wealthy, but what they hadn't predicted was that an era would come in which that wealthy elite elected to rule outside of the framework of government. After all, at the time of the Revolution and the framing of the Constitution, America's wealthiest men were deeply entrenched in politics and served as representatives and delegates. But now, businessmen were building their own financial empires that dwarfed the government in terms of influence and wealth. Politicians, once drivers of social change and the upward transfer of power, were now considered currency to private citizens, bribed and threatened to keep the nation humming along to the tycoons' advantage.

That realignment began with the dawning of a new, post-Reconstruction order characterized by a truce of sorts between the Republicans and Democrats; the parties that had once dueled and murdered one another set aside their battles for personal enrichment. Republicans eventually followed Rutherford B. Hayes's example and turned a blind eye to Democratic treatment of African Americans in the South, allowing the rise of Jim Crow and subjecting generations of black people to discrimination, violence, and disenfranchisement, all so the Democrats would acquiesce to the Republicans' pro-business agenda.

The purchase of the American political system began with the laying of the Transcontinental Railroad, a feat of epic proportions that connected the continent and modernized travel and shipping. In the debate over federal subsidizing, the Central Pacific Railroad Company secured its place in the project in 1861 by handing out the modern equivalent of $13 million of company stock to members of Congress, a brazen bribe one member acknowledged as necessary to "grease the wheels."[9]

The railroads essentially owned the government during this period, as was made apparent in the Crédit Mobilier scandal in 1867, as the construction company working with Union Pacific on the Transcontinental Railroad gifted millions in cash and stock bribes to prominent politicians. The recipients included Schuyler Colfax, the sitting vice president under Ulysses S. Grant; Speaker of the House James G. Blaine; Senator Henry Wilson, who would go on to be the next vice president; and Congressman James Garfield, who became the twentieth president of the United States. In the end, efforts to prove the bribes had influenced votes were inconclusive, as the interests of government and big business had effectively merged.

Public trust in government corroded as the scandals mounted. Grant's administration was hit particularly hard as members were found to have evaded taxes, perpetuated fraud, and committed bribery. Under this avalanche of grift, ironically, Americans' lost faith in government solidified their reliance on business and the wealthy.

Disillusionment also spurred the rise of populism and what would eventually come to be known as the Progressive Era. One of the first harbingers of the populist movement came in the form of charismatic William Jennings Bryan, who won the Democratic Party's nomination in 1896 based on his fiery oration and opposition to the established moneyed interests. To combat Bryan's growing popularity, Republican chairman Mark Hanna engineered the first truly modern presidential fundraising campaign by goading the rich into donating massive sums to nominee William McKinley, citing Bryan's danger as a populist threat and telling the wealthy a donation was tantamount to "helping themselves and their business associates."[10] In the end, McKinley's war chest, padded by special interests and the exceedingly wealthy, amounted to over $7 million (approximately $200 million in modern dollars), an amount so substantial that "no presidential campaign would equal it for nearly half a century."[11]

With campaign contributions and bribes, big business grew so large it effectively dwarfed the United States of America and used the apparatus of government as a support organ. Representative James Weaver of Iowa acknowledged this risk when he warned, "A bold and aggressive plutocracy has usurped the Government and is using it as a policeman to enforce its insolent decrees."[12]

When facing down strikes and labor disturbances, companies could rely on the government to send in troops to squash insurgents, a fulfillment of James Madison's promise in *The Federalist Papers* that centralized government would be there should the working class unite and rise up. Taxes and laws were administered in corporate favor, allowing them to form monopolies and subject laborers to horrific conditions.

By 1881, the writing was on the wall. Journalist H. D. Lloyd outlined the scope of the problem in his article "The Story of a Great Monopoly" in *The Atlantic*, noting that railroads owed more than twice the country's national debt and passed responsibility on to the common people at a rate much higher than the government. He declared their crimes and manipulations tantamount to "sins against the public and private faith on a scale impossible in the early days of republics and corporations."[13] The conclusion Lloyd reached was deeply troubling: "The time has come to face the fact that the forces of capital and industry have outgrown the forces of our government."

The big business of growth and economic expansion wormed

its way into everyday life as the lumbering trusts and businesses interconnected themselves through the stock market. Despite the market's intended purpose as an engine of stability, it was volatile and prone to bouts of wild speculation, manifesting large bubbles that could enrich men beyond their wildest imaginations in the morning and threaten to collapse society by afternoon.

By the late nineteenth century, it wasn't just investors who felt the trembles of the system, but all Americans. Just as Adam Smith had prophesized, the world's markets had grown interconnected, and fluctuations elsewhere made their way home. As bubbles around the world popped, or business reached its zenith, suddenly the country and its people suffered terribly from one crisis or panic after another.

Despite the wealthy touting the market as a stable engine for progress, it has proven to be nothing if not unreliable. From the very beginning, the market has been fraught with panics, depressions, and crashes resulting from malfeasance, overspeculation, and just inherent instability. Following several meltdowns, in post–Civil War America a full-blown depression raged from 1873 to 1879 because of railroad overbuilding and rampant speculation; another depression hit in 1882 because of the decline of railroads; in 1893, a disturbance in Argentina nearly toppled the world order; 1901 saw the first stock market crash during a battle over the Northern Pacific Railway Company; and in 1907 another panic commenced over general instability.

Each of these crises brought suffering upon the American people, whether they had invested or not. They were the victims of capitalists warring against one another and bore the brunt of each wave of instability. The nation was effectively strapped to the market, a ticking, volatile bomb said to be the key to progress and advancement, one that could never be dismantled lest it bring about the collapse of society.

Perhaps it was most evident to the government that such a thing had taken place in 1893 when Democratic president Grover Cleveland faced a crisis that threatened to escalate and ruin the country. As Americans stood in line for food and faced destitution in what looked like a major depression, Cleveland learned the United States was nearing insolvency. With little in the way of options, he met with J. P. Morgan and asked for a loan. The United States of America received $65 million from Morgan and a collection of foreign investors, effectively stabilizing the republic by use of private funds.

If ever there was a doubt as to who was in charge, an individual personally bailing out the US government and saving it from outright failure answered any and all questions as to where real power resided.

★

One of the Gilded Age's most despised characters was Jay Gould, a railroad magnate and financial speculator who openly manipulated people and the financial system to the point where both might break. Infamously, Gould had said he could "hire one half of the working class to kill the other half," and this sociopathic worldview led to his attempt in 1869 to enrich himself by cornering the gold market, an action that resulted in widespread panic and nearly melted down the American economy.[14]

Gould took advantage of any business venture he saw as vulnerable or profitable, regardless of risk or legality. His conquests included Western Union, which he gained control of in 1881 in a takeover aided by Gould's personal paper, the New York *World*. Through the paper, Gould attacked the company and waged a covert war of corporate espionage.

In the past, newspapers had carried the messages of political parties and whetted the appetites of working-class readers for scandalous gossip and wartime intrigue, but Gould recognized the power of media in manipulating thought and reality for individual gain. He used *The World* as a weapon, a new development in how the wealthy might control discourse.

After taking Western Union, Gould saw little need for his paper any longer and pawned it off on Joseph Pulitzer in 1883. Pulitzer employed an army of reporters who investigated corruption while also focusing on popular material such as scandals and horrific crimes—the stuff of tabloid journalism.

Pulitzer soon met his blood rival in 1895 when William Randolph Hearst purchased a failing penny press called the *New York Journal* with the assistance of his wealthy, widowed mother. He quickly stole a chunk of Pulitzer's staff from the *World* and challenged Pulitzer head-on in a contest to "attract the largest number of undiscerning readers."[15]

That same year, as Cubans struggled for independence from Spain, Pulitzer and Hearst took advantage of the crisis to sell newspapers. New Yorkers couldn't get enough of the story, and both publications trumped up tales of suffering and in some cases fabricated incidents completely. To aid them, a deposed junta of Cubans led by Tomás Estrada Palma, the future first president of Cuba, fed the newspapers' propaganda that would then be printed in bold headlines without so much as a cursory fact-check.

Much like what had happened with the Mexican–American War, and what would play out time and time again in future American conflicts, the media created a firestorm that led to warfare. The idea of war percolated in the minds of the American people as they were fed an escalating and tantalizing constructed reality meant to inflame tensions and incite a nationalistic call for arms. By the time the USS *Maine* sank in Havana Harbor on February 15, 1898, the oncoming war was inevitable. Two hundred sixty-six American sailors died after the *Maine* sank under mysterious circumstances, and Pulitzer and Hearst were quick to proclaim that sinister Spanish forces had been to blame—without so much as a shred of evidence.

Experts would later conclude the tragedy had been an accident, likely the result of an interior explosion, but it didn't matter. In that moment, the United States had an incident it could exploit as provocation to enter a beneficial conflict with an overmatched opponent. Reveling in his achievement, Hearst asked his readers, "How Do You Like Our War?" on the front page of the *Journal*'s May 8 edition.[16]

The newspapers weren't solely responsible for the conflict, however, as America was itching for battle. Three decades had passed since the existential crisis of the Civil War had shaken the country; a new war against a common enemy promised a revival of nationalism and white supremacy that reinvigorated the concept of manifest destiny. Arguing for hostilities, the politicians of the age dusted off those old standards of American rhetoric. Senator Jacob H. Gallinger of New Hampshire claimed it was "inexorable destiny" and Senator John M. Thurston from Nebraska urged, "We cannot refuse to accept this responsibility which the God of the universe has placed upon us as the one great power in the New World."[17] Henry Cabot Lodge of Massachusetts said the moment was the "fulfillment of a great movement which has run through the centuries" and that America's Anglo-Saxon blood and divine crusade positioned the nation as a representation of "the spirit of liberty and the spirit of the new time."[18]

Outside of politics, others argued that God himself had set the United States on a collision course with Spain. The popular religious figure Bishop C. H. Fowler told sold-out crowds on a national tour that the Spanish–American War had been a major milestone in Christian history, directly linking America and its white supremacy with the Christian tradition. He declared that the Civil War "made the Anglo-Saxon race fit to be used in the world's evangelization" and that the explosion of the *Maine* "made the Anglo-Saxon race one and set us about our job, namely the deliverance and salvation of nations."[19]

The war itself was a modest affair; Spain was in no place to defend itself on the island of Cuba, and so victory was assured. Regardless, the media aggrandized the fighting with breathless coverage spearheaded by Pulitzer and Hearst—particularly Hearst, who spared no expense in sending a small battalion of reporters and photographers to Cuba in an effort to flood the *Journal*'s pages with exclusive content.[20]

Hearst joined his team in Cuba and irresponsibly inserted himself into the action. He snuck artifacts from the field, wandered too close to hostilities, and endangered himself and others. Once, while gallivanting around the battlefield in his designer clothes, he even got in the way of military operations by "capturing" a group of defenseless Spanish sailors, taking twenty-nine prisoners of war—only to find, when trying to offload them to the proper authorities, that the captain of the USS *Oregon* was so disgusted by Hearst's actions he refused to take the prisoners off his hands.[21]

For all the joy and profit Hearst found in his war, he was severely depressed by the time hostilities ended. He had recognized the moment as his chance to reinvent himself, but to his own displeasure he watched Theodore Roosevelt thrive after pulling a similar stunt by resigning as assistant secretary of the navy to lead the legendary Rough Riders. Hearst lamented his disappointment in a particularly sniveling letter to his mother: "I guess I'm a failure. I made the mistake of my life in not raising the cowboy regiment I had in mind before Roosevelt raised his. I really believe I brought on the war but I failed to score in the war."[22]

Roosevelt, meanwhile, seized the opportunity and prospered wildly, securing the legacy Hearst had craved for himself. He was a quintessential American product, a sickly child who grew into a man who lived by overcompensation and shaped the world by the sheer force of his will to prove his masculinity. Roosevelt did indeed transform himself into a legendary figure in the tradition of warrior statesmen like Andrew Jackson and Ulysses S. Grant, through both his prowess on the battlefield and fawning press. His bestselling memoir *The Rough Riders* was rushed to print in 1899 and presented Roosevelt as a leader capable of inspiring men to "do themselves justice in march or battle."[23]

In lionizing himself, Roosevelt also bolstered the perception of the Spanish–American War as a triumph of American exceptionalism; the conflict and its everyman heroes served as more proof the country was possessed of unconquerable spirit and inspired by divine faith and mission. His writing helped define the war in the minds of the American people, his prose lush and dripping with patriotic luster. He wrote of the Cuban landscape and bands playing "The Star-Spangled Banner," during which "all officers and men alike, stood with heads uncovered, wherever they were, until the last strains of the anthem died away in the hot sunset air."[24]

The scene Roosevelt depicted so beautifully was undoubtedly the birth of the American empire, and the scream of the cavalry trumpets the announcement of a new age and a war machine on an unstoppable march.

★

In his sold-out sermons, Bishop C. H. Fowler had made a case for the Spanish–American War as a holy crusade undertaken by God's chosen people in the fulfillment of the almighty's ultimate plan for the world. The executor of that plan, Bishop Fowler claimed, was President William McKinley: *"President McKinley is a providential man.* Like the prophets of old, he is on an errand. He is the prophet of our times."[25]

McKinley certainly believed himself to be a prophet. When facing a decision about the Philippines, a Spanish colony that had fallen to the United States in the Spanish–American War, McKinley claimed God had visited him in a dream and directed what action to take. He told a group of clergy he had paced the White House in contemplation for days and prayed continually until God had gifted him clarity that he should not give the territory up as it "would be bad business." He declared the divine mission of the United States was to "educate" the Filipino people, a race he saw as unfit for self-government, and to "uplift and civilize and Christianize them," all of it possible through "God's grace."[26] McKinley's "vision" from God was equal parts economic, evangelistic, and white supremacist, a cocktail of ideology that served America's fiscal purposes and fortified the belief that Americans were a superior race of people.

As the politicians of the day discussed the Philippines, they regularly mixed that providential message of manifest destiny with a pragmatic and greedy eye toward the island nation. This was perhaps an unsurprising development, as the territory represented entry into the Asian markets and a new frontier for American financial interests. As Senator Albert Beveridge of Indiana argued in an impassioned speech, "The Philippines are ours forever . . . And just beyond the Philippines are China's illimitable markets. We will not retreat from either."[27] Beveridge trumpeted America's preparedness for the task as an "Almighty God" had marked "us as His Chosen people," a designation God had apparently intended by granting the nation victories in war and the market.

But as much as politicians could see the economic potential in the Philippines, as well as recently acquired Puerto Rico, they hesitated to welcome their peoples into the Union. Just as they had during discussion of the annexation of Mexico, they worried that accepting more people of color into the United States and granting them citizenship would ruin the nation. Senator Benjamin Tillman of South Carolina warned against incorporating "races for which we have no liking," already worried about the "race problem" that free black people presented to society.[28]

The distaste for the people of the Philippines and Puerto Rico necessitated a new strategy of statesmanship the country had never attempted before. The United States, born as a colony of Great Britain and forged under the revolutionary concept that self-government was an inalienable right, a nation that had taken to arms to overthrow its oppressors and styled itself as a beacon for freedom for all peoples, had again, in the sole interest of profit and power, become a colonizer itself.

In both the Philippines and Puerto Rico, America enforced its rule over the people without giving them full citizenship or guaranteed protections. While there, they controlled the functions of government, ensured that United States–friendly politicians and figures prospered, and saw to it that American businesses were given full access to the natural resources of the land and full ability to exploit them for private gain. In this way, the United States of America shaped the world and its economics in its favor and joined the league of colonial nations it had once decried.

Puerto Rico suffered tribulations and America's actions in the Philippines constituted some of the most shameful behavior in the nation's history. Though it was claimed the Filipinos were treated as "wards of the U.S. government," the truth is that America ruled the islands with an iron fist and with little concern for democratic or human rights.[29] The Filipino people had resisted the colonial dominion of Spain, and they continued that resistance once the United States replaced them. Seeking to carry out McKinley's divine vision, the United States attempted to erase Filipino identity, a fate many of the people violently resisted.

In the face of this opposition, America warned the Philippines, "The supremacy of the United States must and will be enforced throughout every part of the archipelago, and those who resist it can accomplish no end other than their own ruin."[30] To enforce that supremacy, the military was given orders to be brutal and unflinching, assured that "it is an inevitable consequence of war that the innocent must generally suffer with the guilty."[31]

American servicemen employed torture as a means of coercion and punishment, including a process called "the water cure," a forerunner to waterboarding borrowed from the Spanish occupation, in which "[the] victim was held down, his mouth pried open with a piece of bamboo or rifle barrel, and dirty or salty water poured down his throat until the stomach swelled to the bursting point."[32] In one particularly awful account, the water cure of a Filipino official played out in ruthless fashion: He was thrown to the floor and filled with water until he was so full it leaked out of his nostrils. As an interpreter screamed at him, "men pounded his stomach with their fists. Water spurted from the man's nose and mouth, and the process began anew."[33]

When torture wasn't sufficient, American soldiers hunted and killed men, murdered with reckless abandon, burned villages, engaged in widespread sexual assault of the female population, and starved the people. In 1901, one of the worst atrocities in American military history took place on Samar as retaliation for an attack in Balangiga. The widespread cruelty set off as General Jacob Smith, the military governor of the island, instructed his men to instill a "wholesome fear" among the people.[34] He gave his men free rein to punish indiscriminately and without evidence. "I want no prisoners," he told them. "I wish you to kill and burn, the more you kill and burn the better it will please me. I want all persons killed who are capable of bearing arms in actual hostilities against the United States."[35] When asked for clarification as to who Smith considered capable of carrying out hostilities, he told his men every male over the age of ten.

Smith's men did not carry out quite the destruction he had ordered but meted out their own harsh justice. In a march across the island, they set fire to hundreds of dwellings; killed nearly forty people, according to US records; and destroyed the infrastructure to the point where disease and famine caused untold deaths. In the campaign to bring American-style civilization to the Philippines, estimates put the total loss of life among the insurgents at sixteen thousand to twenty thousand men; counting civilian deaths from murder, famine, and starvation, the numbers range from two hundred thousand to as many as one million.[36]

Back in the United States, Theodore Roosevelt had assumed the office of president following William McKinley's assassination in 1901. Roosevelt had been commander in chief for less than a year when he addressed the atrocities in the Philippines in a 1902 Memorial

Day speech: "Our warfare in the Philippines has been carried on with singular humanity."[37]

Roosevelt was much less timid about American empire than McKinley had been. Still the swaggering Rough Rider, Roosevelt meant to project America's influence on a much grander and more ambitious scale, a mission he proclaimed in his 1904 State of the Union, which updated the more isolationist Monroe Doctrine of American determinism. He wrote that the wrongdoing and inferior societies of lesser nations would require the United States to exercise "international police power" in righting matters.[38]

Under this new governing philosophy, America assumed its mantle as God's chosen nation to help the poor and helpless peoples, a help primarily focused on strengthening US interests and economic advantages. The concept was an expansion of American exceptionalism, as only Americans could determine which nations required and deserved their benevolent, profitable intervention.

Already the United States had assumed such a relationship with the island kingdom of Hawaii, a relationship cemented when a cabal of American businesses performed a bloodless coup in 1893 so that the islands could be used for their natural resources and primed as a military outpost.

In the years that followed, this trend grew as America continued to intervene in the affairs of "lesser" people whenever it gave them an advantage or if American businesses required the assistance of the US military.

For strategic purposes, Roosevelt supported Panamanian rebels in 1903 who meant to overthrow Colombian rule of the area around the Panama Canal after Colombia balked on talks with the American government. The new nation of Panama was founded on a philosophy of American cooperation, centered on the excavation of the canal, and the installed people who were favorable to American interests oversaw an oligarchical system fraught with deep inequalities.

Many of these campaigns were necessitated by the United Fruit

Company, which had swarmed into Latin America and fully taken over countries that produced bananas and other crops. In these so-called banana republics, the corporation controlled much of the nation's resources and governments, but when there were uprisings or disturbances, the company was quick to ask for military assistance. Over the decades to come, America interceded militarily and interfered in the political affairs of the Dominican Republic, Haiti, Costa Rica, Honduras, Guatemala, Nicaragua, Haiti, Cuba, and Mexico, a staggering legacy of manipulation. This would begin the long and torturous work of constructing an empire engineered to serve American interests around the world at the expense of people and their supposed inalienable rights.

★

As the United States built its empire, the undisputed rule of the corporation took a gruesome toll within the country. To maximize profit, big business overworked their employees, leveraged them against one another, provided little compensation, and required them to labor in dangerous conditions. Industrial workers were pushed to a breaking point.

A labor revolt was brewing as far back as 1877, as railroad workers engaged in collective action that stopped service around the country, including in Illinois, Missouri, New York, and Pennsylvania. It was quoted in Pittsburgh that the uprising might be "the beginning of a great civil war in this country, between labor and capital."[39] On the ground it must have looked like the genesis of a new revolution as workers and fed-up citizens burned buildings, destroyed railroad cars, and caused millions of dollars' worth of damage. The spreading of unrest across state lines was exactly what James Madison had promised the federal government would counteract, and so it was no surprise that President Rutherford B. Hayes dispatched troops throughout the country to do battle with the striking workers.

Particularly disgusted was former president Ulysses S. Grant, who had received copious amounts of criticism for using federal troops to aid freed slaves in the South. He now watched those critics support federal intervention in labor disputes, as well as a new push to build National Guard armories in American cities to stave off uprisings. Grant cringed at this hypocrisy and noted that the national press had "thought it horrible to keep U.S. troops stationed in the Southern States" to protect African Americans but were now fully in favor of "the whole power of the government" being used to suppress a labor strike.[40]

Though the Great Railroad Strike of 1877 was ended by federal intervention, it would hardly be the last labor stoppage or dispute. In 1898 alone there were 1,098 strikes and lockouts; in 1900, 1,839; and in 1901, another 3,012.[41] The workers recognized that organized labor gave them considerably more leverage than attempting to negotiate individually, and so their resulting unions were a means of leveling the playing field and working against the elite to demand at least a living wage and a safer work environment. In this way, unions and collective bodies began to harness the spirit of the American Revolution and were celebrated by their members and communities as embodiments of American principles.

In 1892, another conflict between labor and capital brewed in Homestead, Pennsylvania, this incident revolving around Andrew Carnegie's steel production. The Homestead steel factory was a bleak working environment, described by novelist Hamlin Garland as "a place into which men went like men going to war for the sake of wives and children, urged on by necessity, blinded and dulled by custom and habit; an inhuman place to spend four-fifths of one's waking hours."[42] Carnegie's workers labored around the clock in backbreaking shifts, were paid little, and lived in constant fear of being maimed or killed.

When members of the Amalgamated Association of Iron and Steel Workers union (AA) met with Carnegie's representatives in February of 1892 to discuss a new contract, they saw an opportunity to reach a better deal, as the steel industry was increasingly profitable. They asked for modest raises and were shocked when Henry Clay Frick, Carnegie's right-hand man, responded with an insulting 22 percent cut.

With the two sides at an impasse, Frick escalated the situation by outfitting the Homestead factory like a fortress, surrounding the plant with fences and barbed wire, constructing sniper towers, and armoring the facilities as if preparing for all-out war. Meanwhile, the company sought replacement workers. This escalation got Frick exactly what he wanted: The AA took up arms to protest the provocation.

On July 6, Frick dispatched a private militia to the Homestead factory, made up mostly of Pinkertons, members of a detective agency that had served as hired armies for industrialists and had a long history of murdering and provoking laborers. Frick got the battle he desired as the insertion of the Pinkertons led to a violent clash. The private militia and workers opened fire on one another, resulting in the deaths of three Pinkertons and seven laborers. This carnage prompted Pennsylvania governor Robert E. Pattison, himself a devotee of Carnegie and beneficiary of his political machine, to dispatch four thousand state militiamen to supplement the private army and stamp down the uprising.

Again and again, the government protected the wealthy in their battle against exploited citizens. In 1894, federal troops battled railroad strikers in the streets, slayed thirty people, and arrested their leaders, including future presidential candidate Eugene V. Debs, on trumped-up charges. That same year, Jacob Coxey organized a march of hundreds of unemployed men on Washington, DC, as a means to promote a plan for public works, and was arrested for walking on the grass outside the Capitol as police used clubs to disperse his group.

At the turn of the century, big business was still the undisputed king in the United States. Industrialists openly exploited their workforce and controlled the government, but the discontent of the people was building by the day. Another revolution loomed just over the horizon, as life for an American citizen in the early twentieth century was arduous. In the cities, laborers, particularly immigrants, were pressed into cramped tenement buildings where they lived in disgraceful conditions. A New York labor commission observed: "Refuse of every description makes the floors damp and slimy, and the puny, half-naked children crawl or slide about in it."[43] Those children, if they survived, spent their days toiling in factories. One manufacturer remarked, "The most beautiful sight we see is the child at labor; as early as he may get at labor the more beautiful, the more useful does his life become." Otherwise, they were "scrounging through garbage dumps . . . or in industrial or rail yards looking for coal and wood to heat stoves at home."[44] Their parents worked in backbreaking, demeaning jobs in unsafe conditions for upwards of fourteen hours a day, making little and receiving hardly any time off. They were mangled and killed in industrial accidents, disposed of, and forgotten.

For rural America, fate wasn't much kinder, as agrarianism had been replaced with industrial society, leaving many communities reliant on dangerous trades like coal mining. Men and children alike suffered countless horrors as they sacrificed their bodies and tempted fate in prolonged, grueling shifts, all to power the machine of industry and economic "progress." Their deaths in cave-ins, from accidents, and from asphyxiation became so common that towns and communities grew numb to the tragedies.

There was a sense that capitalism had all but conquered the United States, a feeling the wealthy had gained unalterable control. The market they had constructed served their interests and functioned as the nation's circulatory system, and the government had been bought and sold many times over. And it wasn't as if the infection lay in one party alone: Working Americans were well aware that both the Democrat and Republican parties were servants of the wealthy, especially members of the Senate, which followed the design of the framers by being totally and openly in the pocket of the country's elites.

The rise of the labor unions had been a spark, however, as workers uniting to form a common front had managed to challenge the established order. Following their lead, ordinary Americans began organizing, forming bodies and special-interest groups that lobbied for commonsense regulation and progressive policies to make their lives at least somewhat bearable. Their issues were diverse and wide-ranging, from early feminism and women's suffrage to the regulation of the food industry. They relied on collective action, as well as a new form of citizen journalism called "muckraking" that investigated corruption and social issues and shined a light on the problems of the day.

This spike in social activism led to the Progressive Era, a response to the rise of the ultra-rich and the Gilded Age, a time in which capitalism and irresponsible industry all but destroyed the lives of American citizens. That movement resulted in many of the reforms we have come to depend on: challenging labor practices, demanding safe working conditions, regulating the food we eat and the drugs we take, advocating equal rights and suffrage for women, and pushing for the establishment of what we have come to understand as the concepts of childhood and public education. These reformers worked to make America a safer and more equitable nation in which human dignity wasn't exorcised in the name of reckless profit.

Progressives would not have been able to achieve as much, however, if it weren't for the ascension of Teddy Roosevelt to the presidency. When he took office in 1901, Roosevelt was alarmed by the sway big business held over government. Roosevelt's embrace of the progressive movement arguably stemmed from his affront at the presidency's being subservient to industrialists. Roosevelt wasted no time in bucking the order of the moment and reasserting the power of government over corporations.

Less than three months after McKinley had died, Roosevelt

presented his State of the Union to Congress, an address that promised to continue McKinley's agenda but included a promise to begin doing the necessary work of regulating business, denouncing corporate trusts as "hurtful to the general welfare." Roosevelt believed it was the government's responsibility not to obstruct businesses but to step in when they acted in bad faith.[45]

Roosevelt's mission to reassert government control became a consistent theme of his presidency as he roused progressives, saying, "It behooves Americans to look ahead and plan out the right kind of a civilization as that which we intend to develop for these wonderful new conditions of vast industrial growth. It must not be, it shall not be, the civilization of a mere plutocracy, a banking-house, a Wall-Street-syndicate civilization." To counteract that "Wall-Street-syndicate civilization," Roosevelt used the Sherman Antitrust Act of 1890, a largely cast-aside piece of legislation, and filed forty-four antitrust suits.

The Progressive Era saw many gains on a national level. The passage of the Sixteenth Amendment gave Congress the right to impose an income tax. They established the Federal Reserve System. And the necessary groundwork was laid for the passage of the Seventeenth and Nineteenth Amendments, which respectively established the direct election of senators by the people and the right for women to vote. These reforms transformed the process of government and rectified two of the worst decisions in the founding of the country, the disenfranchisement of women and the construction of the Senate as a means for the wealthy to have unequal representation in Congress.

The movement was, of course, imperfect. Its efforts were chiefly concerned with the plight of white laborers and suffered from tremendous blind spots when it came to segregation and African-American disenfranchisement under Jim Crow, not to mention the constant threat of horrific lynchings and violence. In addition to his white supremacist adventures in Latin America, Roosevelt fell well short in this regard, worrying there might not be a solution to "the terrible problem offered by the presence of the negro on this continent" and continuing his insistence on the preservation "for the white race [of] the best portions of the new world's surface."[46]

Like Roosevelt, progressives were overly concerned with dictating the lives of others. Their efforts to regulate existence within the United States resulted in distasteful and troubling fascinations with prohibition and eugenics, the former rising from rural religious temperance movements and the latter a push to harness the tenets of Darwinist science to engineer a better humanity.

One such proponent of eugenics was New Jersey governor Woodrow Wilson, who campaigned for the sterilization of criminals and the supposedly "unfit," and signed legislation in 1911 that established the Board of Examiners of Feeble-Minded, Epileptics and Other Defectives, a group that decided the reproductive fate of the "hopelessly defective and criminal classes."[47]

In the lead-up to the 1912 election, Wilson became the Democratic Party's nominee and eventually won the office as Republicans splintered under the weight of a showdown between a returning Roosevelt and incumbent William Howard Taft. Taft had previously been Roosevelt's chosen successor, but as Roosevelt soured on Taft's policies he moved further left and grew increasingly liberal in his worldview. In his appearances, Roosevelt began advocating for a policy he called "New Nationalism" that more directly targeted businesses and the wealthy and defined "the struggle . . . of freemen" as being the fight for "the right of self-government as against the special interests, who twist the methods of free government into machinery for defeating the popular will."[48] He proclaimed, "We must drive the special interest out of politics," and sought a more democratic nation in which "the people themselves . . . [were] the ultimate makers of their Constitution."[49]

This zeal for reform cost Roosevelt the Republican Party's nomination, a loss that saw Roosevelt indict his rival Taft as having "completely abandoned the cause of the people" and being guilty of

surrendering "himself wholly to the biddings of the professional political bosses of the great and privileged interests standing behind
them."[50] To continue his battle against Taft and for the American
people, Roosevelt joined the Progressive Party, an upstart political
outfit formed in opposition to both the Democrats and the Republicans, who had been bought and sold by special interests. Roosevelt
successfully undercut Taft's reelection bid, besting him by eighty
electoral votes, but the split of the Republican Party meant the ascension of Wilson, who presented himself as the moderate choice and
a middle ground between Taft's conservatism and Roosevelt's radical
liberalism.

Wilson was a reformer, but of a different sort. He saw the world
as a network of systems of control and believed in elites' exerting
their power over the masses to propel the country forward. He positioned himself as an administrator capable of working the growing
web of government bureaucracy and saw people in much the same
light as the influential engineer Frederick Taylor, whose theory of
management viewed people as cogs in a machine.

Additionally, Wilson was also a wicked racist whose academic
work brimmed with deep and troubling prejudices. As a historian,
Wilson understood the power of stories and narratives in weaponizing the past and influencing the future. His defining work, *A History
of the American People*, aggrandized the Confederacy and glorified the
practice of slavery.

He had an affinity for the pre–Civil War South and heroicized
slave owners, saying their punishments of slaves were "firm but not
unkindly discipline" with a "real care shown for their comfort and
welfare," the slaves themselves treated with "affection and indul-
gence."[51] So great was the bond between slave master and slave that
after word of emancipation hit the South, "great gangs of cheery
negroes worked in the fields . . . with quiet industry, with show of
faithful affection even . . . There was, it seemed, no wrong they fretted
under or wished to see righted."[52]

Wilson was one of the popular proponents of the Lost Cause mythology, a reimagining of the Civil War meant to rehabilitate the South, and painted the scene of a Reconstruction-era South subject to humiliations and the troubling rise of African-American freedom. Their unfortunate rise, Wilson contended, kept "more capable white men" from power.[53]

To combat this injustice, Wilson lauded the founders of the Ku Klux Klan, a group he claimed formed for "private amusement" that carried out "pranks" in the post–Civil War South.[54] These "pranks" by the KKK, as well as the disenfranchisement of African Americans, received praise from Wilson, who reasoned the resurgence of white supremacy in the South after Reconstruction had been "by methods which only an almost revolutionary state of society justified" and that the "forcible interference" in the rights of African Americans had been vindicated, for it had resulted in "an end of chronic revolution."[55]

When he assumed office in 1913, Wilson saw a country primed for greatness, if only it could be exploited and controlled. He wrote that the empire in the dawning of the twentieth century was exemplary, that the Southern states were "readjusting their elective suffrage so as to exclude the illiterate negroes and so in part undo the mischief of reconstruction" as the rest of the nation pulled together in a common understanding of white supremacy and economic domination, an understanding that prepared statesmen for their task of releasing "the energies of the country for the great day of trade and manufacture which was to change the face of the world."

There was no doubt in Wilson's mind he was the statesman America needed. As an intellectual, elitist white supremacist, he possessed unending faith in his own ability to unite the nation and propel it into the future. He once explained that "men are as clay in the hands of a consummate leader," revealing a belief that it was the job of great men to manipulate their people.[56]

His philosophy of government was for elites to create systems that entrapped people and exploited them for maximum efficiency, while his political philosophy was based on the concept of manipulation of narrative and perception. To accomplish both, he relied on new forms of media and science to release those energies and would indeed change the face of the world.

CHAPTER 5

⋆　　⋆　　⋆

The God of Peace

Thomas Dixon Jr. was a preacher of extraordinary ability. He held audiences rapt with sermons on the struggle between good and evil, their battleground the United States of America, a country that held an importance akin to that of Megiddo, the site of the prophesized battle of Armageddon. Like many others, Dixon saw America as a country handpicked by an omnipotent god, and despite internal strife, he believed Americans were a chosen people. In his eyes, the Civil War was an unfortunate wound from which the country had yet to heal. To move forward, to do the work of the Lord, Dixon believed, that rift needed mending.

It was at the turn of the century that Dixon attended a theatrical production of Harriet Beecher Stowe's *Uncle Tom's Cabin* and decided to take action. Dixon was disgusted by the play's antislavery message, enraged by its portrayal of the act of human bondage as a sinister and cruel undertaking. He felt it was his duty as a man of God to right the historical record. His first effort to do so was *The Leopard's Spots:*

A Romance of the White Man's Burden—1865–1900, a novel that retold the story of Reconstruction. In the novel, the Confederacy was a noble attempt to preserve a way of life, and the postwar period was a tragedy in which Southerners were mistreated by criminal Northerners and wicked, newly freed slaves. To follow up, Dixon published *The Clansman: An Historical Romance of the Ku Klux Klan* in 1905 and *The Traitor: A Story of the Fall of the Invisible Empire* in 1907.

Dixon's revision of history sold incredibly well as it served to salve many of the remaining wounds from the Civil War in the eyes of white Americans anxious to revise their racist past. This narrative tidied up the perception of the war by casting blame on African Americans: Whites on both sides, the Union and the Confederacy, had simply been stewards of the country who found themselves in an untenable and regrettable situation. In this Lost Cause mythology, Confederates shed their fascistic philosophy and became gentlemanly protectors of a bygone era and patriots invested in the rights of states. This perspective both buried the Confederacy's white supremacy and justified its continuing existence, creating a history where both sides were possessed of noble motives.

For historical reference, Dixon relied heavily on Woodrow Wilson's unabashedly racist account *A History of the American People* and echoed Wilson's portrayal of the Confederacy as a charming and dignified experiment. Friends since their days as classmates at Johns Hopkins University, Dixon and Wilson learned their history from the same professors and sprung from the same ideological tree. Even after Wilson was sworn in as president, the two continued their friendship and maintained a kind and supportive correspondence. Dixon encouraged Wilson by telling him he'd go down as one of the greatest presidents in history, and Wilson assured Dixon that he was pursuing plans to resegregate the federal government.[1]

Early in 1915, Dixon wrote Wilson with an exciting proposition. A director named D. W. Griffith had adapted his trilogy of novels into a film called *The Birth of a Nation*, and Dixon wanted Wilson, a man who had inspired so much of the story, to have an exclusive look. Wilson knew as president he couldn't attend a screening in a theater, but he offered Dixon the next best thing: a showing in the White House. Dixon was ecstatic. He believed the medium was a new frontier, one that could prove effective for politicians, saying its development represented "the birth of a new art—the launching of the mightiest engine for moulding public opinion in the history of the world."[2]

On February 18, 1915, Dixon, Griffith, and members of the *Birth of a Nation* team dressed in formal attire and shuffled into the White House's East Room, a massive space decorated with chandeliers and usually reserved for state dinners. There were introductions, a great shaking of hands, all of the pomp and circumstance of a major event. The crowd was seated, the lights dimmed, and the movie was projected onto a panel of painted walls. When it was over, the audience roared its approval.

As one of the earliest epic motion pictures, *The Birth of a Nation* is impressive as a technical undertaking. But what Wilson and his White House celebrated that night was unadulterated bigotry. The narrative told in the film is taken straight from Wilson's bastardization of history, a story of America in which whites on both sides of the Mason–Dixon Line struggle to retain dignity even as African Americans tear them apart. Southern families are seen as distinguished, their relationship with their slaves sacrosanct, the parts of African Americans played by actors in ghoulish blackface. After the regrettable fall of the Confederacy, carpetbaggers and freed slaves overwhelm the South, terrorizing the countryside, raping women, invading the legislature, and ruining society with their ignorant and evil ways.

Wilson's histories figure into the narrative heavily. Quotes from his works are cited throughout, and his championing of the Ku Klux Klan is taken a step further, as they are the film's undisputed protagonists. Donning their white hoods and mounting their horses, they ensure that rightful order will be restored and the black menace managed. By the time the film ends, America is one again. The South reasserts white supremacy, with the KKK on guard in case the order is ever troubled.

Dixon later claimed that Wilson told him the film "teaches history by lightning."[3]

The Birth of a Nation was an overwhelming financial and cultural success and solidified in the public consciousness the idea of the Lost Cause. This false mythology disputed the notion that the Civil War had been fought to protect slavery; instead, it framed the war as a noble battle over preserving Southern culture and states' rights, all while scapegoating African Americans.

The Lost Cause ideology rippled through the academic community and found purchase in the worlds of publishing and popular entertainment. The Ku Klux Klan enjoyed a resurgence in which they controlled entire states and gained unbelievable political power. Decades after the end of the Civil War, communities around the country erected monuments to Confederate leaders and generals, many of them in front of courthouses as a not-so-subtle message to minorities that the white supremacy of the Confederacy still reigned through its laws and systems. Organizations like the United Daughters of the Confederacy, which swelled to nearly one hundred thousand members during Wilson's heyday, celebrated their "heritage" by refurbishing overt white supremacy as charming nostalgia and erecting memorials and statues around the country.[4]

Wilson must have been overjoyed. Not only had his vision manifested in dazzling detail, but the world around him was beginning to change according to his whims. His falsified histories had taken hold in the public imagination and were actively affecting reality.

To Wilson, the people represented potential. If they could be united by a Noble Lie, the man who wielded that lie would be unstoppable. Wilson recognized the thrilling prospect that emerging media meant humanity was ready to be united by an orchestrated and compelling vision. All he needed was a means to spread an enthralling lie while crushing voices carrying contrasting viewpoints.

Wilson had believed himself to be the prophet of that lie his entire life. His forays into history and public administration had prepared him not only to construct the lie and fine-tune its rhetoric, but to organize the system that wielded the lie. He saw the United States of America as the perfect incubator to prepare the vision, its history an especially potent womb with its tenuous reliance on espoused democratic ideals and hidden bureaucratic control. At the turn of the century, with the wounds of the Civil War hidden and America purified by the mythology of the Lost Cause, he recognized his opportunity and unleashed his prophecy.

★

As Wilson entered the East Room that night to watch his racist visions spring to life onscreen, his chief political concern was maintaining his promise to keep the United States from joining the Great War raging in Europe. The public largely favored remaining neutral; in the meantime, America was profiting wildly from serving as the world's banker and churning out goods for the warring nations. The prolonged hostilities ensured America emerged as the principal political and economic power; no matter who won the war, all the dominant nations in Europe faced the torturous prospect of digging themselves out of the dust and rubble.

While the United States enjoyed the profits of World War I, millions of Europeans were killed in brutal and dehumanizing fashion. It was a notably modern event, complete with advanced weaponry like machine guns that cut entire armies in two, armored tanks that crushed bones, airplanes that could soar overhead and rain down destruction, and lethal gas that strangled men to death and left them twisted corpses in the bottom of muddy trenches.

But by 1917, prolonged and brutal warfare had tapped British and

French resources, Russia's participation had sparked a revolution, and the discovery of the so-called Zimmermann Telegram had made it apparent that Germany had attempted to entice Mexico into joining the Central Powers and retaking territory lost in the previous century. The time had come, it seemed, for America to join the fray.

Wilson saw an opportunity for America to turn the tide of the war and play an outsized role in the peace process that would outline a new postwar order. Convinced he was a man destined for the times, Wilson wanted desperately to sit at the table where the future would be determined; entry into the chaos represented an opportunity to create a new order on a global scale.

To earn that new order, Wilson needed to renege on his promise of neutrality. To get away with it, he relied on the lessons he'd learned from Thomas Dixon Jr. and *The Birth of a Nation*. Wilson's political philosophy had always revolved around manipulation in the service of a ruling elite, and now he saw the marriage of propaganda and mass media, an evolution of the mythmaking of Andrew Jackson and propagandistic newspapers, as the means to an extraordinary end. To execute this bold new strategy, Wilson turned to George Creel, a sycophantic journalist who had propagated his hero worship of Wilson for years.

On April 13, 1917, Wilson signed Executive Order 2594, officially establishing the Committee on Public Information. He named Creel the head of the committee and charged him with crafting the propaganda necessary to galvanize the home front, win the war, and ultimately position the United States as the de facto world leader heading into the peace process. Wilson desired a "single way of thinking" within the United States, an engineered vision that united disparate interests while stamping out dissenting voices. To win, Wilson said, "It is not an army that we must shape and train for war. It is a nation . . . The whole nation must be a team."[5]

To create that sense of unity and send the country to war, Creel relied on established techniques used to market products. He bragged in his writing that the CPI was "a plain publicity proposition, a vast enterprise in salesmanship, the world's greatest adventure in advertising" that "carried to every corner of the civilized globe the full message of America's idealism, unselfishness, and indomitable purpose."[6]

A true believer, Creel studied the reportage of the time and was frustrated by the negativity emanating from the press. Muckraking investigations into crimes, corruption, and racial strife had formed an accurate but unflattering picture of the United States. Creel believed opinion of the country had soured following the Gilded Age, writing, "Naturally enough, we were looked upon as a race of dollar-mad materialists, a land of cruel monopolists, our real rulers the corporations and our democracy a 'fake.'"

To unite the country, the CPI under Creel effectively buried the country's glaring problems while also vilifying Germany and inspiring the nation to throw its weight behind the Allied cause in Europe. This meant tens of millions of publications in the form of pamphlets, handouts, newspapers, and books, and commandeering the nascent motion picture industry to create movies and newsreels espousing American exceptionalism and portraying the nation as united, brave, and unflinching. Publishers were threatened with ruin should they not toe the national line. Laws were passed that curtailed the rights guaranteed within the Constitution, and critics of the war were jailed.

For that purpose, Woodrow Wilson signed the Espionage Act on June 15, 1917, a bill that prepared the country for war by making it illegal to "obstruct recruitment" or to otherwise aid America's enemies. Nearly a year later, the law expanded with the passage of the Sedition Act of 1918, a fascist piece of legislation that further outlawed all speech considered injurious to the United States and its allies, threatening twenty years in prison for anyone who criticized or disrespected the government, the Constitution, the nation's flag, or the armed forces.[7]

The government used these laws to crush labor unions, socialists, and pacifists who dared criticize the war or the Wilson administration. Over a thousand people were arrested, publications were silenced, and the postmaster general enjoyed dictatorial powers in spying on communications around the country. In a particularly ironic moment, a man named Robert Goldstein was inspired by *The Birth of a Nation* to write his own propagandistic movie, this one called *The Spirit of '76*, that glorified the American Revolution. But because it painted the allied British in a negative light, his film was seized and Goldstein spent three years in prison for the crime of celebrating the genesis of America.

Creel's propaganda overwhelmed the nation and created a firestorm of xenophobic hate and nationalistic fervor. To spur recruitment and sales of war bonds, Creel warned Americans they were besieged with foreign spies and the fate of the nation hinged on their loyalty and hatred of the Germans. Creel flooded schools with propaganda about the history of America and the German threat, instructed teachers on how to indoctrinate their students, and employed Boy Scouts to knock on doors and deliver his propaganda to their neighbors. Over seventy-five thousand public speakers calling themselves Four Minute Men attended public functions and delivered remarks meant to inspire thoughtless loyalty and rouse passions.

Americans turned violent. They stomped dachshunds to death by the dozens, virtually outlawed German culture, and threatened and intimidated immigrants. In 1918, a mob of two hundred men marched German immigrant Robert Prager through the streets of Collinsville, Illinois; beat him bloody; and forced him to sing "The Star-Spangled Banner" and get down on his knees and kiss the American flag. Despite his promises of loyalty, they took him into the woods and hanged him. Eyewitnesses recalled that Prager, who had become a citizen and fashioned himself a fervent patriot, had continually asserted his innocence and his last words were a plea to be buried wrapped in the American flag.[8] Of the incident, *The Washington Post* commented, "In spite of excesses such as lynching, it is a healthful and wholesome awakening in the interior of the country."[9] That wholesome awakening inspired street gangs of "patriots" to perpetrate unthinkable crimes, like the American Protective League, which received the support of the federal government as it spied on citizens, raided their homes and businesses without warrants, and kidnapped people.

As successful as Creel's propaganda was on Americans, even more impressive was its effect on the rest of the world. According to Creel, the war was actually a "world-fight for the verdict of mankind."[10] American propaganda bureaus were opened around the globe and connected via intercontinental cables and newswires that pulsed with finely tuned pro-American rhetoric. In an era where daily life was inundated with the horrors of slaughter and human suffering, Creel's portrait of America as a pinnacle of progress and decency was a shining light.

Creel intended to break the war will of the German people, so he had Allied planes drop leaflets, books, and speeches from the belly of their aircraft as they flew over enemy lines. In some instances, special shells were designed for Allied weapons so that Creel's propaganda could be shot like missiles across the no-man's-land of the battlefield.

This tactic was overwhelmingly effective, and by the time German troops eventually surrendered, they carried with them copies of Wilson's much-ballyhooed Fourteen Points, a supposed plan for a more democratic postwar order, as they requested their terms. Creel had appealed to their exhaustion with the fight and desire for armistice by handing them a plan guaranteeing a new and acceptable world if they would only put down their weapons and trust the Allies. In some ways, the propaganda was even more effective than the bullets.

Creel might have understood he was fighting for the verdict of mankind, but it's hard to imagine even he could have grasped what the CPI might achieve. The main focus of the international propaganda spreading around the globe was Woodrow Wilson himself, the print and motion pictures distributed centering on his speeches and developing call for "democracy" and "self-determination," concepts that were themselves revolutionary but had been stripped of their meaning in practice.

Wilson, after all, was the president of a country founded on antidemocratic principles and dominated by a ruling elite who guided the masses. He was preeminently obsessed with developing systems that further removed the citizenry from government, and was an avowed white supremacist who believed only certain peoples were capable of determining their own fates. But Creel's propaganda positioned Wilson as a champion of human dignity who could save the world from war. Wilson's calls for democracy and self-determination resonated with the people of the world who had yet to become accustomed to propaganda, and to those suffering under the brutal fist of dictators and colonists, Wilson's message rang like deliverance.

When the time came to dictate peace, Wilson boarded the SS *George Washington* and sailed across the ocean to oversee the negotiations. Aboard the ship were American diplomats, the smartest policy experts Wilson could find, and members of the CPI. Along the way Wilson took a break from his preparation and pulled George Creel aside, confiding in the man who had made him a global savior, "I am wondering whether you have not unconsciously spun a net for me from which there is no escape."

Wilson may have doubted himself as he crossed the Atlantic, but when he arrived in Europe he was treated as destiny personified. The crowds that greeted him in France were huge, throbbing masses that deliriously cheered his name, chanting, "Vive Wil-son! Vive Wil-son! Vive Wil-son!"[11] The premier of France remarked, "I do not think there has been anything like it in the history of the world."[12] They lined the streets, screamed from the rooftops, hung out of their windows, and wept uncontrollably as they tossed flowers at Wilson's carriage. For days on end, worshippers built shrines where they prayed to Wilson and God, the two now interchangeable. A schoolchild exclaimed, "I hope Mr. Wilson never dies."[13]

By the time Wilson made it to Italy, he was the most famous man in the world, a full-blown savior upon whom the fate of the future rested. Once more, a president of the United States had willed himself to be an all-powerful deity. In a few short years he had gone from a racist academic to the people's last, best hope. Creel had sold American exceptionalism and Woodrow Wilson to the world and manifested a paradise replete with a messiah.

"WELCOME TO THE GOD OF PEACE," a banner proclaimed.

★

Aboard the SS *George Washington,* Woodrow Wilson wasn't the only person concerned that expectations had been raised too high. The policy experts and negotiators who'd been tapped to represent the United States were panicking because they had no idea what Wilson's slogans meant. They sounded fantastic but offered very little in the way of guidance to rooms full of men lording over a map and trying to decide what the future of the human race might look like.

Wilson remained optimistic. The CPI's selling of him as an ambassador of peace on earth had taken hold and he believed the welcome he'd received from the people of Europe presaged the greeting he'd get in the negotiations. He had long held firm that all of humanity could coalesce if only a man of considerable talents might arise and lead them, and Wilson was ready for his peers in the Allied nations to recognize his worthiness. He delivered to them the gospel of America, a blueprint for economic success and social stability, a framework in which the Noble Lie of democracy was married to the social control of a hidden aristocracy, all of it in the name of what Wilson called "the righteous conquest of the markets of the world."[14]

By many accounts, the reception Wilson received from his fellow heads of state behind closed doors was much chillier than that of the crowd worshipping him in the streets. Many considered Wilson both wildly self-important and frightfully unprepared. He reacted to criticism with disbelief and anger and routinely lectured those around him, further bombarding them with his empty rhetoric. Premier of France Georges Clemenceau, reeling from one of Wilson's sermons, threw up his hands in frustration and asked, "How can I talk to a fellow who thinks himself the first man in two thousand years to know anything about peace on earth?"[15]

While Wilson intended to spread his revelation, the other members of the Allied nations came with concrete agendas. They tolerated Wilson's sermonizing and embraced his slogans to promote the talks as high-minded and ethical, but the actual plans revealed their priorities. From around the world, nations inspired by Wilson's speeches and CPI propaganda came to make their case to the god of peace and realize a new era of justice and democracy. Wilson's repeated stating of his belief in "self-determination" meant many things to many people, but the nations of the world who had been dominated by larger states, exploited for their resources, and subjugated by antidemocratic means took Wilson at his word. They would be greatly disappointed as the talks were devoted almost exclusively to the whims and desires of the major states and paid little mind to Wilson's promises or rhetoric.

The downfall of the Paris peace talks in 1919 was a dogged dedication to the status quo. Wilson and his peers in England, France, and Italy were devotees of the idea that the globe was divided between those capable of self-government and those reliant upon them. In their minds, the world's systems were too complicated for the feeble intelligences of those in "lesser states" and it was necessary for those better educated and better suited for ruling to do the job for them.

One of the chief visionaries and architects of the system, Wilson called it "the great Maze of society" and described the individual as being caught within its walls. While ultimately ignorant of its design, even they would notice "its solidarity, its complexity, its restless forces surging amidst its delicate tissues, its hazards and its exalted hopes." Again, Wilson saw "in the midst of all" a leader "gathering, as best he can, the thoughts that are completed, that are perceived, that have told upon the common mind; judging also of the work that is now at length ready to be completed; reckoning the gathered gain; perceiving the fruits of toil and of war."

Wilson's League of Nations was meant to codify this ideology. The system that had guided the United States would be expanded to harness all other nations and employ the same Noble Lie. To this end, the Allied nations, as representatives of the capable and competent few, would sit atop the League of Nations and manage the affairs of the lesser nations, while the illusion of equality and democracy sated the controlled. Naturally, the Allied nations balked at Japan's recommendation of the Racial Equality Proposal for the League of Nations, a policy that would address worldwide discrimination. Palestine, Syria, Iraq, Rwanda, and other "lesser nations" were transferred from their former rulers to Allied powers, and empire nations like England and France would direct their political and social processes, an anti-democratic setup in which powers could "safely leave while pulling the strings," ensuring their economic and political interests would be "secure."

As France's representative, Clemenceau did not budge from his demand that Germany be punished for the war's destruction. Despite Allied reservations about the effects of punishments, and a belief that a Germany overburdened by reparations and penances might collapse, Clemenceau held firm. The Allies stripped much of Germany's land, levied heavy costs, and demanded they take full responsibility for the war. Believing they had surrendered under Wilson's Fourteen Points, the Germans felt betrayed but were unable to continue the fight.

On June 28, 1919, German representatives trudged into the Hall of Mirrors in the opulent Palace of Versailles and signed the treaty that had been prepared for them. They took full responsibility for the war and agreed to pay a lofty price. In celebration, cannons boomed and national anthems played. It was celebrated as the conclusion of the war to end all wars, but in reality the architects of the peace, who believed themselves to be the most capable and talented of leaders, had set the stage for unimaginable horrors.

Wilson returned home in poor health. He had suffered what appeared to be a small stroke in Europe, but he refused to heed his medical staff's warnings that traveling across the United States to promote the League of Nations would worsen his condition. Despite his efforts, the League was rejected by Congress. Wilson suffered a debilitating stroke that October and was confined to his bed for months afterward while his wife ran the government as an unelected head of state. As debilitated as he was, Wilson continued to plot his return to politics and wanted desperately to run for a third term in 1920. He died in 1924, bitter and still angry that his League of Nations had been rejected, steadfastly determined to rise again to the level of a living god and finally realize his constructed paradise on earth.

★

Though Wilson fell short of his goals, the operation he crafted to win World War I lived on, particularly in the work of Edward Bernays, a CPI member who served in its Bureau of Latin-American Affairs and oversaw much of its operations in the Western Hemisphere. Bernays later made the trip with Wilson and George Creel to Paris for the peace talks and worked to promote the meetings as fair and honorable but received rebukes from the administration when he spoke too openly about propaganda in comments to the press.

To Bernays, however, the concept itself wasn't problematic. In his 1928 book *Propaganda*, Bernays wrote exhaustively on the subject, defining it as manipulation by "an intelligent few" who "pull the wires which control the public mind" in aid of "the executive arm of the invisible government."[16]

Bernays was uniquely positioned to further the subliminal aspects of propaganda by consulting with his uncle, psychologist Sigmund Freud. Bernays took long walks with his uncle and quizzed him on human behavior and the secrets of the newly hypothesized subconscious. Freud believed humans were highly illogical animals piloted by deep-seated fears and insecurities, their actions dictated by internal forces beyond their understanding.

With Freud's theories, Bernays saw an opportunity. If enlightened individuals could understand this subconscious and the irrational nature of people, they could harness them as a means for control and profit, all while leaving consumers unaware of the manipulation. As a salesman, Bernays saw little difference between the selling of politicians and the selling of products; the CPI, after all, was rooted in advertising and salesmanship.

Bernays's realization answered a lingering problem. Following the end of World War I, American industry faced a crisis: War preparation had sparked a revolution in production. Now, in peacetime, factories needed alternate products that could continue the boom. Bernays and his disciples seized this opportunity and constructed a consumer culture that preyed upon the unconscious fears and insecurities of the American people and offered them products that might soothe them.

Advertising and public relations firms sprouted up around the country and probed the human psyche for weaknesses and vulnerabilities. Products were designed with unconscious fears in mind, and ads in magazines and on billboards warned Americans they might be ostracized by their friends or families, or that they might fail financially or socially, if they didn't buy the right brand or good. If they chose the wrong toothpaste, they might die alone. If they served an underwhelming dinner, they might lose their careers and social standing.

In this way, Bernays crafted the modern idea of America, a country haunted by hidden forces and whose citizens' lives are inundated with dangerous manipulations. He popularized smoking, the bacon-and-egg breakfast, and the owning of books as a status symbol, and established lasting brands and American standards like General Electric, the Columbia Broadcasting System, Ivory soap, and Dodge.

Bernays helped usher into the world a new reality in which society came to resemble Freud's concept of the human mind. On the surface was what Walter Lippmann called a "pseudo-environment" wherein citizens bought products based on psychological appeals and voted for candidates who played to their base instincts while blissfully unaware of the constant manipulations brewing right under the surface.[17] It was a consumer-driven extension of Woodrow Wilson's dream for an engineered maze of existence.

This strategy constituted the new world of public opinion, a social science dedicated not to understanding what the electorate and public wanted but to how to convince them to want what the ruling elite wanted to sell them. In Lippmann's definition, public opinion dealt with "indirect, unseen, and puzzling facts" and trafficked in "images of how things behave" that were "simpler and more fixed than the ebb and flow of affairs."[18] Politicians wouldn't bother to explain the actual workings of government, as they had grown too complicated and complex, or foster plans of action to be debated in public. Instead, they would provide the citizenry with easily understandable "stereotypes" the unprepared masses could easily grasp. Soon "truth" as an objective principle disappeared as politicians competed like commercial brands over who could wield the most palatable and inspiring story, an effective means by which to win elections but ultimately a problematic strategy in governing, as Lippmann warned: "These pictures fade and are hard to keep steady; their contours and their pulse fluctuate."[19]

Though Wilson had believed these measures were necessary to

make "the world safe for democracy," the strategies he and Bernays had pioneered came to endanger the very notion of a democratic society.

★

In the postwar period, America again entered a period of aggressive capitalism. Republican Warren Harding, Wilson's successor, believed in "less government in business and more business in government," an unleashing of the market that removed regulations that had been put in place to constrain the businesses that had bled the country dry and terrorized it with regular instability.[20] With this relaxation, and the marketing appeals of men like Bernays, a new culture of consumerism took shape.

The counter to America's burgeoning consumerism lay in Russia, where radicals acting on the same Enlightenment ideals that had inspired Thomas Jefferson and the American Revolution had ousted Czar Nicholas II in 1917. That revolution was met with distrust among the Allies, who from 1918 to 1920 pumped troops into Russia to bolster pro-capitalist forces in the Russian Civil War, including upwards of thirteen thousand from America alone. They fought in vain to defend capitalism, forever pairing that ideology with the Allies and the postwar order they crafted in Paris.

The consequences of their intervention were immense. The Soviets closed ranks and gave way to one of the most murderous regimes in the history of human civilization. They restricted human rights and came to oppose the Enlightenment ideas originally at the heart of their revolution. A generations-long adversarial relationship developed between Russia and the nations that had sought to strangle communism in its crib. Communism promoted unrestrained revolution, an uprising that could spread through the entire world, and Americans committed to the social order under capitalism were deeply disturbed.

During this period, the United States fell into the First Red

Scare; just a few short years after nationalist fervor propelled the nation into war, that societal distrust turned inward. Anything resembling socialism or communism was attacked, including labor unions and collective bodies. A labor strike became an act of treason; one stoppage in Seattle prompted a local paper to declare, "This is America—not Russia."[21] Business owners saw an opening to crush unions, promoting anti-Russian sentiment and warning of "the grasping hand of the Bolshevik."[22]

In this way, consumerism became a patriotic act. Just as Americans had been prompted by George Creel and the CPI to buy war bonds, they were now being told that buying a house or spending their paychecks on conveniences and luxuries would strike a blow in the battle against communism. The papers they read warned them of Russian subterfuge; the movies showed spies ready to plunge the nation into a communist nightmare.

So Americans attacked. On May Day 1919, as labor unions and socialists marched through cities around the country, organized street soldiers disrupted their events. The insurgents beat them, stabbed them, kidnapped them, raided their homes and offices, destroyed their publications and personal effects, and illegally searched their belongings and correspondence. These actions went largely unpunished and were routinely lauded in the press. *The Salt Lake Tribune* observed, "Free speech has been carried to the point where it is an unrestrained menace."[23]

After generations of white supremacy influencing American economics, proponents of capitalism worried the nation's minorities might welcome communism's call for revolution. On July 28, 1919, following the Chicago race riots that killed twenty-three African Americans and injured hundreds, *The New York Times* ran the headline "REDS TRY TO STIR NEGROES TO REVOLT."[24] The story, "Accumulating Evidence," cited anonymous reports of "vicious and apparently well financed propaganda which is directed against the white people, and which seeks, by newspapers, pamphlets and in other ways to stir up discontent among the negroes, particularly the uneducated class in the Southern States."

The Chicago race riot was one of many incidents in what came to be called the Red Summer of 1919, a period in which paranoid and racist whites attacked African Americans around the country, the violence and criminality in some instances assisted by law enforcement and federal troops. African Americans were lynched in public places in a revival of an especially vile American tradition (between 1882 and 1950 some five thousand men and women were lynched).[25] In some cases, hundreds of people would come to the execution. There were picnics. Celebrations. They posed for pictures with desecrated corpses and burning bodies. Postcards were sold. The victims were killed and dismembered, their body parts taken as trinkets and keepsakes.

Of course, racial violence was not limited to one summer, and the targets revealed that fears of socialism were masking desires to undermine the economic ascent of African Americans. Over the course of two days in 1921, white attackers flooded into Tulsa, Oklahoma's Greenwood District, a black community home to a thriving business district, a capitalist success story known as Black Wall Street. The insurgents burned over a thousand homes, destroyed businesses, demolished black churches and schools, and killed at least thirty-six people. In a disturbing twist, the weapons of World War I, intended as tools to protect freedom and liberty, were used to massacre victims. White men set up machine guns to spray the black neighborhoods. In one instance, a plane was outfitted with guns and dropped bombs and incendiaries on their houses. One terrified African-American resident recalled, "There was a great shadow in the sky and upon a second look we discerned that this cloud was caused by fast approaching enemy aeroplanes. It then dawned upon us that the enemy had organized in the night and was invading our district the same as the Germans invaded France and Belgium."[26]

Racial hatred ran rampant even as the country continued to sell itself to the world as a bastion of liberty. Spurred by *The Birth of a Nation* and the rising trends of bigotry, the Ku Klux Klan was reborn and enjoyed more influence than ever before. To achieve this, the KKK realized the necessities of the time and hired a public relations firm, which rebranded the KKK as a nonviolent fraternity.[27] The rebranding worked, and the organization gained political footing throughout the South and in Indiana, where it controlled virtually all aspects of government. It became commonplace to see the KKK in the North, for Confederate flags to wave from coast to coast. In 1925, thirty thousand robed and masked members of the KKK celebrated their rise to power by marching through Washington, DC, the capital of a nation increasingly obsessed with racial purity.

★

American white supremacy boiled over as men and women emigrated from war-torn Europe and the nation's demographics shifted. Just as politicians had argued against the annexation of Mexico in the nineteenth century on the grounds of preserving the supremacy of the white race, politicians in the postwar period advocated restrictions on immigration in the name of racial purity. Representative Robert Allen of West Virginia supported the Immigration Act of 1924 as a "restriction of the alien stream" necessary "for purifying and keeping pure the blood of America."[28] President Calvin Coolidge agreed, saying, "America must be kept America."

Testifying on behalf of the Immigration Act was Harry Laughlin, the superintendent of the Eugenics Record Office in Cold Spring Harbor, New York. Laughlin warned of "immigrant-conquerors" who might take over the country and engage in "race degeneracy."[29]

Laughlin's testimony was taken seriously because the United States was enraptured with the concept of eugenics, the pseudoscience of breeding humans to improve the species. The originator of the idea was Francis Galton, an English scientist and half cousin of Charles Darwin. At the turn of the century, Galton met Charles Davenport, an American who wanted to take Darwin's theories of natural selection and evolution and accelerate them, writing, "What nature does blindly, slowly and ruthlessly, man may do providently, quickly and kindly."[30]

In 1910, Davenport established the Eugenics Record Office, an organization dedicated to studying eugenics and America's genetic stock. Enjoying support from wealthy families like the Rockefellers and Carnegies, Davenport and Laughlin dispatched researchers around the country to investigate the families and generations of people they considered "feeble-minded," later advocating the purging of "the lowest ten percent of the human stock," who were "so meagerly endowed by Nature that their perpetuation would constitute a social menace."

Men like Davenport and Laughlin believed American society to be an actual meritocracy. Like the social Darwinists before them, they went searching for something fundamentally flawed within the individuals who struggled in America; now they could fuse that social theory with genetics. Eugenicists and the state declared war on the "socially inadequate classes," which included "the feeble-minded, the insane, the criminalistics, the epileptic, drug users, the diseased, the blind, the deaf, the deformed, and orphans and paupers."[31]

The idea spread. Doctors in institutions and orphanages maimed and experimented on unwitting patients. Eugenicists openly advocated a racist state in which every citizen would be studied and interrogated from childhood into adulthood, their biological worth weighed and their breeding directed by the government. While everyday citizens engaged in eugenic pageants and bought eugenic propaganda in massive quantities, some proponents openly advocated that unwanted citizens should be killed in gas chambers or poisoned. By 1937, thirty states had passed forced sterilization laws.

Those laws were made possible by the landmark case *Buck v. Bell*, in which the Supreme Court heard the case of Carrie Buck, a twenty-year-old deemed "feebleminded." Buck had been committed to the Virginia State Colony for Epileptics and Feebleminded in early 1924 after a relative raped and impregnated her. Her family committed her to conceal their shame; she was deemed feebleminded and was to be the first person forcibly sterilized under Virginia's new law.

The Supreme Court, including former president William Howard Taft, ruled 8–1 that the state enjoyed the freedom to sterilize its citizens to protect itself from the proliferation of the unwanted. Justice Oliver Wendell Holmes, who later preached his desire to breed a better race, provided the opinion, arguing that society should act to prevent "those who are manifestly unfit from continuing their kind."

In the wake of that decision, over seventy thousand people were sterilized nationwide; the Supreme Court decision has still not been officially overturned. Laughlin and other eugenicists of note remained formidable influencers as the government continually relied on them in instances of sterilization, marriage and breeding restriction laws, and matters of immigration.

A decade later they would be relied on as the defeated nation of Germany saw the rise of a small but aggressive group calling itself the National Socialist Party. In 1933, the Nazi government passed the Law for the Prevention of Hereditarily Diseased Offspring based on Laughlin's design and sterilized upwards of eighty thousand people in a single year. The Third Reich relied on Laughlin's example as they sought to purify the Aryan race and produce a generation of supermen.

Beyond eugenics, Nazi Germany found other ways to follow America's example. Their plans relied on many of the schemes and ideologies pioneered by American leaders: Wilsonian propaganda, state-sanctioned racism and nationalism, genocide in the name of the state, and a cult of mass production, all bolstered by fundamental lies told to the masses.

Wilson's prophecy for the world ultimately failed to produce a new order of peace and prosperity but succeeded in releasing a monster.

CHAPTER 6

★　★　★

The God of War

On a bright, clear Thursday afternoon in the fall of 1929, fifty-four-year-old Winston Churchill took a stroll through New York City to clear his head. Less than five months had passed since a general election had seen Britain's Conservative Party unseated, meaning Churchill had lost his post as chancellor of the exchequer and been cast into the political wilderness. To gather his bearings he'd sailed to North America, toured Canada, and now stood in the epicenter of the New World as he attempted to grasp how the United States, a former English colony, had come to eclipse his dear British Empire.

Recognized by an excited stranger on Wall Street, Churchill was rushed into the visitors' gallery of the New York Stock Exchange, an institution Churchill likened to a casino but credited as the base of growing American influence. He saw it as a temptation that seduced Americans with promises of "unearned" and "easy money," a machine "not built to prevent crises, but to survive them."[1] One of these crises was about to unfold as the market hemorrhaged before Churchill's eyes. That Thursday it lost 11 percent of its value, the future prime minister watching as traders scurried "to and fro like a slow-motion picture of a disturbed ant heap . . . finding no one strong enough to pick up the sure fortunes they were compelled to offer."[2]

That October 24 would come to be known as Black Thursday and signaled the beginnings of the most devastating economic collapse in world history. Just as they had done in past crises, the wealthiest Americans attempted to stabilize the market with an injection of capital. The usual gang of Morgan, Chase, and National City Bank threw in their lots, but their efforts proved futile this time. The following Monday saw a 13 percent drop and then, on October 29, "Black Tuesday," a panicked market attempted to unload its assets and the bottom fell out.

The stock market crash of 1929 was the nasty conclusion of the period of economic fervor following World War I. A succession of pro-business Republican presidents had stoked the capitalist flames and let loose the newly configured consumer market, creating a boom in industry that largely benefited those at the top and seemed as if it might never end.

But as early as March there were troubling signs. Paul Warburg, a veteran banker on Wall Street, warned of an imminent reckoning, saying the market had reached "a saturation point" and that a resulting crash would "bring about a general depression involving the entire country."[3]

Consumers had spent their savings on goods, maxed out their credit, and were saddled with crushing debt. Production was slowing. Employers hoarded capital and stifled buying power among their employees with low wages. In the market, investors were gambling so wildly and perilously a financial writer for *The New York Times* described it as "an orgy of reckless speculation."[4]

President Herbert Hoover attempted to calm the public, but the reverberations of the crash brought the country to its knees. Businesses laid off workers and stalled hiring. Unemployment reached as high as a quarter of the population. Consumer confidence plummeted. Banks collapsed under the onslaught of panicked withdrawals. Around the country starving people waited in bread and soup lines, dug through trash heaps for scraps of food, resorted to stealing fistfuls of coal from the railways to save their families from freezing to death in the winter. The Noble Lie was coming unraveled as the idea of a fair and just society gave way to a cruel, unkind nation. The national identity withered.

As the world's economies had come to be linked, the poison of America's market rippled across the globe, crippling other nations and leading to widespread economic and political uncertainty. With the perceived failure of capitalism and liberal democracy, dejected populations in Europe, still recovering from war, sought alternative philosophies that might lead them out of the chaos and to a return to glory.

One of the emerging contenders for a new direction originated in Italy with the Fascist Party and its leader Benito Mussolini. Mussolini and his fellow fascists believed the world's problems lay in individualism and democracy. They considered democracy and self-determination to be lies, as powerful forces pulled the strings behind the scenes, thinking exhibited in fascist sociologist Robert Michels's concept of the "Iron Law of Oligarchy," which argued that while democratic systems existed for cooperation they would inevitably be co-opted by a ruling elite. Fascists sought to do away with that pretense of democratic freedom and to replace it with a dictatorship.

In Italy, Mussolini sought to restore the glory of Rome and revert sovereignty from the citizen to the state, undoing the individualist shift of the Enlightenment. The state, he believed, stood solely "for the conscience and the universal will of man as a historical entity." An ideal fascist state would then direct the lives of its citizens and marshal their power, much as liberal democracies do in times of crisis and war.

In October 1922, Mussolini orchestrated a coup, mobilizing his paramilitary Blackshirts for a march on Rome that led to King Victor Emmanuel III's granting him power. From there, Mussolini established a dictatorship; dubbed Il Duce, he presided with unquestioned authority. That coup inspired a treacherously ambitious thirty-four-year-old Adolf Hitler to attempt his own takeover in Munich a year later, in November of 1923. He failed, but during his time in prison he wrote his book *Mein Kampf* and grew in stature as a nationalist leader among Germans opposed to the Weimar Republic, which had ruled since the close of World War I.

Of the many nations wounded by the Great Depression, Germany was among the most affected. The terms of the Treaty of Versailles had laden them with substantial war repayments that stalled the economy and inspired a great deal of mistrust in the government. America's financial downfall exacerbated the situation, as the United States had been loaning Germany the money necessary to make its payments.

The rise of the Nazi Party in Germany was due in large part to this political and economic instability. By the time the Great Depression hit the German economy, the Weimar Republic had already survived multiple coup attempts by a variety of extreme political parties, including the Nazis, communists, and anarchists. So fractious and unsound was the order that these groups grew in size until their members were battling each other in the streets as well as inside the halls of government.

Hitler and the Nazis capitalized on the bitter feelings of emasculation and betrayal emanating from Germany's defeat in the Great War. Germans had long felt they were insuperable in battle and only internal treason could explain their failure. This delusion necessitated the myth of "the Knife in the Back," a conspiracy theory that Germany had been betrayed by a combination of unfaithful politicians and Jewish saboteurs. Hitler pushed this narrative while promising that he alone was capable of restoring proper order.

Much of the underlying thought that contributed to Hitler's rise and eventual ascendance to führer of Nazi Germany can be found in German tradition and philosophy. Just as the United States had co-alesced behind the idea of manifest destiny in the early nineteenth century, Germany in the twentieth century looked to the Romantic period for inspiration and purpose and, similar to the Americans, came to see the white race as the embodiment of the universe's will, a race of men destined to conquer and lead.

Likewise, the philosophy of Nazism was directly related to the myth of American exceptionalism and its inherent white suprem-acist ideology. In fact, Nazism was inspired by and maintained a direct line to prominent American movements and popular figures, such as Lothrop Stoddard. The author of the 1920 book *The Rising Tide of Color Against White World-Supremacy*, a bestseller in the United States that received positive reviews and the ringing en-dorsement of President Harding, Stoddard was an inspiration to the racist foundation of Nazi Germany. He defined world history as a racial struggle rightfully dominated by the Aryan race, and as the twentieth century took form, Stoddard saw that dominance threatened by changing demographics and internal strife among white nations. He called World War I a "white civil war" and warned that a "weak-ening of white solidarity" that allowed people of color to gain power and outbreed them could "produce the most disastrous consequences."[5] Stoddard's theories were held in such high regard that when he visited Germany in 1939, he was given exclusive meetings with Heinrich Himmler and Hitler himself.

Another American with profound influence on Hitler was Madison Grant, a close personal friend of Herbert Hoover's who played a piv-otal role in crafting America's exclusionary Immigration Act of 1924. Grant's *The Passing of the Great Race* warned that the Aryan race was weakening itself by intermarrying with other racial groups—a practice he called "race suicide"—and advocated that "defective in-fants" and adults of "no value to the community" should be murdered to provide relief for society.[6] Hitler called it his bible.

But perhaps no American was held in higher esteem or considered more influential in the formation of Nazi thought than automobile magnate Henry Ford. In an interview with the *Chicago Tribune,* Hitler declared that he regarded Ford as a potential fascist president in the United States and admitted a desire to "send some of [his] shock troops to Chicago and other big American cities to help in the elections."[7] Heinrich Ford, as he was called, was so admired by Hitler that a portrait of him hung in the Nazi leader's office.

Ford's influence on the Nazis began during World War I, when Ford went on a peacemaking tour of Europe and reported that a member of the excursion told him the conflict was the result of Jewish manipulation. Ford returned and began publishing long and paranoid conspiracy theories in his newspaper, *The Dearborn Independent.* These pieces included excerpts from *The Protocols of the Elders of Zion,* a document that purported to reveal secret meetings between Jewish powerbrokers who sought world domination by leveraging white nations against one another. In truth, *The Protocols* were fake: The unknown author, most likely a Russian at the turn of the century, lifted large sections from a French satire of political machinations by white politicians called *The Dialogue in Hell Between Machiavelli and Montesquieu.*

Ford's promotion of these theories helped spread anti-Semitic sentiment through the United States. His work also found considerable welcome in Germany; it was collected, translated, and printed in 1922 under the title *The International Jew: The World's Foremost Problem.* Ford's dubious collection of half-baked conspiracies and misunderstood satires was taken for gospel truth by Hitler and his fellow Nazis.

For his contributions, Ford was granted the Grand Cross of the Supreme Order of the German Eagle in 1938 and was rumored to support the Nazis politically and financially. Allegations surfaced later that the Ford Motor Company helped the Nazi war machine and took advantage of slave labor. Though Henry Ford apologized later in life for his role in spreading anti-Semitism, the die had been cast. Hitler had his philosophy and the Nazis their very own manifest destiny to call them to purpose.

★

In 1932, New York governor Franklin Delano Roosevelt captured the Democratic nomination for president of the United States, declaring in his acceptance speech that he intended to end an "era of selfishness" and undo the damage of "false prophets" of speculation and easy wealth.[8] His attack on these prophets continued as he won the presidency and promised a "new deal" for the American people as "the money changers" had "fled from their high seats in the temple of our civilization." "We may now restore that temple to the ancient truths," Roosevelt said, directly challenging the notion that the wealthy and powerful were crowned by God. "The measure of the restoration lies in the extent to which we may apply social values more noble than mere monetary profit."[9]

Restoration was far from a sure thing as Roosevelt took office. The American economy had cratered and public faith in the United States as an institution was eroding. Roosevelt's New Deal sought to revitalize that faith by throwing the full weight and power of the nation into the business of healing. Banking and investing were reformed and government funds focused on creating new programs to put the unemployed back to work. These programs included the Civilian Conservation Corps and the Civil Works Administration, which sent Americans around the country to work on infrastructure, including the construction of dams, bridges, irrigation, parks, schools, and libraries, and to assist farming and rural communities that had been hit hard in the Depression. With the invention of Social Security, the most vulnerable populations would be provided for, including senior citizens, the unemployed, the disabled, and endangered children.

Arguably Roosevelt's greatest achievement in the unfurling of his New Deal wasn't necessarily its effect on the economy but rather on the populace. Economists have debated the effectiveness of Roosevelt's programs in restarting the economy, and a considerable consensus has emerged that it was a combination of his efforts and the start of World War II that saved the country. But the mobilization of the unemployed and the desperate might have preserved civilization outside of economic considerations by vesting citizens in a new, working vision of the United States, a proposed cleansing and reformed version of the American Noble Lie. Roosevelt's greatest task was to repair the wound of economic depression while ensuring that the story of America and freedom were not supplanted by the poison of fascism.

When Roosevelt became president in 1933, unemployment and frustration had brought many workers to the brink. Disgruntled and emasculated men were recruited into fascist organizations either overtly influenced by Nazi ideology or tangentially related. Of these, perhaps no organization was more overt than the German-American Bund, a group that had been given the blessing of Germany's Nazi Party in 1933 to represent them in America. After internal struggles, former autoworker Fritz Kuhn assumed leadership of the group in 1936 with the explicit goal to grow the Bund on a "platform bedecked with swastikas and Stars and Stripes."[10] Around the country, the Bund opened camps to train its members and indoctrinate their children with Nazi propaganda and teachings, an ode to the Hitler Youth. In 1937, Kuhn, standing in front of a Nazi banner, announced his mission to "save America for white Americans," an echo of the calls of past politicians, including former presidents.[11] On February 20, 1939, the Bund held a rally in Madison Square Garden staged to resemble an assembly of the Third Reich. The event attracted over twenty thousand attendees who chanted totalitarian slogans, gave Nazi salutes, and cheered as anti-Semitic, fascist speeches were delivered in front of a backdrop that featured a portrait of George Washington and an array of Nazi swastikas.

Another fascist organization was the Silver Legion, a paramilitary group that took its cues from Hitler and Mussolini as they marched in shows of strength and planned the military overthrow of the United States. Led by writer William Dudley Pelley, who believed he and Hitler were destined to rule the world, the Silver Legion was distinctive for its uniforms: silver shirts adorned with the letter *L*, blue corduroy pants, and a blue cap. At its peak the Legion swelled to nearly fifteen thousand members and enjoyed secret support from Nazi interests.

But for all of the explicit organizations, there were other more prominent and subtle fascistic voices. One of the most influential figures was Father Charles Coughlin, a priest who enjoyed a radio audience of roughly thirty million Americans and voiced admiration for Hitler and Mussolini while decrying Jews as "the Mystical Body of Satan."[12] Coughlin organized his own political movement, the National Union for Social Justice, that enjoyed the support of millions of Americans.

No fascist organization held more influence than the America First Committee, which seemed in the late 1930s to be a developing, viable political party. The AFC was dedicated to maintaining neutrality in World War II and walked a fine line between advocating isolationism and cooperation with the Axis powers. The vanguard of the AFC was aviator Charles Lindbergh, the American hero who piloted the *Spirit of St. Louis* in the first solo transatlantic flight in 1927 and who had become one of the most famous and revered men in the country. Lindbergh had been heavily recruited by the Nazis and was invited to inspect the burgeoning Luftwaffe in 1936 and 1938, an endeavor that led to his being awarded the Commander Cross of the Order of the German Eagle by high-ranking Nazi Hermann Göring.

As Germany ravaged Europe, Lindbergh was sympathetic to the Nazi cause and openly lauded Hitler as "a great man" who had "done much for the German people."[13] In an article printed in 1939, Lindbergh called to Americans as "heirs of European culture" to reject a war he worried would "destroy the treasures of the White race." Instead of fighting the Nazis or Fascists, Lindbergh advocated an alliance to defend white supremacy, warning, "It is time to turn from our quarrels and to build our White ramparts again . . . a Western Wall of race and arms which can hold back either a Genghis Khan or the infiltration of inferior blood." This alliance, Lindbergh was sure to point out, required cooperation between Germany, France, England, and America.

Although the America First Committee was dealt a mortal blow when Japan attacked Pearl Harbor in 1941, Lindbergh continued his crusade unabated. In a speech in Des Moines, Iowa, he finally named the forces he believed responsible for the new world war: a conspiracy forged between the Roosevelt administration and the Jews, whom he called the "greatest danger to this country" with their "large ownership and influence in our motion pictures, our press, and our radio and our government."[14]

Later, in a Lindbergh appearance at Madison Square Garden, a reporter described the reaction of the crowd as "a deep-throated, unearthly, savage roar, chilling, frightening, sinister and awesome."[15] Soaking up the adoration, Lindberg "smiled like an adolescent as the mob stood to its feet, waved flags, threw kisses and frenziedly rendered the Nazi salute."

But the war had begun in earnest. The United States entered the fray and fought to make the world free of overt fascism; calls for cooperation with Nazism fell by the wayside. The German-American Bund retreated into the shadows; the Silver Legion members were rounded up and arrested. Father Coughlin lost his national pulpit. Lindbergh ceased his quest to form an alliance among the world's white populations and attempted to repent by lending his services to the air force in Europe.

History largely forgets the viable fascist movement that grew in the United States as the American Myth disinfected and scrubbed clean the country's authoritarian underpinnings and cast the United States as the hero and savior of the civilized world.

★

In the wake of World War II, the story of how Hitler and the Nazis came to power would, like so many other integral and important narratives, be truncated and simplified. Popular memory held that Hitler, a charismatic orator and dynamic figure, hypnotized the German population and that Nazism was an aberration, a blip of evil totally isolated and removed from prevalent society. But, as always, the true story of how the Third Reich was constructed, facilitated, operated, and eventually destroyed is much more complicated and, unfortunately, far more replicable than some might be comfortable admitting.

Certainly individuals were swayed by Hitler's enigmatic rhetorical appeals, but the phenomenon of Nazi Germany would never have been possible had the party not received widespread support from powerful institutions within Germany who saw them as useful tools for profit and power. With the support of wealthy and powerful Germans looking to use the fascists for their own ends, the Nazis made use of the nation's most prevalent and influential media to flood Germany's conscious and unconscious minds with propaganda designed to portray Hitler as a timeless champion and to fuel the people's sense of a looming threat. To fine-tune these appeals, Joseph Goebbels, minister of Nazi propaganda, looked to the groundbreaking work of Edward Bernays and American propaganda during the First World War, a campaign that many Nazis believed had facilitated Germany's defeat. Goebbels and his associates learned from the glorification of Woodrow Wilson and his marketing as a god of peace, as well as the mobilization of the Allies in World War I, the power of simple repetition of slogans and phrases, creating in Germany a life where it was virtually impossible to escape the ceaseless drone of party rhetoric. In the footsteps of the Committee on Public Information, the Nazis outfitted public squares with loudspeakers, issued millions of radios to the people, and papered the country with an exhausting amount of propaganda, an effort that Albert Speer credited as creating "a technical means of domination."

Propaganda captured Germany for the Nazis, not any particular talent by Hitler, who was notorious for his indecisiveness and created within the party a dysfunctional and unpredictable air that fortunately helped bring along its demise. Following American trends, Goebbels was able to twist reality and convince Germans they were part of a righteous cause, a historical movement with footing in a grand tradition, all of it particularly powerful as the populace was frightened and desperate for direction. Goebbels crafted around Hitler a cult of personality that lent him the power and presence of a living god. Part of this effort involved the co-opting of a white-identity religious movement called Positive Christianity that promoted Jesus Christ as an Aryan and the very first anti-Semite. This faith pushed the biblical story of Christ throwing the moneychangers out of the temple as the first action in a war on Jews, a war that Hitler himself would dedicate himself to, writing, "I believe that I am acting in accordance with the will of the Almighty Creator: by defending myself against the Jew, I am fighting for the work of the Lord."

Later history portrayed the Nazis as staunchly antireligious, but they actively took over the standing religions and absorbed their power, mirroring how generations of Americans had glorified their crimes through the myth of holy inspiration. As they grew in stature, Nazis displayed their swastikas next to Christian symbols in order to associate the iconography until they became one and the same. That takeover came full circle in 1937, as Hanns Kerrl, the Nazi Reichsminister of church affairs, addressed Germany's clergy and declared, "National Socialism is the doing of God's will . . . The Fuehrer is the herald of a new revelation." No longer was there any need for Positive Christianity or faith of any kind other than the belief that Adolf

Hitler now embodied the will of the German people and the will of the Christian God.

In this way, Nazi Germany became a religious and secular cult. Citizens intertwined their identities with the fate of Hitler and ceased questioning his constant contradictions, his obvious shortcomings, and even the realities of his brutal and genocidal regime. They worshipped him as their political and religious leader and, as a cult, would take their lives as their constructed reality came undone. Like Wilson, Hitler had used propaganda and engineered consent to transform himself into a living god and his ambitions into a national crusade.

The vision that Hitler gave his followers was shaped by his perception of the United States, a nation he saw as having pioneered the type of racist, stratified society he hoped to achieve and improve upon. His plan resembled the Confederate States of America, which he praised as "the beginnings of a great new social order based on the principle of slavery and inequality."[16] Hitler lamented that the Civil War had led to the disintegration of the Confederacy but still admired how Jim Crow and legal segregation had created an ironclad racial hierarchy in the United States, leading him to believe in the possibility of a new world of white supremacy immortalized in law as well as violence.

By that same standard, the Nazis held America in high regard for its contributions to white supremacy. In his 1934 book *Völkisch World History*, Albrecht Wirth called the founding of the United States "the strongest prop" for "the struggle of the Aryans for world domination"; Wahrhold Drascher's *The Supremacy of the White Race* named it "the first fateful turning point" in the rise of white global dominance.[17]

Before the outbreak of the Second World War, Nazis turned repeatedly to America for inspiration in the construction and operation of their empire, and explained the United States' partnering with the Allied powers as symptomatic of Jewish manipulation. Hitler even took the time to write in one of his last missives before his suicide that he had never wished for a war against "either England or America."

American eugenicists assisted and continued to inspire the Nazis as they constructed their system of racial purification. Nazis patterned their laws after those that had gained acceptance in America, most written by eugenicist Harry Laughlin. For his contributions, Laughlin enjoyed fame and notoriety in Germany, as well as an honorary degree from the University of Heidelberg. While Germany sterilized over three hundred thousand people, American eugenicists visited regularly to observe their process. Following one such excursion, William W. Peter, secretary of the American Public Health Association, dreamed of a similar system, saying, "An overtaxed world waits hopefully for the result of the recent great enterprise in Germany, which shall enrich human life."[18] As a special guest of the Third Reich, Lothrop Stoddard, whose work influenced the eugenics campaign in Germany, observed judges determining citizens' reproductive fates and wrote that they were "weeding out the worst strains in the Germanic stock in a scientific and truly humanitarian way."[19] Just as had been the case with Carrie Buck, the murder of innocent people was framed as a merciful charity.

Likewise, Americans obsessed with eugenics and social Darwinism saw them as the natural progression of science and reason, particularly those who held their own deep-seated prejudices. In a shocking 1938 poll, 61 percent of Americans told Gallup they thought Jews were either "entirely" or "partly" responsible for their persecution.[20] Later that year, 67.4 percent told *Fortune* they supported turning away refugees from Europe.[21] Laura Delano Houghteling, President Roosevelt's own cousin and wife of the US commissioner of immigration, fought vigorously to keep Jewish children from being admitted into America, saying, "20,000 charming children would all too soon grow into 20,000 ugly adults."[22] John Trevor, a friend of Madison Grant's and a prominent anti-immigration advocate, warned that the influx of refugee children amounted to a "foreign invasion."[23]

Those voices would win. Even as Nazi persecution of the Jews grew ever more apparent, the United States turned its back on refugees. In 1939, this denial took a tragic turn as the MS *St. Louis,* a German ocean liner filled to the brim with over nine hundred Jewish refugees, was denied asylum. Many of the refugees on board were later killed in the Holocaust.

On a broader scale, Hitler gained much of his worldview by observing liberal democracies and their treatment of minority populations. The concept of the concentration camp was borrowed from the British Empire, which had used mass prisons to tame their colonies. For systematic genocide, he looked to America's dispatching of the Native American population in the nineteenth century, an act of ethnic cleansing accomplished under the same Romantic banner of manifest destiny.

As the world uncovered the horrors of the concentration camps, it began to view the Nazis as an aberration of history, a brief fever that had bloomed from nowhere and threatened to consume the body proper. The Allies, who fought bravely against the menace, were likewise crowned as the saviors of the Earth, their espoused principles of liberty and human dignity seen as the antidote for the fascist disease. Lost in this narrative, however, were the ties that bound American society to Nazi Germany, and with them the haunting yet necessary truth that fascism was not just an isolated phenomenon limited to early twentieth-century Europe but a pervasive human condition that could take poisonous root on any continent at any time with any people.

★

In August 1941, prior to the United States' entering the war, President Roosevelt met with Winston Churchill, now prime minister of the United Kingdom, aboard the HMS *Prince of Wales* battleship in Newfoundland to draft a values statement for the postwar world.

Released on August 14, the Atlantic Charter enumerated eight principles that would be stressed after "the final destruction of the Nazi tyranny."[24] These values were meant not just to link the United

States and Britain but to serve as a beacon for other liberal democracies opposed to fascism and totalitarianism. According to the charter, these nations would be dedicated to a world in which countries would not seek territorial gains. All territory changes would be according to the wishes of the people enjoying the right of self-determination. Trade opportunities and access to necessary raw materials were to be shared among the nations in an effort to improve the living conditions of their people, an improvement that included a freedom from "fear and want," as well as a general peace and a disarmament of the world's armies.

It was a vision in line with the stated principles of liberal democracy, a plan for a better world forged from the wreckage of Nazi Germany and an order that had failed because of greed and inequality.

There were immediate signs that such a vision would never come to pass. As possessors of large swathes of colonies around the world, the British were unwilling to embrace all-encompassing "self-determination," a concept that would mean the dismantling of the British Empire. As the world bore witness to the worst conclusion of eugenics and imperialism, the British still saw the world as divided between those capable of self-governance and those who needed the steady hand of more adept stewards. Beset by uproar from British politicians that the empire's colonies were incapable of self-governance, Churchill addressed the House of Commons less than a month after the release of the Atlantic Charter to quell concerns, assuring them that the problem of Nazism was "quite a separate problem from the progressive evolution of self-governing institutions in the regions and peoples which owe allegiance to the British Crown."[25]

With the Allies confronting the Nazis and protecting the world from spreading fascism, it has become easy to overlook the flaws of the victorious nations and instead cast them in all the glow and glory of triumph. Certainly their sacrifices and bravery should be commended, but it would also be dishonest to discuss the makings of the post-Nazi order of the world without acknowledging the foibles of its architects. Despite their avowed dedication to the tenets of liberal democracy, these leaders were guilty themselves of fascistic tendencies, routinely disguised behind democratic rhetoric. Even as the Allied powers met to discuss ideas like freedom and open societies, the United States had imprisoned over a hundred thousand Japanese Americans in concentration camps in a horrifying move deemed constitutional by the Supreme Court.

The Allies also welcomed the Soviet Union to their struggle after Nazi Germany betrayed their nonaggression pact in June 1941. Under the iron rule of Joseph Stalin, the USSR had been guilty of crimes against humanity on a similar scale to the Nazis, estimates putting the number killed under Stalin's reign of terror at anywhere from six to twenty million people.

But as the Big Three met in a series of conferences, their faults and crimes were largely laid aside as they debated and constructed a world of their choosing. Roosevelt took a lead role in envisioning a new era of world peace maintained by an organization he called the United Nations, a successor to the failed League of Nations. Roosevelt suggested the UN be constructed almost identically to the original *trias politica* of the United States government, with three wings: the General Assembly, the Executive Committee, and the Security Council. Just as the framers of the US Constitution had done, the UN presented the illusion of democracy and representation to the world while maintaining control for the elite. In this case, the Executive Committee allowed the largest nations to oversee operations. Churchill especially saw the need for the illusion as it was "undesirable" to dictate without at least "letting the other countries express their opinion."[26] Stalin balked at even the perception of equality, asking Roosevelt, "Do you want Albania to have the same rights as the United States?"[27]

To preserve peace, a task that Roosevelt admitted might only be possible by use of force, he proposed a system he called "the Four

Policemen" in which the United States, Britain, Russia, and China would oversee the disarmament of the rest of the world, including every weapon beyond a simple rifle. Then those four nations would maintain their own spheres of influence and quash any potential threat the moment it might emerge. It was, in theory, a shared domination of the entire world.

The Four Policemen concept was a large and daunting proposition, but the Allies were enamored with the possibilities. With disarmament, the world could avoid another threat like Nazi Germany while focusing on improving the quality of citizens' lives. The UN provided a space for smaller nations to make their voices heard, while the powers governed world affairs to their liking. That equilibrium, however, was only possible if the Allies maintained their uneasy alliance and tenuous sense of trust. As Churchill noted at their meeting in Yalta, "The peace of the world depends upon the lasting friendship of the three great powers."[28] The Four Policemen theory, as well as the viability of the UN, was contingent on powerful nations' trusting one another and putting aside their long-held suspicions and ambitions.

By the time the UN was ratified in 1945, those hopes were already disintegrating: Roosevelt had died, and the Allies had fallen back into their patterns of subterfuge and distrust. Meetings were rife with tension over postwar spoils. Churchill wanted to ensure the survival of the British Empire. Stalin held up negotiations until he was allowed to maintain control over Poland. The United States, now helmed by Harry Truman, had just dropped nuclear bombs on Hiroshima and Nagasaki in a show of force that the Soviets perceived as a clear-cut message.

By the time Truman heralded the organization as "better machinery" and equated its potential failure with a betrayal of "all those who have died," the concept of the Four Policemen had transformed into the basis for the Security Council. The major nations enjoyed permanent seats and ultimate veto power, an arrangement that ensured the UN would be virtually ineffective as the Allies wrestled with one another for decades to come.[29]

Though Allied leaders were busy plotting their moral future, the prosecution of the war on the ground was anything but upstanding. Like their partners the Russians, American troops committed thousands of sexual assaults as they wrested territory from Axis control. Though those numbers would be disputed, there's little argument to be made as to the total and widespread destruction perpetrated against the people of Japan. Adopting a punishing strategy designed by swaggering colonel Curtis LeMay, the United States Air Force chose to carry out total war and drop incendiary bombs to set fire to Japanese cities composed primarily of combustible materials.

Months before the nuclear destruction of Hiroshima and Nagasaki, an equally insidious operation and devastation took place. On March 9 and 10, 1945, over three hundred B-29s dropped incendiary bombs on Tokyo as the citizens slept in their homes. Over the course of the evening, a quarter of Tokyo was destroyed and 83,000 people killed. The capital burned so hot that entire neighborhoods burst into flame from the heat alone. People were burned to a crisp; survivors recalled how they watched people "falling to the ground and dying like human torches," their bodies "black as charcoal," the burning so complete they were unable to tell the difference between "arms and legs or pieces of burnt wood."[30]

For their participation, the bombing squads received certificates welcoming to them to the "royal and rugged order of EMPIRE BUSTERS" for having "helped to clear the Tokyo slums and having aided in the spring plowing."[31] *Time* magazine, reflecting on the bombing, called the strategy a "dream come true" and celebrated that "properly kindled, Japanese cities will burn like autumn leaves."[32]

The disregard for the lives of the Japanese people had been fermenting in the United States since the bombing of Pearl Harbor. Much like the Nazi Party's dehumanization of the Jews, Americans had been immersed in propaganda depicting the Japanese as sub-human terrors, often in the form of rats or vampiric creatures. Popular culture directed at adults and children alike portrayed a world in which the Japanese could be hiding behind any corner, ready and willing to massacre the American populace. This hatred enabled the unlawful internment of the Japanese in the United States and per-mitted a poisonous racism to emerge and direct domestic and mil-itary policy. General John L. DeWitt, one of the leading proponents of that internment, was quoted as saying, "We must worry about the Japanese all the time until he is wiped off the map."[33]

This sense of the Japanese threat was shared among America's political and military leaders, and to aid in their mission of disabling their foe, they disregarded any notions of morality and turned to the burgeoning field of nuclear physics to create a weapon to bring the war to an end. In the process, they ushered into being a new era of world domination by other means, as well as a new kind of war that consistently brought humanity to the very brink of annihilation.

★

On April 12, 1945, President Franklin Roosevelt was resting in his vacation house in Warm Springs, Georgia, when he complained of a headache and slumped over in his chair. That afternoon he died of a cerebral hemorrhage, bringing to an end an unprecedented twelve-year term as president of the United States in which Roosevelt had steered the country through economic ruin, existential crisis, and a ghastly war. His successor was Vice President Harry Truman, a rela-tively unknown politician who had only been vice president for a little over three months. In that time he had met sparingly with Roo-sevelt and was kept almost completely in the dark regarding the workings of the administration.

As he took the office, Truman was told that the United States had developed a new groundbreaking weapon, but it was nearly two weeks before he was briefed on the specifics of the atomic bomb. Unbeknownst to Truman, a massive mobilization of military and scientific minds had been undertaken in 1942 to harness burgeoning atomic science to develop a weapon capable of bringing the war to a timely close. Originally, the race to invention had been fueled by fears that the Nazis might produce a bomb, but now, in the face of Germany's imminent collapse, the weapon served as an answer to the problem of continued Japanese belligerence.

On July 16, a mere three months after Truman's swearing in, members of the Manhattan Project gathered in the Jornada del Muerto desert in New Mexico for a test code-named Trinity. The very next day, the Allies met in Potsdam, Germany, for their final wartime conference. With Roosevelt's death, the partnership was already in danger of collapse. This distrust was fueled by Truman's ignorance of foreign affairs, which allowed hard-line advisors in the State Department and affluent members of a cabal of intellectuals who would come to be known as "the Wise Men" to guide the new president on Soviet relations. These advisors touted a pragmatic approach that eschewed ideology in the name of gamesmanship. The strategy appealed to Truman, who, as a senator in 1941, had told *The New York Times* that his perspective on the budding Russian–German hostilities was that the United States should "help whichever side seemed to be losing" to "let them kill as many as possible."[34]

In the midst of this turmoil, the Allies plotted the occupation and rehabilitation of Germany, including a split of Berlin that maintained separate sectors of influence. As the plans were being drawn, the alliance was already endangered by Truman's maneuvering, particularly his determination to keep the atomic bomb a secret from Stalin. Believing the Soviet leader displayed "a rather unfriendly attitude" toward the United States, Truman chose not to disclose the whole truth about the bomb, keeping its specifics among the United States, Britain, and Canada and choosing only to tell Stalin he possessed "a weapon of unusual destructive force."[35] Unbeknownst to Truman, Stalin was already well aware of the existence of the bomb, as he'd learned the particulars from spies he had implanted in the project.

What the United States would do with this weapon of "unusual destructive force" was anything but certain. Many close to Roosevelt and within the Manhattan Project had fiercely advocated for a humane strategy to bring the war to a close without resorting to the mass murder of innocent people. Alexander Sachs, a confidant of Roosevelt's, had suggested in 1944 that once the bomb was ready for use "a rehearsal demonstration" for scientists and religious leaders from around the world could be conducted. That way, its destruction could be expressed to the Axis powers, and Germany and Japan could surrender or else face "atomic annihilation."[36]

Some scientists who had helped design the bomb called for a "demonstration" for representatives from the United Nations to take place in a "desert or a barren island."[37] To make use of the technology and drop it on an unsuspecting population, they argued, not only would be cruel but would undermine the credibility of the United States and deal a potentially fatal blow to its benevolent persona.[38]

These concerns were not shared by members of the military who saw the unexpected dropping of a bomb as necessary for their purposes in war and continued geopolitical strategies. Major General Leslie Groves, the director of the Manhattan Project, admitted in his memoirs he never understood calls for a demonstration and was only concerned with "the importance of the effect on the Japanese people and their government of the overwhelming surprise of the bomb."[39] To boot, military planners were eager to "assess accurately the effects of the bomb," an interest only served if the weapon were to be used in an act of war against an intact city brimming with living, breathing citizens.[40]

With the decision made, a committee drafted a list of potential targets for destruction, a list that was created with the intention of maximizing psychological trauma and physical devastation. Initially the list included the metropolis of Kyoto, but Secretary of War Henry Stimson spared the city as he had honeymooned there before the war. In its place, the city of Nagasaki would be considered.

On August 6, a B-29 bomber called *Enola Gay* cruised over Hiroshima, an industrial city on Honshu Island, and dropped a bomb nicknamed "Little Boy" from 31,000 feet at eight fifteen A.M. The intended target was the Aioi Bridge, but the bomb exploded directly above the Shima Surgical Clinic, instantly killing thousands and incinerating the city in a hellish firestorm. The resulting mushroom cloud rose to over 35,000 feet as Hiroshima burned. Over 60 percent of the city was destroyed, the majority of its buildings reduced to rubble, the intensity of the blast reducing the world to ash and evaporating unsuspecting citizens.

Estimates put the death toll in Hiroshima, following the explosion and radiation poisoning, between 90,000 and 166,000.[41] In Nagasaki, bombed three days after the obliteration of Hiroshima, an estimated 60,000 to 80,000 perished. Japan would ultimately surrender, but only after the United States had subjected its people to some of the cruelest actions ever perpetrated by a nation-state.

Japan was not the only target of the bombings, however, as the display was intended to impress upon the Soviet Union the might of the United States militarily. Remarking on the destruction of Hiroshima, Stalin said the bombing had "shaken the whole world. The balance ha[d] been destroyed."[42] Russian foreign minister Vyacheslav Molotov, a key figure in Allied negotiations, later said the bombs were "not aimed at Japan but rather the Soviet Union" and intended as a warning should the Soviets consider testing US resolve.[43]

Before the war had even ended there was a developing sense among American and British leadership that war with Russia was inevitable and all efforts should shift to preparing for that battle. A plan code-named Operation Unthinkable was even considered, wherein the United States and England might launch an attack on the Soviet Union, but an open assault was ruled out in favor of clandestine operations.

The brain trust advising President Truman and guiding US postwar policy routinely stressed pragmatism and an abandonment of espoused principles. As early as 1945, Truman directed covert operations and intelligence maneuvers against the USSR, a strategy that would later take shape as the Truman Doctrine in 1947, a policy of containment that stressed US intervention around the globe whenever Russia was perceived as seeking additional territory. Though sold as containing the menace of communism, it served a dual purpose of protecting the American spheres of influence and maintaining American political and economic dominance.

To this end, Truman addressed Congress and asked for $400 million to aid Greece in its civil war against communist forces, even though the government was guilty of ghastly human rights abuses. Truman explained the crimes away by saying, "The Government of Greece is not perfect . . . The Greek Government has been operating in an atmosphere of chaos and extremism. It has made mistakes."[44]

Those mistakes, as well as so many others, would be ignored, as the main priority was battling Russia on the geopolitical stage. By 1948, the United States was funding covert operations around the globe and funneling money and resources into the hands of anyone who fought communism, including former Nazi collaborators and war criminals. One more egregious example was Operation Paperclip, an effort by US forces to smuggle over one thousand Nazi scientists and technicians into the United States to integrate Third Reich weaponry and technology into American weapons and its eventual space program.

As Harry Rositzke, the former CIA head of Russian operations, explained, "We knew what we were doing. It was a visceral business of using any bastard as long as he was anti-Communist . . . the eagerness or desire to enlist collaborators meant that sure, you didn't look at their credentials too closely."[45]

The United States forfeited any claim to the moral and philo-sophical high ground as the Cold War took shape in favor of military and political advantage. The fight to defeat Nazism and rid the world of explicit fascism had granted an opportunity to redefine the human experience and possibly usher in an era of peace and prosperity that made good on the principles of freedom and democracy championed by America, but the temptation of global and financial hegemony was too great.

In one of the defining documents of the dawning of the Cold War, the second-highest-ranking US diplomat in Russia, a man named George Kennan, sent what came to be called "the Long Telegram" in February of 1946. The missive was an analysis of the Soviet Union by Kennan, who believed the philosophy of revolutionary communism meant Russia would continue to trouble capitalism wherever it ex-isted. This, according to Kennan, necessitated a policy of "contain-ment" to prevent it from spreading around the world. In this way, the Soviet Union reflected the United States, its survival predicated on the health of its perpetual revolution and its ability to spread across the globe.

Kennan's recommendation served as a cornerstone of US foreign policy for the next several decades, but the emphasis on his strategic proposal has long obfuscated much of his message. Kennan believed that many of Russia's actions were defined by an ingrained anxiety: The Russians had been continually double-crossed and acted upon, whether it was during their civil war, when Allies had tried to strangle the USSR in its crib, or when the Nazis had betrayed their pact and slaughtered their people.[46] Despite his worries, Kennan maintained faith that "peaceful and mutually profitable coexistence of capitalist and socialist states is entirely possible," and his sugges-tions were not limited to foreign policy. To win the struggle against communism, he stressed, the United States would have to change.

His suggestions included the need for Americans to educate themselves regarding Russia and its people and to shun propagandistic, militaristic preconceptions. He also argued that America's success in the postwar world would be defined by its own progress and whether the nation lived up to its principles.

"World communism," he wrote, "is like a malignant parasite which feeds only on diseased tissue." The battle would be determined by adherence to ideology and whether America continued to improve the lives of its people. Kennan wrote: "Every courageous and incisive measure to solve internal problems of our own society, to improve self confidence, discipline, morale and community spirit of our own people, is a democratic victory over Moscow worth a thousand diplomatic notes and joint communiques."

The postwar world needed America, as a champion of liberal democracy, to be the counterbalance to Stalin's despotic regime, a beacon of freedom that could inspire the world and better the lives of its peoples. Kennan believed the future depended on these ideas and America's ability to realize and embody them. "Finally," he wrote to close his message, "we must have courage and self confidence to cling to our own methods and conceptions of human society. After all, the greatest damage that can befall us in coping with this problem of Soviet Communism is that we shall allow ourselves to become like those with whom we are coping."

CHAPTER 7

★　　★　　★

A Mindless Juggernaut

On Sunday, July 17, 1955, Walt Disney opened his theme park by welcoming his guests and proclaiming, "Disneyland is your land. Here age relives fond memories of the past, and here youth may savor the challenge and promise of the future. Disneyland is dedicated to the ideals, the dreams, and the hard facts that have created America, with the hope that it will be a source of joy and inspiration to all the world."[1]

The event was televised live by the American Broadcasting Company in a program cohosted by Art Linkletter, Bob Cummings, and Ronald Reagan. Following Disney was his nephew, who testified to his uncle's spirituality and then asked for a silent prayer. Next was California governor Goodwin Knight, who effusively praised Disney and his new wonderland, dedicating the park "with the knowledge that we are the fortunate ones to be Americans, and that we extend to everyone everywhere the great ideals of Americanism, brotherhood, and peace on Earth, goodwill towards men."[2] "The Star-Spangled

Banner" played as members of the armed forces saluted and raised the flag. A massive parade began down Main Street, USA, the hub of the park constructed to resemble an idyllic American town. There was a military flyover and military bands. Interspersed among them were contingents of characters from Disney's popular films and costumed men and women who appeared to represent every era from the history of the United States, from settlers to astronauts in space suits.

Disneyland itself was designed to resemble this clash of eras and cultures, with time travel made as easy as walking from one attraction to the next. When ABC transitioned from the parade to a tour of the grounds, actor Ronald Reagan, his most recent role that of a rough-and-tumble cowboy in *Cattle Queen of Montana*, welcomed viewers to Frontierland as a nineteenth-century fort opened its gates to guests. Inside was an experience that brought myth to life. There were cowboys, saloons, wagon trains, relics of the Old West. Living history stepped forward as an actor portraying Davy Crockett, a hero spun into a mythical figure, arrived wearing his trademark coonskin cap and carrying his trusty rifle "Old Betsy." He apologized for being late, his traveling companion explaining they had been ambushed by "redskins . . . just itching to lift [their] scalps." Asked how he escaped, Crockett joked about killing them with his rifle, to the delight of the assembled children. He then sang a cheerful song about Old Betsy and the slaughter of Native Americans as men and women in costume danced with their own firearms.

Despite the network's polish, the opening was fraught with problems and nicknamed "Black Sunday." And as guests delighted in the pageantry, seven miles of gridlocked traffic lay just outside the kingdom's walls. Offscreen, Sleeping Beauty Castle caught fire. Thousands of people snuck into the park or were admitted using counterfeit tickets, leading to food shortages. The July heat was so intense, and the poured asphalt so fresh, that guests sank into the streets and sidewalks. Several of the rides were either inoperable or forced to close due to dangerous conditions.

One of the few parks to impress that day was Tomorrowland, a vision of a coming age where Americans would regularly travel to the moon and live peaceful lives made better by new and wondrous inventions. It was a dream of a world made safe for innovation and progress, a land of aspiration. To highlight that dream, particularly the role of atomic science in making it a reality, ABC interviewed Disney's scientific consultant Dr. Heinz Haber, a popular figure who hosted several educational programs for Disney, including *Our Friend the Atom*. To bring science to life, Dr. Haber motioned to a display of several mousetraps holding Ping-Pong balls intended to replicate a nuclear reaction. Haber's young son then threw a ball into the traps, resulting in a shower of motion.

Though the television host had introduced him as "a gentleman of considerable renown," the truth was that Dr. Haber, before being rebranded by Disney as their friendly face of science, had been a Nazi who flew missions for the Luftwaffe in World War II. He had been identified in Operation Paperclip as a Nazi scientist worth recruiting for American purposes and had played a role in the burgeoning field of space travel.

In direct contrast to the lighthearted broadcast, and the smiling host at his shoulder, Dr. Haber's post-experiment monologue struck an ominous tone. As the camera tightened on the former Nazi's face, he directly addressed the children watching at home. He told them atomic power was "an important part of [their] future," but warned, "*If* you grow up, be certain that you use it wisely."

★

Never before in the history of the world had such utter annihilation been a real possibility. With the invention of the nuclear bomb by the United States in 1945, and Russia's subsequent explosion of their first bomb four years later, the proposed partnership between the Allies of World War II had quickly imploded. This collapse set the stage for a defining struggle in which total eradication of the human race loomed over everyday life like an oppressive tempest. Though Americans now held the ability to destroy the very world with the press of a button, the American Myth maintained that they were the heroes of history.

The Cold War was an ideological, economic, and military struggle that lasted five decades and relentlessly threatened humankind's safety and sanity unlike anything before. It reaped untold damage on the political, economic, and social futures of people around the globe while unleashing traumas and inspiring distrust that would have consequences even for generations born decades after its end. It was a devastating outcome following the defeat of Adolf Hitler and the Nazis: a complete and total collapse of the envisioned world order crafted by Franklin D. Roosevelt, Joseph Stalin, and Winston Churchill. It was a mortal blow to the Enlightenment revolutions that birthed both America and Soviet Russia, and possibly the death knell of liberal democracy in the modern world.

Though the Cold War is often framed as a battle between two cultures, it's important to step back from this framing of history. The conflict did not lie between the peoples of the United States and Russia but between their political and military leaders—or, more specifically, hard-liners who stocked the political and military bodies. The hostility was not inevitable. There were individuals and movements inside both countries that opposed the antagonism and warmongering but were overrun by their respective states. That the Cold War has come to define what an American is and what America stands for is a tragedy still unfurling in real time.

The conflict began because the nuclear bomb presented a novel problem. Its destructive power was so great that for the first time, military leaders had at their disposal a tool they might never use. The only analogous comparison would be chemical warfare, which had been condemned, but even poisonous gas was limited and could be neutralized with preventative measures. Relatedly, the battle over control of the world was twofold: a hard war based on weapons and destruction that could instantly kill millions, and a soft war predicated on possession of moral authority. This entirely new struggle necessitated an entirely new strategy.

In the wake of World War II, the American military bucked tradition and refused to demobilize. Past wars had seen a drawing down of efforts and provisions as soon as peace had been declared, but with the threat of the Cold War, drawing down simply wasn't an option. Instead, the United States continued mobilization with arms development and war planning, resulting in a growing symbiotic relationship between the military and the dominant sectors of American life. The result: a nation both philosophically obsessed with and economically dependent on war.

One of the architects was Curtis LeMay, the man responsible for burning Tokyo and its people to a crisp. LeMay was a swaggering warmonger who chewed cigars and barked his orders, and, like the pragmatists who had ingratiated themselves with Harry Truman, LeMay valued results over ethics and ideology. "All war is immoral," he said. "If you let that bother you, you're not a good soldier."[3]

In fighting this battle, LeMay and his peers looked to nascent organizations like the RAND Corporation to study the standoff for potential strategies that might help the United States. RAND was one of many private-sector think tanks opening around the country dedicated to scrutinizing the modern world for new avenues of political and economic gain. With the Cold War, RAND and other actors believed the answers might be found in the developing field of game theory, a strain of thinking focusing on "games of strategy" and approaches meant to reap a "maximum of utility" or a "maximum of profit."[4] Though game theory's origins lay in economics, its worldview could supposedly be implemented in every possible situation. The method was to study the behavior of rational actors in contact with other rational actors to calculate the possibilities and outcomes and then determine what decisions were most likely, a descendant of Taylorism and Wilsonian management that reduced existence to numbers and devalued humanity in favor of cold, hard rationality.

Game theorists likened the Cold War to a scenario called the Prisoner's Dilemma, where two competing forces acted according to their own interests and, in the meantime, neutralized one another. On paper, the strategy seemed sound. By pursuing its own advantage, producing weapons of war, and behaving strategically and rationally, the United States would, at worst, hold the Soviet Union in check. If the Russians blinked, America gained. An arms race—in rational terms, anyway—was the smartest play.

In practice, however, it drew both nations into an artificial state of play. As Lloyd Shapley, a Nobel Prize–winning game theorist, told his colleagues at RAND, "In attempting to apply game theory to (say) economic or military behavior, we of necessity introduce into the class of relevant economic or military situations the prospect of being required to play a game."[5] In other words, instead of addressing the very real horror of nuclear war, the United States and Russia became singularly focused on winning strategy inside a synthetic environment.

To win the game, deadlier weapons were invented; stockpiles grew; militaries developed first-strike strategies, second-strike strategies, and instantaneous response protocols; and nuclear warheads were buried in secret silos around the country. The prospect of deterrence hinged on nuclear brinksmanship, a strategy Thomas Schelling, another Nobel Prize–winning game theorist, defined as "the deliberate creation of a recognizable risk of war."[6] In this "game" it was decided the best play when chained to another person and approaching a cliff was to aggressively head for the cliff and hope the other person's response would be to recoil in abject fear.

But what happened if the other actor decided on running at oblivion themselves, which game theory showed was more than likely the most rational play?

The solution was to prepare for actual war in order to convince

Russia to back away from the edge. It was a new phase of Cold War thinking, a definitive transition from staving off nuclear war to making the rational case for prosecuting nuclear war. America's military thinkers and leaders mulled the possibility that to keep Russia from diving off the cliff of nuclear destruction, the United States needed to be prepared for the possibility of initiating nuclear destruction while continually proclaiming itself the moral executor of the world.

The most prominent prophet of this aggressive stance was Herman Kahn, a RAND member notorious during the Cold War for his rambling lectures and oversized personality. Kahn was notable for his ability to rationalize the irrational, to look into the depths of nuclear apocalypse and frame the slaughter of millions as sound strategy. At RAND he'd floated the possibility of an "alternative to peace," positing that, contrary to previous thought, a nuclear war might be "limited" and winnable.[7] Kahn looked at the numbers with the same rational detachment as had the technicians behind the destruction of Tokyo, Hiroshima, and Nagasaki. In the event of an actual nuclear war, he believed, millions would die and the consequences would be dire, but when looking at the aftermath, including "genetic mutations" from the radiation, he argued the costs might be "horrible" but "far from annihilation."[8]

Kahn's book *On Thermonuclear War*, a bestseller read by every major political and military figure in America and probably Russia, approached nuclear war as a thought experiment. He calculated how many hundreds of millions would perish in a nuclear exchange, estimated how long it would take for populations and economies to recover, and presented his theory of a winnable nuclear war. He admitted "human tragedy would be greatly increased" but argued that increase "would not preclude normal and happy lives for the majority of survivors and their descendants."[9] In his lectures he goaded shocked crowds, asking, "It is possible, isn't it, that parents will learn to love two-headed children twice as much?"[10]

Behind the scenes, the United States relied on nameless and anonymous figures to punch the numbers and weigh the advantages of vaporizing an entire country, all the while stepping in front of cameras and proselytizing the inherent goodness of its mission and character. To win the moral peace, it seemed, one had to be willing to wage hellish, immoral war.

★

On the evening of January 17, 1961, Dwight D. Eisenhower addressed the nation for the last time as the president of the United States. His eight years in office had been marked by economic prosperity and cemented America as one of the two dominant superpowers in the world. The address could have been a fond farewell littered with a litany of achievements, but Eisenhower had worn out his staff of writers in drafting a foreboding speech.

As he warned of the threat of the Soviet Union, Eisenhower quickly turned to the equal hazard of militarism in facing that threat. He spoke of a "permanent armaments industry of vast proportions . . . felt in every city, every state house, every office of the Federal Government," and cautioned "an alert and knowledgeable citizenry" would be required to "guard against the acquisition of unwarranted influence, whether sought or unsought, by the military-industrial complex."[11]

His concern was partly economic, as the defense budget had ballooned and threatened to drown the country in debt, but in his eight years in office, Eisenhower had also witnessed a disturbing trend take hold. The military and its symbiotic satellites of weapons manufacturers, private contractors, and war planners had grown in influence to the point where Eisenhower had raged two years earlier that defense considerations and planning had come to be marked by "political and financial influences rather than military considerations alone."[12] The Cold War and its novel problems had allowed them to grow beyond defense and blossom into an economic and political body that overshadowed all others and, as agents of profit, demanded constant growth. Sociologist C. Wright Mills observed that they had created an "emergency without a foreseeable end," a state where "war preparedness is felt to be the normal and seemingly permanent condition of the United States."[13]

Before Eisenhower recognized the dangers of such a state, he had played an integral role in creating it. As chief of staff of the army, he had penned a memo titled "Scientific and Technological Resources as Military Assets" that examined America's victory in World War II and admitted, "The armed forces could not have won the war alone."[14] He credited the mobilization of the country's industry and scientific community; Eisenhower believed that for the military to be successful in the postwar world, "the Army must have civilian assistance in military planning as well as for the production of weapons."

To this end, a peacetime mobilization began: The military funded uninterrupted manufacturing of arms and an unending parade of think tanks dedicated to war planning, and America's universities and top academics were tasked with focusing their research on creating new weapons, strategies, and disciplines meant to win the conflicts of the future. Soon after its birth, the process took on a dark momentum all of its own.

Though Eisenhower was one of the most decorated and revered military figures in American history, he had been raised a pacifist and recognized the value of peace. In March of 1953, two months after he took the oath of office, he had seen an opportunity for an early and diplomatic end to the Cold War following Joseph Stalin's death. Ten days after assuming power, Stalin's successor Georgy Malenkov had signaled to the United States a desire for a cooling of tensions.

In what came to be known as his "Chance for Peace" speech, Eisenhower criticized the "burden of arms draining the wealth and labor of all peoples," saying, "Every gun that is made, every warship launched, every rocket fired signifies, in the final sense, a theft from those who hunger and are not fed, those who are cold and not clothed."[15] The state of permanent war, he believed, had cost too much money, robbed the people of better lives, and kept the best minds of the generation from inventing the future. Even the man who had put the machine into motion recognized the social, political, and personal advantages of being the man to bring it to an end.

Though the heads of state were dedicated to ending the Cold War, they were essentially powerless. Hard-liners in both countries held too much sway and the momentum was too formidable. In the United States, the military-industrial complex had already taken root in the system and was inextricably intertwined with the economy and the government. For both nations the specter of war was a means by which to control their populations and stave off necessary reform. In 1955, Malenkov was forced out by Nikita Khrushchev and his associates. Unable to achieve peace, Eisenhower found himself the steward of an array of tyrannical programs that ran counter to every principle he had sworn to uphold.

Those programs were made possible by the establishment that had exploited Harry Truman's incompetence following Franklin D. Roosevelt's death in 1945. That group of pragmatists had steered America's course by eschewing principles and instead focusing on attainment of power by any means. Few people embodied this mindset more than Allen Dulles, who served as Eisenhower's director of the Central Intelligence Agency.

Dulles's CIA transcended its mission as an intelligence-gathering body and became one of the most sinister and underhanded actors in the modern world. To succeed in the Cold War era, the CIA constantly overstepped its bounds, committing crimes both domestically and around the globe. After decrying rumors of Soviet "brain-perversion techniques" in 1953 that were "so abhorrent to our way of life that we have recoiled from facing up to them," Dulles authorized widespread clandestine operations that experimented on, tortured, and dosed unwitting American citizens with drugs like LSD in order for the United States to perfect its own brand of mind control.[16] To carry out what Congress would later call "extensive testing and experimentation" on Americans, the CIA kidnapped subjects, paid addicts with heroin, and, in an action code-named "Operation Midnight Climax," employed sex workers to seduce men into entering government-funded brothels, where they were unknowingly given psychedelic drugs as hidden operatives observed their reactions and sexual activities behind one-way mirrors.[17]

Abroad, the CIA undermined democracy and the right of self-determination, both tentpoles in America's propaganda, whenever elections were perceived as unfavorable to the US government or business interests. In this way, global affairs became a game of chess between the United States and Russia as both nations continually interfered in the politics and lives of the people, treating them and their destinies as pawns to be maneuvered and ultimately sacrificed.

Theoretically, America was dedicated to the principles of freedom and democracy, but in the nonwhite world it tolerated fascism if fascist leaders were capitalists who kept their populations in check while cooperating solely with America and its corporations. This created a system where despots could plunder their countries, eliminate individual rights, and even commit mass killings and atrocities as long as they knelt at the altar of the United States and capitalism. To this end, the CIA was wielded as a tool to spread white supremacy and corporate dominance throughout the world.

In 1953, the CIA and British intelligence engaged in widespread social manipulation and orchestrated a coup in Iran that deposed Prime Minister Mohammad Mosaddegh in favor of Shah Mohammad Reza Pahlavi, who tortured and killed his political opponents. Mosaddegh, on the other hand, had threatened British Petroleum's hold over Iranian oil.

Democratically elected Guatemalan president Jacobo Árbenz interfered with United Fruit, and due in part to Edward Bernays and corporate America's interference, the CIA armed and trained revolutionaries in 1954 and provided them with the propaganda necessary to install dictator Carlos Castillo Armas. The resulting genocide killed tens of thousands.

In 1961, Congo's first prime minister, Patrice Lumumba, who touted "neutralism" in the Cold War but was portrayed as a Soviet puppet, was overthrown and killed in favor of United States–backed dictator Mobutu Sese Seko, who executed and tortured his opponents while building a totalitarian government that stole billions from its people.[18]

After years of facing CIA-funded opponents, Salvador Allende finally won the presidency of Chile in 1970. This set off a chain of events that led to the United States' backing General Augusto Pinochet, a ruthless despot, and helping him overthrow Allende.

As national security advisor to President Richard Nixon in 1970, Henry Kissinger remarked on the Chile coup that he did not "see why we need to stand by and watch a country go Communist due to the irresponsibility of its own people." Once more, an American official professed the long-held belief that only certain people were to be trusted with the right of self-determination.[19] In these matters, it was no coincidence that the countries involved were primarily composed of nonwhite populations. These other races, much in the vein of how nineteenth-century white supremacists viewed Mexicans in the annexation debate, were simply not considered intelligent or capable enough to guard the gift of freedom and representative government. If they were to choose communist, socialist, or left-leaning representatives, or otherwise challenge the unfettered rule of private corporations, then they were seen as threats to American dominance and obviously the victims of Russian manipulation.

This philosophy came to encompass both political parties within America and established a permanent, unelected, and largely anonymous class of rulers in the military, intelligence, and foreign policy wings of government, the members of which rarely changed regardless of what party enjoyed electoral success. When John F. Kennedy entered office in January of 1961, he was surprised to discover several operations that had begun with the Eisenhower administration had carried over, including ongoing activity in Southeast Asia that had been in place since the Truman administration.

One of the actions Kennedy inherited from Eisenhower was the Bay of Pigs Invasion, a disastrous attempt by the CIA to overthrow Fidel Castro, the communist leader of Cuba. Eisenhower approved the plan in 1960 and sank millions into the recruitment, training, and arming of anti-Castro forces. By the time Kennedy was briefed, the invasion was less than three months from launch. In April, the operation failed in spectacular fashion and America was immediately implicated, revealing to the world the dirty and unethical actions Dulles's CIA had been perpetrating for years.

The Bay of Pigs was yet another move in the game between the United States and Russia. Castro and the communist foothold in Cuba, just miles from the US mainland, were considered vital assets in Russia's strategy, and so Khrushchev and his cadre of hard-liners approved a plan in 1962 to protect the island with nuclear weapons. When the gambit was discovered, it created a thirteen-day crisis that threatened to end in the extinction of the human race.

At the heart of the Cuban Missile Crisis was the problematic discipline of game theory, an immoral and unethical strategy made possible by America's continued belief in its own moral and ethical superiority. Because the United States and Russia had decided to play a game and were opposing one another in a synthetic contest, they operated as if they intended to start a war when neither side desired one. Despite Russian anxiety and US posturing, there were no plans to invade Cuba. In discussions with Soviet leadership during the tensions, Khrushchev explicitly stated, "We didn't want to unleash a war. All we wanted to do was threaten them, to restrain them with regard to Cuba."[20] When the situation escalated, he admitted, "This may end in a big war."

As Kennedy navigated the crisis he was besieged by military

leaders demanding escalation. There were calls for bombing, to invade Cuba, to launch a preemptive strike, all actions that Russia later confirmed would have led to war. One of the loudest voices in the room was Curtis LeMay, then the air force chief of staff. In debating strategy he relied on planning developed by game theorists and called Kennedy's unwillingness to begin World War III "appeasement."[21] When a U-2 spy plane was shot down and its pilot Rudolf Anderson was killed on October 27, LeMay prepared a counterstrike that would have surely led to the deaths of millions. Kennedy ordered him to stand down, causing an enraged LeMay to wail, "He chickened out again."[22] On Sunday, October 28, when the crisis was averted and peace had been won, a war-hungry LeMay suggested to a stunned meeting that the agreement to avoid nuclear apocalypse presented an opportunity to gain advantage, asking, "Why don't we go in and make a strike on Monday [the twenty-ninth] anyway?"[23]

The military thinking predicated on game theory had created in the United States and Russia a movement so strong that it grew larger than its actors. Both Kennedy and Khrushchev felt the game escaping their grasps as it gained an energy all of its own. In back-and-forth communiqués between the leaders, Khrushchev seemed increasingly distressed and Kennedy begged him to "show prudence and do nothing to allow events to make the situation more difficult to control than it already is."[24]

In the end, what saved the world and its peoples from nuclear destruction was a crucial decision by Kennedy and Khrushchev to choose not to play the game. During the crisis, Kennedy chose simply not to act, defusing the escalation necessitated by theory. Finally, once the game had been neutralized, Kennedy and Khrushchev chose, in the throes of the worst crisis the world had ever seen, to act counter to game theory strategies and trust one another.

Though the United States and Russia were able to escape the apocalyptic trap they had set for themselves, the principles of game theory and the nihilistic pragmatism that fueled and inspired it had already infected the nations and begun to eat them from the inside out. In addition to the game being played on the global stage, there were many more games being played within the countries' borders, and though peace had been won for the moment in this contest, a much larger and lengthier game was just beginning.

★

The singular obsession of the Cold War altered the United States forever. To best Russia in all facets of life, America came to be defined by its opposition and twisted itself into a caricatured, smiling projection of the artifice of capitalistic success. Under that veneer festered dystopian measures of cultural and political control; attempts to purge the political body of contrary and independent thought; and further subjugation of vulnerable populations.

From the end of the Korean War in 1953 to the assassination of John F. Kennedy a decade later, America retained a façade of peace and homogenization. It was a period where an absence of war hid war without end, and a time in which white Americans, particularly white men, came to enjoy the bounties of postwar prosperity while ignoring (or supporting) the rampant political, social, and economic inequality that defined the next two decades.

In the collective imagination, and in future nostalgia, it was the apex of the American experience and the last moment before everything fell apart. The truth, however, is that much like the opening of Disneyland, where pageantry and joy graced the camera's eye, growing chaos and unchecked flames raged just out of view.

If America was going to answer the moral challenge of the USSR, it was going to need to be reworked and reimagined, particularly as its past paralleled the defeated Nazi regime. This was another battle of propaganda in the same vein as George Creel's work in rebranding the United States during World War I and was meant to stave off cultural criticisms by Russia, whose main weapon of attack was high-lighting the hypocrisy of a nation touting equality and freedom while maintaining a segregated society based on racial hierarchy.

Historian John Higham mourned this effort and its effects on American history and perception, deriding it as "the Cult of the American Consensus" in *Commentary* magazine in 1959. Higham had watched over the course of the forties and fifties as his colleagues disinfected the country's record of events; deemphasized struggles of race, class, and politics; and seemed to rejuvenate and rehabilitate the nation as they stressed "the continuity of American history, the stability of basic institutions, the toughness of the social fabric."[25] In the wake of World War II, it was desirable to distance the United States from its sociopolitical ties to fascism and authoritarianism. Historians and everyday people had long accomplished this feat by tying together the Revolution and the Constitution, reimagining manifest destiny as a heroic undertaking, recasting the Civil War as an unfortunate disagreement that ended in rebirth, and framing the Industrial Revolution and the march of capitalism as a triumph rather than marked by interminable oppression.

This championing of capitalism, as well as the Cold War's being framed as a showdown between communism and the free market instead of oppression versus liberty, was boosted by the booming postwar economy and created a new consumerism that heralded un-bridled capitalism as the antidote to looming communism. Capitalism and its twin forces of production and consumption had become synonymous with the world-shattering concept of personal freedom from monarchial tyranny—or, as reporter Joseph Barry put it in *House Beautiful*, "the freedom offered by washing machines and dish-washers, vacuum cleaners, automobiles, and refrigerators."

Capitalism and America were now completely interchangeable, leaving little room for anything but full-throated support of markets free of oversight. In reaction to Cold War paranoia, the Second Red Scare gripped the nation and transformed it with widespread fear of

Soviet subterfuge. Conservative forces targeted all left-leaning bodies within the United States, including communists, socialists, labor unions, and a number of left-leaning individuals, particularly all remnants of Franklin D. Roosevelt's New Dealers.

The targeting of government workers revealed the agenda. Mirroring Soviet political purges, figures like Senator Joseph McCarthy, joined by young and ambitious politicians like Richard Nixon, brandished investigations like modern agents of the Inquisition, claiming falsely that the government had been infiltrated by Soviet agents. These claims were based primarily on rumors and gossip among conservative circles, many of them exemplified in the salacious Beltway book *Washington Confidential*, written by conservatives Jack Lait and Lee Mortimer, a bestseller that described an infected DC where "sex-starved government gals" were recruiting "colored men" and "meek male clerks" to wreck America from the inside out.[26] It's important to note that the perpetrators of this proposed conspiracy to bring down the United States on behalf of the USSR were professional, independent women, African-American men, and gay men: individuals who threatened the unbridled dominance of straight, white men.

Using fear of feminine independence, miscegenation, and the specter of unchecked homosexuality, the Republican Party and conservative forces demonized liberalism and set to work clearing the government of the people who had worked to realize and sustain FDR's New Deal policies. They were targeted as traitors, removed from their positions, and, in some cases, imprisoned. Suffering a large share of the harassment were LGBTQ+ Americans caught in what has come to be known as "the Lavender Scare," a period of paranoia and discrimination that equated their sexual orientation with personal deficiencies and communist sympathies.

Helping in this task was Federal Bureau of Investigation director J. Edgar Hoover, who had been abusing his powers to illegally interfere in events for years. In the postwar era, Hoover doubled down on his investigations and harassment of American citizens, all of it part of his admitted goal to "exploit cold war fears" to maintain the FBI's "wartime gains."[27]

Under Hoover's watch, the FBI violated laws to investigate federal workers, academics, and law-enforcement officers. Its agents scrutinized their politics, relationships, and sex lives, and actively sought their removal for anything Hoover personally deemed deviance. The FBI broke into homes, tapped phones without warrants, falsified and forged documents, and lied about sources. Hoover had even engineered a plan in 1948 for "mass detentions of political suspects in military stockades" where individuals considered insufficiently American and capitalist in ideology could be placed in "a secret prison system for jailing American citizens" and habeas corpus could be eliminated.[28]

This secret machinery hummed under the surface of the consensus as American society grew more homogenized. The window of acceptable politics lurched to the right and the New Deal/FDR era, now demonized and equated with the communist threat, quickly receded in favor of super-capitalism and aggressive nationalism.

Antonio Gramsci, a political prisoner in Benito Mussolini's Fascist Italy, had spent his imprisonment from 1929 to 1935 studying how his country had come to be dominated by fascistic thought. He determined that ideology had permeated all facets of political, social, and personal life, and coined the term *cultural hegemony*. Now, in America, the cult of the consensus had overtaken the populace in the shadow of the Cold War and come to define what America meant by means of overt political and legal suppression, as well as a quiet, subtler means of myth manipulation, social pressure, and a constant barrage of propaganda that defined Americans' perception of reality.

It was a consequence of the flourishing field of popular culture and mass media, a by-product of the proliferation of movies, television shows, and commercial advertisements, which, by the end of the fifties, were an inescapable facet of American life disguised by the veil of personal choice. Advertising firms continued the Freudian messaging pioneered by Edward Bernays, playing on the subconscious insecurities of consumers, while many of the movies, television shows, and print publications of the time portrayed an America whose institutions were sound, its social order fair and unquestionable, and its history marked by exceptionalism.

Government played an important role in this shaping of reality presented by mass media. In 1952, the Television Code told broadcasters that all content must preserve respect for God, law, and the customs of the country while vilifying sex, drugs, and criminal activity. Broadcasters were responsible for "decency and decorum," a charge they met by agreeing not to air, under threat of penalty of fines or of losing their licenses, "profanity, obscenity, smut and vulgarity" or "attacks on religion." When Americans turned on their televisions, they were greeted with a dream world where all was right in the country, its values were sound, and any attempt to say otherwise would be punished.

That punishment for violating expectations of portraying the American Myth would be exemplified in the motion picture industry, which was hit hard during the Red Scare. Left-leaning people were vilified by McCarthy's investigations and eventually blacklisted after being betrayed by actors like Ronald Reagan, who served as an informant for the FBI. In the wake of that purge, a cadre of conservative actors, directors, and figures in Hollywood created the Motion Picture Alliance for the Preservation of American Ideals, an organization that filled the vacuum and held sway over further production for several years. Members included Reagan, John Wayne, Walt Disney, and Gary Cooper, a who's who of the cultural figures who came to define the era's mythmaking through film. In 1947, a pamphlet authored for the group by a young Ayn Rand was distributed throughout Hollywood. It explicitly defined the motion picture industry as a propaganda arm for American interests, outlining several do's and don'ts, including the need to promote industrialists and the wealthy while downplaying the collective, all of it in an effort to promote that "Americanism and the Free Enterprise System . . . are inseparable, like body and soul."[29]

With this dominance of mass media, Americans were inundated with living, breathing myth. Both political parties peddled American exceptionalism and avoided anything approaching criticism. On the TV and on movie screens, the past was being radically altered as Westerns transubstantiated the genocide of Native Americans into a heroic act of self-defense and war films crafted additional much-needed daylight between heroic Americans and Nazis. By decree, good would always triumph over evil.

★

On May 17, 1954, the Supreme Court ruled unanimously in the matter of *Brown v. Board of Education* and declared segregation in public schools unconstitutional. There was cause for celebration, but for racist, pro-segregation Southerners it was a cataclysmic event that uprooted their perception of reality.

Segregationist Southerners had maintained an incredible delusion that the stratified racial hierarchy between whites and African Americans benefited and was enjoyed by both races. As editor R. Carlton Wright wrote in his paper *The Columbia Record* in 1933, the institution of "white supremacy" was "no longer in danger" as African Americans had settled into their role of secondary citizens.[30]

This was a continuation of the slavery-era rationalization and Lost Cause lie that there existed a familial love between slaveholders and their property, an illusion that meant any disruption had to have been the result of outside manipulation. To this end, white supremacists reacted to the *Brown v. Board* decision and the coming civil rights movement with predictable paranoia, believing the North was again interfering with a time-honored tradition.

Like the First Red Scare following World War I, unrest in the African-American community was blamed on Russian interference.

Segregationist figurehead Governor George Wallace of Alabama drew a direct line between agitation and Russia, telling his supporters, "The President wants us to surrender this state to Martin Luther King and his group of pro-communists."[31] Jim Johnson, head of Arkansas's White Citizens' Council, a white supremacist political organization, and later associate justice of the Arkansas Supreme Court, asked, in the throes of the push for equal rights, "Don't you know that the communist plan for more than fifty years has been to destroy southern civilization, one of the last patriotic and Christian strongholds, by mongrelization, and our negroes are being exploited by them . . . ?"[32]

To combat this "exploitation," white supremacists in the South again took up the banner of the Confederate States of America and resisted efforts to desegregate their schools, including a massive riot at the University of Mississippi that killed two and injured three hundred. When African Americans engaged in systematic protest in an effort to secure civil rights, white supremacists brutalized them, murdered them, bombed their homes and churches.

The racial violence was nothing new. White supremacy in the South, and across the country, had always been reinforced by the threat of fascistic viciousness and intimidation. What was new, however, was the mass media, which came to broadcast pictures and videos of the violence to a populace that had been previously all too happy to ignore tragedy as they carried on with their lives.

White America's tranquil fantasy unraveled as every night on television there was a stark and undeniable contrast between the African Americans fighting for their rights and their oppressors brutalizing them to maintain power. It made for a simple and immediately recognizable narrative: Images of peaceful protestors attacked by dogs, sprayed with fire hoses, and pummeled with clubs and bricks played on the evening news while leaders like Martin Luther King Jr. preached a policy of civil disobedience that married open, peaceful rebellion with the Christian religion, powering the movement with spiritual morality.

Mass media and television news played an outsized role in another defining moment of the era that fractured the consensus: the Vietnam War, during which broadcasts were filled with scenes of a bloody conflict in Southeast Asia, black-and-white statistics of Americans dying in combat, and the occasional editorial from trusted newscasters who questioned the logic and morality of the war. With only a handful of available channels, there was no place for viewers to hide or alternative perspective to seek out.

Every night a national crisis played out on live television.

Like the civil rights movement, the Vietnam War was a prime example of the considerable gap between the purported principles of America and its political actions. Much as had been the case in other Cold War maneuvers, American support for South Vietnam over North Vietnam was based on political pragmatism, and the use of force undermined a legitimate revolution and the will of the people. Again, the United States, itself a product of colonial revolution, a state outwardly dedicated to freedom and self-determination, was fighting to deny those principles in action to support undemocratic forces and deny the oppositional ideology of communism a win at any cost.

It is telling that Ho Chi Minh, the revolutionary leader of North Vietnam, was a true believer in the message of American principles. In 1919, as Woodrow Wilson and Allied leaders in Paris had plotted a future safe for democracy and self-determination, Ho had donned formal attire and attempted to present Wilson with his own eight-point plan that addressed his concerns in Vietnam and continued French rule. Like so many other people from smaller nations, Ho was ignored. Decades later, he had appealed to Harry Truman, invoking Roosevelt and Churchill's Atlantic Charter.[33] In 1945, when declaring independence for Vietnam, Ho directly alluded to the Declaration of Independence, saying, "All men are created equal," and sounding the hope that "Allied nations" that had "acknowledged the principle of self-determination and equality of nature, will not refuse to acknowledge the independence of Vietnam."[34]

Ho's faith in the propaganda of the liberal superpowers proved tragically misplaced. Belief in self-determination only extended as far as white-majority nations that explicitly supported free markets. Furthermore, Ho's revolution was considered unacceptable by the military planners because he had reacted to the United States' dismissal by turning to communism, necessitating intervention. Military planners believed North Vietnamese forces could be subdued with precise strategy and planning. They convinced President Lyndon B. Johnson, who worried he might lose his administration's goal to remake the economic and social order over "that bitch of a war on the other side of the world," to swallow the bitter pill and order the rational operation to commence.[35] To justify the suppression of a populist revolution that ironically and heartbreakingly mirrored America's own founding, Johnson cited a "love of liberty" that dictated the United States "pay any price to make certain that freedom shall not perish from this earth."[36]

Directing the war was Secretary of Defense Robert McNamara, who had used the same technical rationale to revitalize the Ford Motor Company as he had to plan Curtis LeMay's murderous bombings in World War II. To defeat North Vietnam, McNamara devised a scientific approach designed to break the rebellion but found the statistics and figures he had come to rely on "made no sense."[37] No matter how many bombs were dropped, no matter their efficiency, they failed to subdue the spirit of the revolution. Like so many game theorists, McNamara had failed to consider the human element.

Governed by rationality and imprisoned by political pressures, the United States found itself fighting a brutal and unnecessary war that was both unwinnable and without purpose. Hostilities raged for another decade, costing the lives of nearly sixty thousand Americans, approximately three hundred thousand South Vietnamese soldiers, over eight hundred thousand North Vietnamese soldiers, and an estimated half a million civilians. Both sides resorted to brutality, including the torture of enemy combatants and sickening war crimes. The madness of the Vietnam War laid bare a fundamental and mortal flaw in the American system: The rationality and pragmatism that had taken hold in the prosecution of World War II and then Vietnam was antithetical to a free and open society.

The tyranny that had necessitated revolution in 1776 had again reared its head, only now America had assumed the role of oppressor.

At home, a revolutionary movement took hold in nearly every corner of American life. There were the oppressed peoples, among them African Americans and their civil rights movement, women and their burgeoning feminist ideology, and the LGBT community coalescing in a movement of their own. Joining them was a new generation of white liberals rejecting their parents' consensus and culture of conformity. It was a coalition unlike any seen before.

This newfound questioning of tradition and authority had roots in an emerging strand of philosophy known as existentialism, which held that meaning could only be found through the efforts of the individual. Considered in the wake of the Holocaust, which many believed had shattered the idea of world events' being controlled by the actions of an omnipotent and righteous god, existentialism, as defined by French philosopher Jean-Paul Sartre, was marked by the idea that "man is condemned to be free," a condemnation that meant people were "responsible" for everything they did and every meaning they defined.[38] This meant that the bedrocks of society, including political, historical, social, and religious traditions, not to mention the cult of consumerism, were virtually meaningless, as individuals had to take charge of their own existences and decide for themselves what was meaningful, what was right, and what was wrong.

The revolution questioned the condition of the United States and the culture of conformity, as well as widespread efforts to subjugate the people of the world. For historian Theodore Roszak, who studied the revolution and its challenge of the status quo, it represented a critique of the "technocracy" that had developed in the United States and cast the people as "subjects of purely technical scrutiny and of purely technical manipulation" that turned them into cogs in an inorganic machine. Within that machine, he believed, people were capable of great wrongdoing, an explanation that drew a direct line between the atrocities of the Third Reich and the United States.

The counterculture charged that Americans had confused their own illusions with reality and, as writer Charles Reich presaged, "Americans ha[d] lost control of the machinery of their society."[39] Reich observed "the central fact about America . . . is the discrepancy between the realities of our society and our beliefs about them," a discrepancy that had loosed "the apparatus of power," which had "become a mindless juggernaut, destroying the environment, obliterating human values, and assuming domination over the lives and minds of its subjects."[40]

Reich's portrayal of a runaway, inhuman culture of greed and power struck a chord with a generation who looked around them and saw a society that made less and less sense by the day. The illogical narrative of the myth, betrayed daily by readily available scenes of oppression and murder, hinted at a larger disorder that cried out for attention, and spurred a movement that threatened to escalate into the kind of full-scale revolution the Founders had so feared.

That revolution, however, would never be fully realized, in part because the forces of the status quo embraced the more moderate aspects of the movement while destroying the elements that might overtake the ruling norm. To accomplish the latter, J. Edgar Hoover's FBI launched a massive effort code-named COINTELPRO to spy on counterculture groups, violate their civil liberties, infiltrate their ranks, sow disorder and spread disinformation, and, in many cases, intimidate them into silence. It began in 1961 with a "disruption program" targeting the Socialist Workers Party but expanded to the antiwar movement and civil rights movement, as Hoover and other political leaders believed the unrest was a communist plot.[41] The movements, Hoover maintained, were testimony to "how unified, organized, and powerful an element the Communist movement [was] in the United States," and, if left unchecked, it might spread "to college campuses around the country," a prospect that, Hoover charged, "must not be allowed to happen."[42]

To defend America, Hoover and others like him sought to snuff out the revolutionary fervor that valued liberty and human dignity, the founding principles that had established the United States in the first place.

As the FBI attempted to destroy the counterculture, American business saw an incredible opportunity. The expression of the self in the gathering revolution opened the door to a new type of marketing that exploited the idea of self-expression through consuming. Advertisements used the inherent hipness of the counterculture, a movement marked by youthful art and subversive aesthetics, promising conforming Americans that they too, for a price, could be free of societal pressures, turning products into "devices of liberation."[43] In this way, blue jeans, rock 'n' roll music, alternative clothing, and recreational drug culture were mined for profit and turned into meaningless expressions of empty revolution.

Marketing firms and consumer scientists were quick to conceptualize this absorption of the counterculture because the techniques were already in development before the breaking of consensus. In 1956, Wendell Smith published an article presenting his idea of "market segmentation," a new approach to marketing that focused less on mass efforts and turned toward "smaller or *fringe* market segments" that could represent lucrative niches once products were "tailored to a specialized population."[44] The emergence of the counterculture was a godsend for companies looking for these niches. They targeted specific groups, particularly the young, white members of the protest movement, negating their need for actual revolution by replacing it with material satisfaction.

The coalition was winnowed as many white liberals left their partners in the lurch to seek out their own fortunes and their own power. The institutions and consumerist culture had succeeded. Dangerous protests, bloody street battles with National Guardsmen, attendance at time-consuming university sit-ins and teach-ins, and wrestling with personal and societal privilege had been rendered obsolete.

★

There was no greater living metaphor for the tumult and disorder of the 1960s and '70s than Richard Milhous Nixon. The son of Quakers who forbade drinking and war, he grew into a violent alcoholic responsible for the deaths of thousands in cruel and illegal bombings. A politician who outwardly presented himself as the champion of law and order, he operated his administration as a crime syndicate and wreaked havoc before ever taking his oath of office. Nixon was a living contradiction who perfectly and depressingly represented the disparity between America's sparkling, star-spangled veneer and the smoldering devils brimming just under its surface.

First and foremost, though, Richard Nixon was a salesman, one who learned his trade in his family's grocery store. His early political career was marked by the types of gimmicks preferred by nascent marketers, giving away home goods like clocks and toasters to people who answered their phones "Win with Nixon!"[45] As vice president in 1959, he engaged with Nikita Khrushchev at the American National Exhibition in Moscow in an event called "the Kitchen Debate." As the two sparred over the fundamentals of the Cold War, the salesman couldn't help himself: Gesturing to a model American home, Nixon attempted to sell Khrushchev on the luxuries of American consumerism, asking, "Would it not be better to compete in the relative merit of washing machines than in the strength of rockets?"[46]

Nixon grasped better than anyone at the time the synergetic relationship between politics and consumerism, and particularly the use of spectacle in mass media to sell politics as a product, and how products supplemented personal identity. Despite accounts of popular history that portray Nixon as having been victimized by television's growing influence over politics, Nixon had embraced the medium well before the oft-discussed televised debate with John F. Kennedy in 1960. As a member of Joseph McCarthy's Red Scare committee the decade before, Nixon had established himself as a personality in his dogged pursuit of communists and had turned his investigation of supposed traitor Alger Hiss into a televised event. In 1952, as a scandal over a secret political fund threatened Nixon's place as Eisenhower's nominee for vice president, he took to the airwaves for his infamous "Checkers speech" and shamelessly used his family as props to save his political life.

Following a time in the political wilderness, Nixon reemerged in 1968, when he sensed an opportunity to profit from emerging changes in a Republican Party that had veered far right in reaction to the civil rights movement and antiwar counterculture.

Previous Republican presidential nominee Barry Goldwater, pushing segregation and libertarianism and describing liberals as "collectivists who ask our permission to play God with the human race," had lost his bid for the presidency to Lyndon Johnson but given the party a new identity.[47]

Philosophically, Ayn Rand, the young writer who had developed guidelines for Hollywood filmmakers, had come into her own as an author and intellectual leader. She presented her concept of objectivism to conservative politics, a train of thought that echoed capitalist godfather Adam Smith and argued it was imperative for individuals to be greedy and self-centered. In her blockbuster *Atlas Shrugged*, she told the story of a future dystopia where giants of industry were forced to rebel from a collective, decayed society. Book critic Granville Hicks lambasted the story in *The New York Times*, saying it was clear that the book was "written out of hate," a criticism future chair of the Federal Reserve Alan Greenspan dismissed by saying, "Parasites who persistently avoid either purpose or reason perish as they should."[48]

Perhaps the most influential figure in the rebirth of Richard Nixon was actor-turned-FBI-informant-turned-politician Ronald Reagan, who by this time had won the governorship of California on the platform of "send the welfare bums back to work" and a promise to "clean up the mess" of the antiwar movement.[49] As the face of conservatism, Reagan waged aggressive war on "beatniks, radicals, and filthy-speech advocates," groups he labeled "criminal anarchists and latter-day fascists."[50] Reagan told a confidant, "I'm convinced we win when we defy the little monsters," and his star skyrocketed during the turbulent sixties as he positioned himself as a cheerful warrior for the old guard.[51]

Nixon believed he could supplant Reagan as the face of the counterrevolution, and to do so he again relied on television and mass media. He surrounded himself with "merchandising men and technicians," members of the campaign and witnesses to the operation, likening the strategy to the production of a television commercial.[52] For this endeavor, he tapped a young television producer named Roger Ailes who believed actual politics, being boring and too complicated for the average American, made for bad television, or, in his words, "a horseshit show."[53] Ailes fabricated televised events meant to make Nixon look like a leader at a town hall, the questions as carefully chosen as the audience members. Ailes oversaw their selection and placement to preserve a delicate balance of seeming diversity and white superiority, all the while espousing racist views when the cameras were off.

On television, Nixon was presented as a tested, honest leader capable of uniting the country and bringing the war in Vietnam to an end. Behind the scenes, however, he was anything but. As LBJ neared a peace in Vietnam that Nixon and his campaign believed would deliver the White House to Vice President Hubert Humphrey, Nixon ordered his men to "monkey wrench" the peace talks, essentially an act of treason that ensured thousands more would die.[54] Believing himself to be the only man capable of righting the ship of state, Nixon lied, cheated, and stole in an effort to win and keep hold of the presidency by any means, including intentionally dividing the country.

Nixon applied the concept of market segmentation to the field of politics, and with this, election strategy and American politics were seized by a new breed of consultants, pollsters, and technicians who prized game theory strategies and niche-marketing principles. Nixon was more than willing to slice the electorate into marketing niches to profit off of frustration stemming from the turbulence of the 1960s and political exhaustion in the white population. Images from the civil rights movement, as well as disorder in the streets, had manifested a sense of crisis and instability that frightened white voters. Violence against civil rights supporters in the South and the mess in Vietnam, a mess perpetuated by Nixon himself, had moved many, but they wished for a return to normalcy, and Nixon was more than happy to return to them the illusion of order.

Targeting disaffected Democrats, Nixon crafted "the Silent Majority," or, in his later remembrances, his "new American Revolution."[55] On the surface of this strategy was a depiction of an America "enveloped in smoke and flame" where hardworking citizens heard "sirens in the night," saw "Americans dying on distant battlefields abroad . . . Americans hating each other; fighting each other; killing each other at home."[56] Nixon paid lip service to the civil rights movement and questioners of the war but assured voters tired of their actions that they weren't "racists or sick," they were "forgotten Americans," and that the counterculture's efforts had gone too far.

Latent racism allowed Nixon to gain the support of Southern Democrats and moderates disenchanted with LBJ's civil rights legislation. Strategists had noticed the opening for Republicans to win over these segments in 1970 with Richard M. Scammon and Ben J. Wattenberg's publication of *The Real Majority,* an investigation of America's political center that found Democratic support of civil rights had provided an opening as white voters, even those professing liberal views, were still inherently racist. They said the "middle voter" was a woman "from the outskirts of Dayton, Ohio" with "a mixed view about civil rights."[57]

To moderates, Nixon made the case there were "two extreme groups . . . those who want instant integration and those who want segregation forever."[58] There was room, he suggested, for a "middle course" that opposed flagrant white supremacy while wishing for an end to African-American protest. Nixon and Republicans reinvented how Americans discussed race, largely eliminating open racism and replacing it with coded words and symbols where prejudice could be easily denied and prejudiced people could believe their prejudiced ideals were justified and benign.

In the South, Nixon appealed to the white supremacists themselves, assuring them in private he would "lay off pro-Negro crap."[59] In his speeches for Southern audiences he employed racist dog whistles, prejudiced appeals hidden behind rhetoric in order to enjoy deniability, to signal his sympathies while criticizing "hypocritical" Northerners who asked, "Why don't those Southerners do something about their race problem?" while engaging in their own discrimination.[60]

For his efforts, Nixon convinced "Dixiecrats" like white supremacist Strom Thurmond, who had previously strayed from the Democratic Party to form their own pro-segregation group, to leave the Democrats and align themselves with Republicans. This ideological shift came to define American politics for decades to come and secure for the GOP a stranglehold over white voters in the South by means of orchestrating what would come to be known as the Southern Strategy. In building his vaunted Silent Majority, Nixon created an alternate American reality where the civil rights movement and counterculture had succeeded in eliminating racism and securing necessary reform while ensuring racism's survival and the negation of that reform.

Voters bought in and bought in big. Richard Nixon the Product, guaranteed to assuage racist guilt and reestablish white supremacist consensus, had been sold to the American people, and buyer's remorse would be the least of their concerns.

★

Like the rest of his political life, Richard Nixon's inevitable downfall played out on the airwaves of broadcast television. His collapse was self-inflicted and caused by an unnecessary assortment of crimes. In the Watergate scandal, which sealed his political fate, Nixon had followed the intelligence community's lead and created his own squad of extralegal henchmen, nearly all of whom were either ex-CIA or employed by the agency, to spy on his opponents and undercut their efforts. For Nixon, protecting his own political power had become synonymous with national security, and so it had to be protected with the same pragmatic approaches the safety of the people deserved. His paranoia was his undoing, however, as breaking into Democratic National Committee headquarters on the night of June 17, 1972, to install illegal wiretaps proved unnecessary. Nixon went on to win that election without the need for interference, taking every state but Massachusetts.

The investigation into these crimes and others that Nixon and his cronies had committed was a national sensation, as *The Washington Post* and *The New York Times* competed for readership by reporting on the astonishing twists and turns along the way.

By the time the Watergate hearings began on May 17, 1973, the people were more than ready to tune in and watch the show like it was the latest, hottest soap opera.

Jim Lehrer, one of the hosts of the gavel-to-gavel coverage, welcomed viewers by admitting, "We are doing this as an experiment," and seemed resigned to the fact that the nation's grave constitutional crisis might, here and there, "be in competition with a late, late movie."[61] To compete, the coverage came complete with dramatic music, graphics, detailed sets, and experts who could explain the minutiae to viewers at home. The hearings on the impeachment of a criminal president were being treated like a sportscast or the latest episode of *Dragnet.*

The members of the committee vamped for audiences at home, performed for the cameras, and became household names. Like politicians in the pre–Civil War Congress with the advent of national print media, they were well aware of their constituents and the national audience watching at home. There were quotable lines, theatrical revelations. Again, as Lloyd Shapley had warned his fellow game theorists, playing a game lent everything the feeling of artificiality.

To save his neck, Nixon kept up appearances and pretended he had nothing to worry about even though he had been caught dead to rights. Just as he'd done with the Checkers speech, he stared into television cameras and assured the people at home he had done nothing wrong. His vice president, Spiro Agnew, who happened to be facing his own criminal investigation, joined him in weaponizing the mass media. In outright lies meant to twist reality and sow seeds of doubt, Agnew and Nixon accused the media of ratcheting up conspiracies against them for profit, framing the media and journalists as enemies of the people. Agnew delighted conservatives when he said, "Perhaps the place to start looking for a credibility gap is not in the offices of government in Washington but in the studios of the networks in New York."[62]

For his defense, Nixon was more than willing to position his own survival as a battle between two narratives of American life, the consensus that had served white America well and the reality of injustices endured by those who had fought for the civil rights movement and the counterculture. Just as he had done in his electoral bids, Nixon framed his own fortunes as those of "real" Americans who were being opposed by vast and sinister forces that threatened to derail him and, by extension, the United States of America.

But Agnew resigned in disgrace, as would Richard Nixon. A

creature of incurable paranoia, the president had taped his crimes and provided his detractors with a word-for-word record of his transgressions. When it became apparent his cause was futile, Nixon collapsed in what appeared to be a nervous breakdown. He paced the halls of the White House late at night, extremely drunk and muttering to himself. In a meeting with congressmen, he terrified the room when he groused, "I can go in my office and pick up a telephone, and in twenty-five minutes, millions of people will be dead."[63]

The man who had promised order became a liability. Aware that Nixon had previously drunkenly ordered an aborted nuclear strike on North Korea in 1969, the secretaries of defense and state sent word throughout the administration that any order to launch nuclear weapons by the president must first be approved by them, an unconstitutional and chilling command. The night he signed his resignation, Nixon broke down and sobbed uncontrollably with Henry Kissinger, asking his secretary of state, the man who had carried out the indiscriminate war crime of bombing Cambodia, to sink to the floor and pray with him.

When Nixon walked onscreen the next day to leave the White House for the final time, there was no trace of the dangerously unstable and emotional man who'd signed away his presidency. He smiled for the camera, read a final statement, exited to applause, climbed aboard the presidential helicopter, and flew into the clouds. It was like a television show where the criminal had been caught and all had been set right with the world. Gerald Ford quickly pardoned Nixon, signaling that the slate had been wiped clean and inviting Americans to believe the long national nightmare was over.

The message was clear: The country's disease had been cured. Racism had been eliminated, the illness of conformity and militarism overcome. A rogue president had been reined in. Americans could go to bed that night and sleep soundly knowing all was well and assured they were ready to savor the challenge and promise of the future.

CHAPTER 8

*　　*　　*

The Cult of the Shining City

A little over two months after taking office as the fortieth president of the United States of America, Ronald Reagan addressed a gathering of AFL-CIO leaders on March 30, 1981. The speech was meant to bridge the divide between the antilabor Republican Party and the most powerful union in the country and test whether the growing sphere of the Silent Majority could continue to make inroads. In that effort, Reagan reiterated the campaign message that had won him forty-four states in the election: cutting taxes, curbing spending, and the importance of faith, family, and community in restoring the country.

"Now, I know that we can't make things right overnight," Reagan said in closing. "But we will make them right. Our destiny is not our fate. It is our choice . . . You and your forebears built this Nation. Now help us rebuild it, and together we'll make America great again."[1]

Chaos erupted as Reagan was escorted out of the Washington Hilton. In a matter of seconds an aspiring assassin emptied his revolver, shooting and paralyzing Press Secretary James Brady and striking a police officer and a Secret Service agent. After being shoved into the presidential limousine, Reagan was discovered to be bleeding from a wound under his arm. With a bullet burrowing near his heart, the newly minted president was in grave danger.

The shooter was a disturbed twenty-five-year-old man named John Hinckley Jr. who wanted to kill Reagan to impress actress Jodie Foster. Hinckley attempted the assassination as his final effort to earn her affection. In June of 1982, Hinckley was found not guilty by reason of insanity, a verdict won by his defense lawyers as they proved his "anchors" to reality had "slipped away" as he progressively grew more and more lost in a fantasy world where reality and popular culture twisted into oblivion.² After interviewing Hinckley for over forty hours, renowned psychiatrist Dr. William T. Carpenter testified that he had been stricken with "ideas of reference," a condition in which people "interpret in a highly personal and idiosyncratic way . . . what may be commonplace events."³ In this case, Hinckley had manufactured his own reality after several fanatical viewings of Martin Scorsese's 1976 film *Taxi Driver.*

The protagonist of *Taxi Driver* is an alienated New York cabbie named Travis Bickle portrayed by Robert De Niro, a character Hinckley's lawyers said he identified with, and through that connection, he began picking up "in largely automatic ways many [of his] attributes."⁴ The movie depicts America as a dangerous society rife with crime, racked with amoral greed, and overflowing with lonely and isolated people, perhaps none as lonely or isolated as Bickle. While cruising the trash-strewn city in his cab, Bickle watches the decline of a great country while wishing for "a real rain" to "come and wash all this scum off the streets."⁵ Eventually, after being spurned by the object of his obsession, he attempts to assassinate a presidential candidate but eventually settles for the bloody rescue of Jodie Foster's underage character Iris from a life of prostitution.

Scorsese captured the film's bleak American setting by filming during the summer of 1975 at the height of New York City's sanitation strike. The labor stoppage preceded a crisis caused by the city's dire financial condition. Advised by Ayn Rand devotee and then–chairman of the Council of Economic Advisers Alan Greenspan, President Gerald Ford initially denied requests to intervene. Greenspan had drawn a line in the sand, saying there was "no shortcut to fiscal responsibility" and that default was "virtually inevitable."[6] New York would eventually be saved but lose autonomy as corporations and banks demanded unfettered influence and austerity measures that cut jobs and services.

The fiscal crisis certainly wasn't limited to New York City. The legacy of the tumultuous decades of the sixties and seventies, not to mention the hangover of the Watergate scandal, had saddled America with an insurmountable paranoia and crushing disillusionment. *Taxi Driver* scriptwriter Paul Schrader felt this burden deeply as he wandered the derelict streets of New York. He found refuge in the pages of the book *An Assassin's Diary*, written by Arthur Bremer, the man who shot and paralyzed Governor George Wallace in 1972. Bremer's troubled rantings inspired Schrader's creation of Travis Bickle, which inspired John Hinckley Jr. to attempt to assassinate Ronald Reagan, an actor who had graduated to the role of president of the United States, an ouroboros of stupefying proportions.

Reagan's survival of this bizarre attempt on his life helped lay the groundwork for his status as a living myth in the eyes of many Americans. The sixties and seventies had seen waves of chaotic violence, but his endurance seemed to mark a turning point, a glimpse at hope for a despondent nation.

Perhaps things were turning around.

Perhaps he had been spared for some greater purpose.

On April 28, a rejuvenated Reagan appeared before Congress to deafening applause. His first priority was to quell concerns that something was inherently wrong with the United States. "You've provided an answer," he told the American people who had written him get-well letters and prayed for their ailing president, "to those few voices that were raised saying that what happened was evidence that ours is a sick society."[7] America, he promised, was full of good and decent people and continued to be an exceptional society and the hope of the world.

Having convinced the nation of its soundness, he immediately pivoted and marshaled his goodwill in promoting his plan to radically alter the American economy.

Like so many others, Reagan looked at the events surrounding his shooting and delivered order from the chaos. Experiencing his own ideas of reference, Reagan believed his survival was proof of a higher purpose and evidence of a higher calling.

★

The Reagan Revolution of the 1980s now feels inevitable, but following the disgraced presidency of Richard Nixon, it seemed at the time as if the Republican Party might never recover. President Gerald Ford's turn as president was largely an afterthought, a custodial role so unremarkable that Ronald Reagan challenged the incumbent's nomination and was only bested at the 1976 Republican National Convention due to the behind-the-scenes work of future secretary of state James Baker and an assembly of delegate wranglers, including a relatively unknown operative named Paul Manafort.

The party was unstable and lacked a definitive identity. Nixon's carving up the electorate by means of segmentation and flexible ideology that borrowed freely from liberals had garnered electoral success while hollowing out the party's philosophical core. There was little ideological difference between Republicans and Democrats in the aftermath of Watergate.

In the following years, a party in desperate need of identity took a hard right turn inspired by elements outside the party that exerted pressure and eventually remade Republicans in their own image. Perhaps no transformation embodies this more than the surreal conversion of the National Rifle Association from a nonpolitical sportsman's club dedicated to gun safety and marksmanship to one of the most influential and destructive lobbies in history. Prior to the 1970s the NRA had welcomed reform of gun laws and rarely cited the Second Amendment. But in May 1977, at an event called the Revolt at Cincinnati, the organization was taken over by a group of hardliners who galvanized the organization's militant opposition to any and all gun control laws.

Another grassroots movement spearheaded by a woman named Phyllis Schlafly rose to prominence in the fight against the proposed Equal Rights Amendment, which guaranteed equality for women. The ERA enjoyed widespread and bipartisan support until Schlafly launched a resistance by leveraging traditional gender roles and appealing to middle-class and wealthy white women who had been well served by the patriarchal system and were reluctant to afford privileges to women of the lower classes and other races. Schlafly's developing base was warmly welcomed by Republicans as they changed course and the party turned opposition to the ERA into a party principle at the turn of the decade.

The emergence of a pro-gun base and a split among white women along the lines of the ERA and eventually abortion, which had been a largely settled issue but was reignited during the culture wars by white evangelicals, created new opportunities for segmentation. Disciples of Nixon seized this opening and created a new identity that merged free-market ideals, the authentic core philosophy of the party, with controversial and hot-button wedge issues to create a categorically reactionary conservative movement.

The takeover of the party happened largely behind closed doors. Young Republicans staked their claim by using the underhanded, pragmatic Nixonian philosophy of victory by any means. Elections of Young Republicans and College Republicans, in many ways the infrastructure that girded the Republican Party as a whole, were the sites of power plays and crooked takeovers by ambitious young men like Roger Stone, a proud trickster with ties to Nixon; future George W. Bush guru Karl Rove; and prolific strategist Lee Atwater. These upstarts reignited the party and represented a philosophical and strategic bridge from the devastated era of Nixon to the triumphant Reagan Revolution, building off the clashes of the 1960s and '70s that had defined their youths and framing politics as a battle for cultural survival.

They built a broad majority by pairing tested rhetoric that favored emotion over facts; appealed to white, patriarchal anxiety; pressed sensitive and controversial wedge issues to divide the people; and modernized the Southern Strategy by updating Republican, racist dog-whistle appeals. As a member of the Reagan administration, Lee Atwater gave insight into the latter strategy in a now-infamous interview with Alexander Lamis for his book *The Two-Party South*, explaining the evolution. "You start out in 1954 saying, 'Nigger, nigger, nigger,'" he said, admitting overt racism had grown untenable and Republican politics now demanded more nuance. "By 1968 you can't say 'nigger' . . . So you say stuff like forced busing, states' rights . . . You're getting so abstract now [that] you're talking about cutting taxes, and all these things you're talking about are totally economic things."[8]

This approach whitewashed inherently racist beliefs, allowing white voters to advocate for their continued dominance while enjoying the rhetorical distance from explicit white supremacy, hiding the bigotry and tribalism behind mundane-seeming issues.

The strategy worked. Republicans began referring to race without ever directly mentioning it, focusing instead on words and phrases like *busing, welfare queens,* and *hardworking Americans.* In 1980, Ronald Reagan appeared at the Neshoba County Fair in Mississippi, assuring Southern voters, "I believe in state's rights . . . And I believe that we've distorted the balance of our government today by giving powers that were never intended in the constitution to that federal establishment."[9]

As president, Reagan continually framed racist policy from a purely economic and social standpoint, creating "color-blind racism," or exclusionary laws and stances that had been crafted as fair in nature but were designed with African Americans and other minorities in mind.

Republicans now had a proven strategy. They had crafted a new coalition of segments of the population that could revitalize their party by appealing to populist movements while obscuring their unpopular underpinnings, primarily their top-down economic principles. It was enough to mobilize a political force that could survive and thrive in a post-Watergate world, even if the message was a toxic sludge of paradoxical ideals and created a powder keg of anger and prejudice. But what happened next, to the detriment of all, was that that political strategy evolved from a pragmatic approach to a doctrine of radical religious faith.

★

Shaggy-haired, academic in tone, and the product of commune-based Christianity, Francis Schaeffer made for an unlikely evangelical influence. He loomed large over the movement, however, and his 1976 magnum opus *How Should We Then Live?* served as a rallying cry to spark renewed interest in religion's place in the political sphere.

The book was Schaeffer's history of the world, a survey beginning in ancient Rome and culminating in the turbulent present. Schaeffer presented a disturbing picture of decaying Western civilization that framed political and social chaos as having been caused by the waning influence of Christianity. As a warning from the past, he argued the fall of the Roman Empire was not "because of external forces such as the invasion by the barbarians" but due to a lapse in moral and unifying clarity based within scripture.[10]

In this narrative, the discord of the modern age, with its riots, wars, political failures, and widespread turmoil, was a symptom of secular humanism, a consequence of postmodern and relativist thought that Schaeffer likened to "intellectual suicide" and called "the paths of death." Democratic philosophy, and by extension a truly free and democratic society, were thereby extremely dangerous. Political dominion by Christianity and the establishment of a theocracy was the only true option if civilization was to survive.

To accompany the book, Schaeffer filmed a ten-part documentary that was screened widely in churches and Christian classrooms and attracted droves of viewers. The concept provided a fresh and enlivening perspective to a population desperate for answers. The rise of secularism and loosening of puritanical constraints in the sixties and seventies, a social revolution that saw the challenging of sexual mores, familial roles, and the hierarchies of power, had terrified evangelicals, and Schaeffer's work submitted a pleasing and readily acceptable answer to their lingering questions. Liberalism was to blame for the prevalent chaos, and if left unchecked, it could destroy the United States of America and deliver the world unto a new Dark Age.

Among Schaeffer's many converts was a Virginia-born preacher named Jerry Falwell. A natural orator, Falwell had founded the Thomas Road Baptist Church in Lynchburg in his early twenties and grew the modest house of worship into one of the country's largest and most influential bases of evangelical power through televangelism, a new form of mass media religion that married the medium of television with charismatic preaching. Televangelism proved an effective means of spreading the message as it peaked in the 1980s, with almost twenty-five million Americans, or nearly a tenth of the population, tuning in to religious programming.[11]

During the civil rights era, Falwell used his pulpit to loudly support continued segregation. "The facilities should be separate," he preached. "Where God has drawn a line of distinction, we should not attempt to cross that line." Eliminating segregation, which he believed was ordained by God, would lead to disaster and would "destroy [the white] race eventually." In an effort to combat desegregation and liberal progress, men like Falwell built empires of white Christianity that mobilized millions of voters, raised endless riches, and, in many cases, continued the tradition of segregation.

They pushed their congregations to take their children out of the public schools and enroll them in private Christian academies where the curriculum reinforced their faith and the classrooms were free of minorities. Like their Confederate forebears, they twisted the gospel to paint the North and desegregated society as apocalyptic and antithetical to the word of an angry, racist God. Though Christian principles of morality and fairness had informed the strategies of civil rights leaders like Martin Luther King Jr.—Falwell repeatedly questioned King's "sincerity"[12]—these white evangelical leaders directed their parishioners to an ideology emphasizing personal benefit, cultural isolation, and a rabid dedication to conservatism.

The gospel was intentionally distanced from social justice and pivoted to advocating for self-empowerment and the worship of wealth, long undercurrents in churches awash in white supremacy. The Christian Right adopted a belief in capitalistic success as denoting God's favor, particularly following pastor Norman Vincent Peale's influential book *The Power of Positive Thinking*, which turned the faith on its head by promoting faith and piousness as a means to "achieve a happy, satisfying, and worthwhile life" and gain "expanded influence."[13] Peale's sermons were self-help and self-enrichment lectures amplifying conservative causes while demonizing New Deal liberalism and "super-duper social improvements."[14] For his contributions to the prosperity gospel and his role in transforming evangelicalism, Peale gained converts among the wealthy, like real-estate mogul Donald Trump, whose first wedding Peale officiated. In 1984, Peale was awarded the Presidential Medal of Freedom by Ronald Reagan, who gushed, "Few Americans have contributed so much to the personal happiness of their fellow citizens."[15]

A decade earlier, the Christian Right had believed the man to represent them might be Jimmy Carter, a humble peanut farmer from Plains, Georgia, who unseated Gerald Ford in 1976. Though he was a Democrat, Carter was most assuredly Southern and quite open about his Christian faith. Carter had not joined Falwell and others in the post-MLK split, however, and couched his support of civil rights in the gospel. Because of these differences Carter eventually left the Southern Baptist Convention while continuing to teach Sunday school throughout his post-presidential life.

Carter's brand of Christianity stood in stark contrast to that of the Christian Right. While Falwell's ilk was sanctimonious and battled the world around them, Carter turned inward in reflection and asked Americans to consider their own personal responsibilities. In his much-maligned "Malaise speech" in 1979, Carter posited that the threat facing the country was "nearly invisible" and constituted "a crisis of confidence" that could be seen in "growing doubt about the meaning of our own lives and in the loss of unity of purpose for our nation."[16] He admonished the culture at large, accusing it of "self-indulgence" through "consumption." The nation's capital, and its elite class of rulers, had become "an island" and represented a gathering threat. For the future he laid out a choice for the American people between two distinct paths, one "that leads to fragmentation and self-interest . . . a mistaken idea of freedom, the right to grasp for ourselves some advantage over others," and the other a hard-won rededication to shared society.

His appeal was earnest and thoughtful, a secular sermon of duty and reckoning with the American Myth, but it wasn't what politics demanded from a president of the United States. In the age of mass media the presidency more closely resembled the televangelists haunting the airwaves, who could symbolically exorcise the country's demons and motivate their flocks, than Carter's humble rural preacher. Carter's refusal to play this game opened the door for Ronald Reagan, a handsome celebrity with decades of acting experience. In his closing argument before the 1980 election, Reagan declared there was "no national malaise" and "nothing wrong with the American people." [17] What he offered was absolution, a utopian vision of America as "that shining city on a hill" that had been the subject of Christ's Sermon on the Mount and part of America's lore since its settlement.

From the beginning of his political existence, Reagan peppered his speeches and appearances with references to religion. In declaring his candidacy for president in 1979 he called for a "spiritual revival" while touting tax reform and a pro-business agenda, and criticizing women joining the workforce. [18] When accepting the party's nomination at the 1980 Republican National Convention, he asked the attendees to "begin [their] crusade joined together in a moment of silent prayer" and ended his address by saying, "God bless America," and firmly enshrining the phrase and concept in the modern American lexicon. [19]

Reagan made an incredible ally for the Christian Right, but for all of his public proclamations of mainstream religious faith, Reagan's own strand of Christianity was rooted in the occult and shaped by his time in California surrounded by showbiz personalities trafficking in New Age ideas. Though late-night hosts loved joking about his wife Nancy's association with astrologers and psychics, even members of Reagan's inner circle were troubled by the degree to which the Reagans relied on them. Donald Regan, Reagan's chief of staff, characterized Nancy as having "a dependence on the occult" and admitted in his memoir of his time in the administration that "the highest affairs of the nation" were being directed through and at the mercy of consultations with Nancy's spiritual advisors, including appearances by the president, his speeches, and even "negotiations with a foreign power," which necessitated the Reagans' communicating highly classified information to advisors outside the government. [20]

Bizarre and superstitious ideas shaped Reagan's worldview and, through him, infected the political discourse and warped shared reality. In his years as an actor, he had been steeped in conspiracy theories and myths, maybe none more conspicuous than his faith that Americans had been preordained by divinity and history as a chosen people. Touting the principles of manifest destiny, Reagan told students at William Woods College in 1952 that he saw America "in the divine scheme of things . . . as a promised land."[21] As proof, he relayed to them "a legend" concerning the Declaration of Independence and how, as the Founding Fathers struggled with their conviction to affix it with their signatures, a stranger appeared in the room and demanded, "Sign that document, sign it if tomorrow your heads roll from the headsman's axe. Sign that document because tomorrow and the days to come your children and all the children of all the days to come will judge you for what you do this day."[22] According to this legend, the mysterious speaker was the force that inspired the signing that founded the country, and once the deed was done he simply disappeared, as if he were a ghost.

Reagan repeated this legend again and again. At the first Conservative Political Action Conference (CPAC) in 1974, Reagan addressed the Republican faithful by saying, "You can call it mysticism if you want to, but I have always believed there was some divine plan that placed this great continent between two oceans to be sought out by those who were possessed of an abiding love of freedom and a special kind of courage."[23] Again, he supported his belief in the divinity of America by turning to the legend of the mysterious figure at the signing of the Declaration of Independence: "Some years ago, a writer, who happened to be an avid student of history, told me a story about that day in the little hall in Philadelphia . . . I confess, I never researched or made an effort to verify it."[24]

The story was inspiring, but the legend of divine interference in Philadelphia was completely fabricated and had originated in a book called *Washington and His Generals; or, Legends of the Revolution*, an 1847 volume of popular myths authored by writer George Lippard. Lippard was a close friend of Edgar Allan Poe and wrote countless tales for a living that featured invented instances of the supernatural during the American Revolution and capitalized on the previous success of Parson Weems's myths about George Washington and his cherry tree.

The "avid student of history" who introduced Reagan to the myth and framed it as factual was an occultist named Manly P. Hall. Hall gained fame and notoriety in midcentury California and was a favorite of Reagan's and among New Agers who flocked to his lectures and appearances to learn about "symbols," "long forgotten truths," and myths in the vein of the supposed lost continent of Atlantis. In his work, Hall claimed to divine "the emblematic figures, allegories, and rituals of the ancients," which obscured a "secret doctrine concerning the inner mysteries of life."[25]

He maintained that the United States of America and the concept of freedom had been the orchestrated plan and "the secret dream of the great classical philosophers," who knew, before Christopher Columbus, "of the existence of our Western Hemisphere and selected it to be the site of the philosophic empire."[26] According to Hall, America represented the spiritual and philosophical heir of ancient Greece, Rome, and a long and illustrious line of secret societies that had worked behind the scenes to bend world events in order to build the United States into that shining city on the hill.

Another influence on Reagan was Hal Lindsey, a Christian conspiracy theorist who wrote a number of books outlining his belief that Americans were living in the End Times as depicted in the Christian Bible's Book of Revelation. Lindsey was a bestselling author and injected the Christian Right with a premillennial angst that the Cold War was not just a geopolitical struggle but a clash between the literal embodiments of good and evil, a showdown between champions of God and his eternal nemesis Satan. In a film version of his book *The Late, Great Planet Earth*, a popular movie featuring Orson Welles, Lindsey appeared wearing denim on denim to deliver his portent of doom: "I believe what we're seeing today is the fulfillment of these ancient prophecies . . . I believe that we are racing, on a countdown, to the end of history as we know it."[27] In his book he predicted the Cold War would escalate into "the last war of the world" and usher in an apocalypse wherein "Christ [would] return to prevent the annihilation of all mankind" by the Beast of the Soviet Union.[28]

In the 1980s, Reagan's muddle of occultism and premillennial apocalypticism merged with the Christian Right's belief in white supremacy and fear of societal collapse. This formed a new faith maintaining that the United States of America had been founded by the grace of a Christian God and the ingenuity of a long line of learned, elite, ordained white men. According to this ideology, America was the last, best hope for mankind, the steward for the Second Coming of Jesus Christ, and the foundation for the kingdom of heaven on earth.

Following his close call with death in March of 1981, believing divine intervention had saved his life, and his presidency to be the culmination of centuries' worth of toil, suffering, and cosmic predestination, a grateful Ronald Reagan was more than ready to assume his prophesied role as an instrument of the will of this new, American god.

★

When the Reagan administration was initially organized in 1981, one of the first orders of business was the distribution of a book entitled *Mandate for Leadership: Policy Management in a Conservative Administration.* Weighing in at over a thousand pages, the tome was prepared by the Heritage Foundation, an upstart conservative think tank, and prescribed specific and exhaustive policies for every department that constituted "a blueprint for the construction of a conservative government." According to the Heritage Foundation, that construction required a massive tax cut for the wealthy, the establishment of a new arms race, and the erasure of progressive measures for racial and economic fairness, among other actions meant to extinguish the gains made by Franklin D. Roosevelt's New Deal.[29]

The Heritage Foundation became a de facto governing body, a

group of unelected, unaccountable, and largely anonymous figures, their own vice president defining them as the "intellectual shock troops of the conservative revolution."[30] Much like how the United States military had delegated and contracted its planning to the RAND Corporation following World War II, the Republican Party, beginning with Reagan, shifted responsibility for government planning and operations to for-profit bodies like the Heritage Foundation. The party also enlisted a virtual army of pollsters, strategists, and other private organizations, and focused on public perception, essentially turning the GOP into a smiling, handshaking mascot for deeply conservative policies hidden behind exhaustively fine-tuned and misleading rhetoric.

Reagan was born to play the part. For decades he had been stepping in front of the camera to deliver prepared lines that forwarded the propaganda of free-market ideals and American Myth, particularly in his star turn as the face of the General Electric Company, which required him to travel the country making patriotic, pro-business speeches. Each night he was handed the following day's lines so he could prepare, a continuation of his process as a B-list actor. Notoriously uninterested in the specifics of the job of president of the United States, he kept few hours in the Oval Office and refused to dive into policy. His briefings were often prepared as movies or cartoons lest he lose interest altogether. When pressed for details on his plans, he often stammered or made them up out of whole cloth, or, if possible, handed the microphone over to someone else. He lied so consistently and shamelessly about his achievements it became central to his public persona.

Soviet leader Mikhail Gorbachev called Reagan "intellectually feeble."[31] Republican senator William Cohen lamented, "With Ronald Reagan, no one is there. The sad fact is we don't have a president."[32] Speaker of the House Tip O'Neill, whom popular history reframed as a reluctant and constructive collaborator with Reagan, said the president "lacked the knowledge he should have had in every sphere" and "was an actor reading lines, who didn't understand his own pro-grams." O'Neill added, "I hate to say it about such an agreeable man, but it was sinful that Ronald Reagan ever became president."

These deficiencies were hidden by an extensive public relations operation that constructed around Reagan an immaculately orches-trated and executed cult of personality that managed his image by controlling the press and presenting him as the embodiment of the mythical America that so many Americans had been conditioned to believe in. Reagan's teams harnessed the airwaves in a way no other president had ever dared to, resulting in what *Time* magazine labeled the "TV presidency."[33] Through "a new level of control over the me-chanics of modern communication," a strategy of "staging news events for maximum press coverage," and "the timing of announcements to hit the largest television audiences," the Reagan administration re-defined how a White House operated and managed the public imag-ination.[34]

Enabling this was an accomplice in the American press. As Jimmy Carter had noted in 1979, Washington, DC, and its ruling elite had become an island removed from the rest of the nation. Members of Reagan's administration trafficked in the same social circles as the journalists and opinion makers: They drank together, they attended the same parties, and their lives and fortunes became inextricably intertwined. The twisted journalism that resulted, the permanent circle of favors for favors, trading of information for access, constituted its own ecosystem in which the president would be portrayed in a positive light. With the new Hollywood president, American media began covering politics as if it were an enter-tainment, replete with characters and story lines. Journalists became indebted to the administration for its continual release of news items to fill their columns and time on the evening news. It was simply easier and more economically feasible to parrot the talking points rather than tackle a living, breathing myth, a daunting fact that rel-egated the press, in the words of *New York Times* columnist and editor James Reston, to the position of "transmission belt" for the presidency's messaging.[35]

For Reagan's reelection campaign in 1984, the official strategy laid bare the pursuit: *"Paint RR as the personification of all that is right with or heroicized by America,"* the goal being to plant the "subliminal" idea that *"a vote against Reagan"* is *"a vote against mythic 'America.'"*[36] If Reagan remained relentlessly positive and constantly preached the inherent goodness and infallibility of the United States, critics of his policies would be seen as critical of the country itself. To be a viable candidate, politicians would first have to kneel at the altar of American exceptionalism, acknowledge there was nothing intrinsically wrong with the country, constantly speak to America's past as a mythic arc of moral righteousness, and frame campaign issues as momentary blips in an otherwise unblemished narrative.

The lines Reagan read were largely crafted by a speechwriter named Peggy Noonan, who searched for "the grammar of the Presidency" and decided that an ideal president should sound like Franklin D. Roosevelt, the very man whose policies he was seeking to dismantle.[37] His addresses weaved in elements of spiritual stories to interlock the United States and Christianity, fragments of addresses by past presidents, and a revised history that pardoned America of its sins and restored its veneer of morality and invincibility.

Reagan's campaign and communications strategies succeeded. In 1984, following a sustained effort to lace him into the living, breathing American Myth, Reagan nearly swept the electoral map and destroyed former vice president Walter Mondale, a respected stalwart of the party who only managed to win his home state of Minnesota and the District of Columbia. Reagan's team had discovered that America was ready to leave the tumult and strife of the 1960s and '70s behind and embrace the cult of exceptionalism. Even though the Republican Party had felt particularly endangered following the resignation of Richard Nixon and the stain of Watergate, Reagan's revival of consensus and insistence on denying still-pressing cultural matters created an overwhelming conservative majority that hobbled its adversaries. By tying the Democratic Party to the actions of the counterculture—which now, in the age of Reagan, were appearing less and less like a necessary movement and more like unpatriotic, subversive tantrums—it undermined their electoral chances by casting them as un-American.

One of the more pressing matters in Reagan's revival was the correction of the perception of the Vietnam War as a stain on a long history of military dominance. Reagan changed the perception of Vietnam as an unjust and flawed war, moving the focus to the men who had fought there and laying the blame of defeat on a military that had been unwilling to win the war and an American public whose protests of the war amounted to a betrayal of the troops serving overseas. The approach was an echo of the Third Reich's "Knife in the Back" myth, reigniting the American belief that it was a chosen country that could never be defeated when united. Anyone questioning war or the actions of the United States was effectively branded as traitorous and dangerous to American interests.

Reagan minted this myth while presenting the Medal of Honor to Vietnam War hero Roy P. Benavidez, saying veterans of the war "came home without a victory, not because they'd been defeated, but because they'd been denied permission to win."[38] He reiterated that the lack of victory was the fault not of America's troops, an army of warriors on the side of God, but of the government and society that had held them back.

Two years later, Roy Benavidez, the hero Reagan had used to build his new myth, reappeared in the news, making public that the Reagan administration had denied him benefits as part of a cut to veterans' services.

Reality didn't matter, however, as the myth playing out on television drowned it out. Following Reagan's reframing of Vietnam with a new myth of national betrayal, there was a surge in public displays of patriotism. Across the country, cities held celebrations to rectify a fictional wrong constructed by the president. In May of 1985, New York City held a massive parade for veterans of Vietnam with floats, ticker tape, all the trappings needed for a patriotic revival.

On the same front page of *The New York Times* as its coverage of the parade was a story that Reagan's deregulation of the media had allowed conservative mogul Rupert Murdoch to purchase multiple television channels in the United States. With his ownership of the *New York Post* and this new collection of outlets, he was touted as a prominent new influence whose reach could now be felt in one in every five American homes.[39]

★

Cultural wars and revisionist history aside, the main goal of the Reagan administration was to radically alter the economy. Following the passage of the Economic Recovery Tax Act of 1981, the bill that would begin that transformation, Reagan held a press conference at Rancho del Cielo, the Reagan vacation ranch outside Santa Barbara. Dressed like an aging cowboy, the president strode out to a wooden table in front of a gaggle of reporters and took a disapproving glance at the pervasive fog obscuring his property's majestic views. "Since this is the first day of this kind of weather, of this fog, since we've been here," he told the press, "I shall refrain from saying you all are responsible for bringing it up with you. The sun has been shining brightly here."[40]

Even though the optics had taken a dispiriting turn, the appearance was what mattered. A lighting rig cut through the mist and lit the president signing into law a massive tax cut. It had been sold to the American public as a means to shared prosperity but was nothing more than a slashing of taxes for the wealthy and a license to steal.

What came to be known as "Reaganomics" was actually the handiwork of a collection of supply-side economists who believed the most important actors within the economy, by many levels, were the producers and the wealthy, who were to be treated as a class of wealth priests whose instincts and self-interest served as extensions of a capitalistic god. Reagan himself had very little understanding of the principles and, as with most of his other policies, had no interest in diving deep into the minutiae. The rhetoric that supply-side economics was tantamount to freedom and that taxes and regulations constituted economic slavery was more than enough for the actor to take his stage and proclaim, "Government is not the solution to our problem; government is the problem."[41]

In the past such an appeal might have been a populist rallying cry for democratic change, but Reagan was selling the power of the wealthy and their businesses to control the government for the people, echoing the tenets of the Gilded Age. Shifting resources, Reagan starved the parts of the federal government that benefited individuals and redirected them, while also freeing the wealthy and corporations to allocate wealth according to their own self-interest.

Following Reagan's lead, the broader society came to equate free markets with freedom and to fetishize wealth and influence. Americans began engaging in conspicuous spending as profits soared for the highest earners, echoing the climate that precipitated the Great Depression. Greed, which had been lauded as patriotic during the Cold War, was now tantamount to godliness. In popular culture the wealthy were viewed as heroes, their exploits and lavish consumption documented on early reality television shows like *Lifestyles of the Rich and Famous*. As they cruised through the seas in their decked-out yachts and soared above in their private jets, the wealthy moved through the world as if they belonged to another race. Ridiculous figures like Donald Trump, a swaggering real-estate mogul who lived an oligarchical life beset with gaudy gold fixtures, were elevated to embodiments of the American dream.

The government was relegated to assisting the market and all pretense of oversight or management disappeared. The new belief was that the principles of capitalism as envisioned by Adam Smith would lead to businesses' regulating themselves, improving safety and environmental standards, as well as providing better salaries for their workers. By acting selfishly, the market would somehow organically become more ethical and humane.

Unfortunately, that would prove untrue, as supply-side economics was a sham. The very idea of "free markets" was never real; behind the scenes, the government was actively choosing winners and losers by allowing established institutions and individuals to further consolidate wealth and freeze out competitors. One of the most notorious cases was the rise of Walmart, a discount retail store that grew so powerful in this environment that it spread across the country and destroyed small-town America one small business at a time. The market Reagan created was cruel and unforgiving to all but a chosen few who could kill smaller competitors while wielding enormous political influence.

Though Reagan and his supporters spoke glowingly about reducing the size of government, under his administration it actually tripled in size. Federal debt skyrocketed. By 1982, even the most devoted Reaganites were disillusioned, including David Stockman, the director of the Office of Management and Budget, who had been a true believer before admitting "the Reagan Revolution was impossible—it was a metaphor with no anchor in political and economic reality."[42]

Deregulation and the privatization of government functions wreaked unbelievable damage. In the Defense Department there were multiple scandals from what was described as an "eight-year feeding frenzy" that resulted in what Senator David Pryor of Arkansas called "a shadow government, a government by contract."[43] Several members of Reagan's administration were implicated in corruption wherein Republican donors and insiders were given massive contracts to handle the government's business. Meanwhile, social programs that helped the poor and disadvantaged were decimated, leading to a rise in homelessness and crime.

The criminal and unethical behavior wasn't relegated only to government; the religious movement that had won Reagan his power coursed with corruption. The televangelists who had preached the value of wealth and capitalism were by the day succumbing to their own scandals. Jim Bakker, a disciple of Jerry Falwell's, had built an empire for himself and his ministry that included its own cable channel and theme park, but a scandal involving "diamonds, minks, Mercedes, sex, sin, and betrayal" brought him down, even as Reagan's administration was "less than eager" to investigate the crimes of one of Bakker's most conspicuous supporters.[44] Falwell worked to minimize the damage from scandals like this, placing blame on a supernatural enemy and urging believers not to "let Satan win the day."[45]

It seemed the devil's handiwork was everywhere. Cultural critics claimed popular music was filled with evil messages meant to brainwash the nation's youth. Tabloid journalists warned Americans that their neighborhoods and communities were swarming with devil worshippers and kidnappers waiting to snatch their children. News programs pushed tales of demonic activity and claimed the devil and an army of demons could take possession of viewers' bodies at any moment. With HIV/AIDS, assistance to sufferers of a massive public health crisis was denied as the disease was treated like a biblical plague on a nation of sinners.

Crime and poverty were made into evidence of this moral rot, sparing better-off Americans from having to consider the effects of gutting the social safety net. Efforts to combat crime placed the onus on the individual instead of on society, prosecuting drug addicts as criminals instead of addressing social conditions. Those being punished were predominantly the poor and African Americans, which, within this mindset and in keeping with the Lost Cause mythology, hinted at some sort of personal failing in these communities. William Bennett, an influential conservative who served as secretary of education for Reagan, laid blame on the people, citing "moral poverty."[46] The devil made a convenient scapegoat. Instead of facing the existential crisis of capitalism, the glorification of greed, and a history rife with abuses, missteps, and manipulation, conservatives could point to an external threat responsible for society's ills.

That message was especially potent considering the corruption of outwardly pious political and religious leaders. Even the believers could be corrupted, and all Americans needed for proof was to follow the news. In this way, Republicans were able to reframe the consequences of their policies, the widespread poverty and dysfunction they had created, and turn them into focuses of moral crusades they alone could lead.

Like John Hinckley Jr., America had come unmoored and grown lost in a fantasy world where actual problems had become so complicated and complex that simple solutions would replace them, even if those solutions were obviously fictional. It was a matter of faith, of unending belief in something despite overwhelming signs to the contrary. In the minds of its citizens, the United States of America had been established as the force for good in the world, an agent of a Christian God, and Americanism, a blending of American Myth and worship of capitalism, had manifested as a national religion with its own tenets and doctrine.

It didn't matter that the president of the United States was obviously disengaged from the rigors of the office, that the new economy created vast divides in wealth and class, that inaction in the AIDS crisis was a breathtaking cruelty, or that the war on drugs and the mass incarceration epidemic reflected a ghastly unfair and prejudiced society. Any development that contradicted America's infallibility or the virtuousness of unrestrained capitalism, that sought to interrupt this faith, would be summarily dismissed. Any critic would be labeled an apostate and agent of a lurking evil that sought to bring down the shining city on a hill.

★

Meanwhile, many of America's interventions and operations around the world were coming back to haunt it. Having been under the control of Shah Mohammad Reza Pahlavi since the United States–orchestrated coup in 1953, Iran revolted in 1979 and turned to

Muslim fundamentalist Ayatollah Ruhollah Khomeini to craft an Islamic state. Blowback in Iran would not prevent the United States from further interference, however, as the Reagan administration remained active in South America and the Middle East. It was so active that its policies often contradicted one another, with disastrous consequences.

In El Salvador, the United States trained and funded death squads they considered a "lesser evil" than leftist revolutionaries.[47] These death squads were taught by American personnel in American bases to fight a Vietnam-style counterinsurgent war, a strategy they pursued by roaming the countryside and killing entire villages indiscriminately. Similarly, as the Soviet Union toiled in an unwinnable war in Afghanistan, the United States provided aid and weapons to Islamic guerillas, planting the seeds of future terrorism against America.

In one of the most damning incidents of Reagan's presidency, the administration engaged in the Iran-Contra scandal, a mess that saw Israel facilitating the sale of American weapons to Iran to fund Nicaraguan Contras, counterrevolutionaries opposing the Sandinista government. Though Reagan called the Contras "the moral equivalent of our Founding Fathers," they were guilty of atrocities, including planned attacks on civilians, mass killings, torture, and rape.[48]

One of the more consequential foreign policy decisions undertaken by the Reagan administration was their cooperation with Iraqi dictator Saddam Hussein, a partnership that saw the rise of terrorism as a geopolitical tool, facilitated two wars, and destabilized the Middle East. It began in 1980 when Iraq invaded Iran and the United States chose to secretly side with Hussein, as he was seen as a strong candidate for the now-familiar role of American-aligned dictator.

To help Hussein and injure Iran, America provided intelligence, money, weapons, and even the chemicals he eventually used to gas Iranian targets. Despite publicly condemning Hussein's decision to pursue chemical warfare and leave entire towns asphyxiated and destroyed, calling it "horrible, outrageous, disgusting," the Reagan administration was fully aware of the plan.[49] Five years earlier—and almost exactly twenty years before the start of the second Iraq War, which used those exact weapons as reasoning for intervention—a CIA report stated "Iraq ha[d] begun using nerve agents" they deemed effective and capable of turning the tide of the war.[50]

Not long after the invasion, a thirteen-year-old Iranian boy named Mohammad Hossein Fahmideh wrapped himself in explosives and detonated under an approaching Iraqi tank, killing himself but halting an attack. Ayatollah Khomeini blessed Fahmideh as a heroic martyr and instituted a religious decree that anyone committing suicide as an act of war would follow Fahmideh in martyrdom. This opened the door for waves of Iranians to commit suicide to help in the war's prosecution, but the idea spread through the Muslim world as a means to attack an overwhelming enemy. The United States felt the first sting of this new weapon in 1983, when a pair of truck bombs destroyed barracks in Beirut, Lebanon, killing 241 American soldiers.

Faced with an unexpected attack that could not be traced back specifically to any country or state, America eventually left Beirut. When Iraq invaded its neighbor Kuwait seven years later, it presented an opportunity to respond against a traditional foe in the form of a rogue state. The lead-up to this invasion was more complicated, however, as Hussein had just received millions of dollars' worth of technology and weapons from the United States as he built up his invasion forces. The two nations maintained intelligence sharing after the Iran–Iraq War and communicated consistently by back channels, Hussein continually reassuring President Bush that his aggressive speeches and actions were merely posturing to contain Islamic forces within the region. A contingent of American leaders even visited Hussein and flattered him, leaving the dictator with the impression the United States would not interfere should he invade Kuwait.

On the US side, Hussein's actions presented both a problem and an opportunity. The occupation of Kuwait meant that Iraq controlled a large percentage of the world's oil supply, and with Saudi Arabia nearby, further adventuring would mean a dominant monopoly. Reacting with force would signal to Muslims that the United States could marshal a coalition of Western powers to quell potential uprisings, and in the process, a victory might go so far as to erase the lingering stench of defeat in Vietnam.

A propaganda campaign was launched to sell Hussein as a Hitlerian dictator who might attempt to conquer the world. To this end, George H. W. Bush, now president, began equating the Kuwaiti situation with America's past crusades, saying it had the greatest "moral importance" since "World War II."[51] He accused Hussein, a leader he had supported financially and politically for years, of "brutality" worse than any "Adolf Hitler ever participated in."[52] To put a human face on the tragedy and complete the transformation of Hussein from trusted US ally to demagogue, the public relations firm Hill & Knowlton worked with a Kuwaiti lobby. Together they orchestrated a tearful and harrowing performance by a Kuwaiti girl named Nayirah who lied in testimony before lawmakers, saying that Iraqi soldiers had slaughtered her people and massacred babies. Nayirah was later revealed to be the daughter of Kuwait's ambassador to the United States, her appearance arranged by Congressman Tom Lantos, who enjoyed significant financial support from the Kuwaiti lobby.

When the United States declared war in January of 1991 it was with the backing of thirty-four other countries, including the Soviet Union. Bush heralded the operation as a "new partnership of nations" that constituted "a new world order" where "the nations of the world . . . can prosper and live in harmony."[53] By defeating Hussein and liberating Kuwait, Bush meant to finally sedate the Middle East while resurrecting Franklin D. Roosevelt's long-dead policemen strategy for maintaining world order and peace.

Learning from their mistakes in Vietnam, the United States military limited the press's ability to cover the war and provide unflattering stories, instead following the Reagan model of supplying ready-made and favorable materials. The American press obliged, regurgitating military propaganda and providing breathless coverage that lionized the military and presented the United States as an unquestionably heroic force. There was no history or context to be found. Past partnerships between Saddam Hussein and Reagan and Bush were obscured. It was not mentioned that a large share of Iraqi weapons and vehicles had been manufactured in part by American companies like General Electric, Lockheed Martin, or any number of military contractors. Reports of Scud missile attacks neglected to mention that those weapons had been bought with American tax dollars. For viewers watching at home, the Persian Gulf War, despite its massive civilian casualties in Iraq, the destruction of necessary infrastructure, the unspeakable environmental damage, and its questionable origins, was presented as an overwhelming success and packaged like a blockbuster movie.

The war was a ratings bonanza, especially for the original cable news network, CNN, as it featured twenty-four-hour content. Americans were transfixed by the coverage, the product likened by critic Mark Harris to "a miniseries and the Olympics," the presentation "complete with play-by-play, instant analysis, background features, martial theme music, computer animation, elaborate maps, and retired generals as expert commentators."[54]

What had started with Ronald Reagan had now come full circle. The day-to-day actions of the United States of America had been packaged and sold back to the American public as a television show with a cast of good guys and bad. Past foreign policy mistakes and the sacrificing of ideals were laundered and scrubbed clean of the stain of hypocrisy and effectively commoditized. With world events playing out on their television screens, all of it appearing to be divorced from them, Americans began to feel as if their government and the course of human events were a spectacle to be watched, an entertainment beyond their control.

★

A cornerstone of George H. W. Bush's envisioned new world order was renewed cooperation between the United States and Russia, a partnership crafted during World War II and subsequently lost to the terror of the Cold War. With the Persian Gulf War, that alliance seemed on the verge of resurrection. With the reinvigorated arms race, Ronald Reagan had challenged America's enemy to a new contest of economic chicken, and Russia had blinked first. There was no means by which the "Evil Empire" could match the reckless spending of Reagan, and the economic engine of communism had long since sputtered. After nearly a decade of cataclysmic war in Afghanistan, Russia shrunk back from the world stage and stopped interfering in geopolitical affairs. The Berlin Wall fell in 1989 and the United States was left virtually unchallenged in its hegemony.

The eventual fall of the Soviet Union was sealed in 1985 when moderate Mikhail Gorbachev took the reins of power. Gorbachev rejected the cult of personality that had sustained Soviet politics for decades and was averse to the totalitarian tactics of his predecessors; members of his own family had been oppressed and tortured in political prisons. He openly criticized past leaders like Joseph Stalin, saying they were "guilty of enormous and unforgivable" crimes, and promised a new era of reforms in government and transparency.[55]

These reforms upended the Soviet Union. As the ruling elite had exerted maximum control on all facets of society, including journalism and popular culture, they had effectively manufactured through propaganda an artificial reality in which Russian citizens participated in relative conformity, a dream state where citizens could see all around them that society was in decline while their leaders constantly lied to them. Over time this duplicity created a surreal existence where objective reality had ceased to exist and was replaced, instead, with a chronic, throbbing numbness. "Facts" and "history" changed so often it was impossible to keep track.

As Gorbachev allowed scrutiny and dissent, citizens of the Soviet Union woke from their dream. Their news suddenly swelled with reports of the corruption they had always known was there but had never been allowed to discuss. Their movies and television shows changed and began depicting cultural decline, including personal isolation, widespread violence and substance abuse, and the erosion of communism as an ideology with the ability to unite, inspire, and maintain political order. The cultural hegemony that had held the country together for decades was beginning to unravel.

In truth, the communist dream of Karl Marx and Vladimir Lenin had been, much like America's revolution, corrupted from the start, used by a ruling elite to maintain inequality while controlling a population, a twisted perversion of its outwardly espoused ideals. It had been a deeply hierarchical system that had only lasted as long as it had because of cultural manipulation and the threat of totalitarian punishment. Communism had ceased to work because its ruling class had captured its revolutionary spirit and limited it for maximum control.

As the Soviet Union fell apart, the nation's elites tried to salvage the authoritarian state. A group of conservative hard-liners formed a military coup in August of 1991 and detained Mikhail Gorbachev in his Crimean vacation home, releasing on television a statement blaming Gorbachev's health for his abdication. Such moves were commonplace in the USSR, and in the past the cabal might have been successful, but this time the people refused to go along. Led by anti-Soviet president Boris Yeltsin, the public took to the streets, resisting the propaganda, and the coup failed. Gorbachev returned, if only to shepherd the end of empire.

On Christmas Day 1991, Gorbachev tendered his resignation and the Soviet Union came to an inglorious end. In his final statement, Gorbachev admitted, "I am leaving my post worried. But also I hope, with faith in you, in your wisdom and spiritual strength. We are the legatees of a great civilization, and it now depends on each and every one for it to be reborn to the new contemporary and worthy life."[56]

For seven decades the Soviet Union had existed as a superpower and the counterbalance to American dominance, a force of might through collectivization, and now it died, in a writer's words, "stripped of ideology, dismembered, bankrupt and hungry."[57] It had pushed the world to the brink of nuclear destruction and forced a polarized environment in which smaller nations had been held hostage by the threat of global genocide. Now, as the new millennium loomed, it passed quietly in the cold, dark night.

Covering its demise was Ted Koppel of ABC News, reporting live from Saint Basil's Cathedral. Koppel's show *Nightline* broadcast the final lowering of the hammer and sickle at the Kremlin while playing the strains of the "State Anthem." Interviews with Russian citizens were marked with a strange anger toward Mikhail Gorbachev. They were grateful for the prospect of freedom but resented his programs that had thrust them into the light. Many already seemed nostalgic for the safety of oppression.

President George H. W. Bush addressed the nation that evening, congratulating and thanking Gorbachev for his work while casting a long glance at the future and his vision of a new world order. "We stand tonight before a new world of hope and possibilities and hope for our children," he said, "a world we could not have contemplated a few years ago."[58]

When *Nightline* took its first break at 11:53 P.M., a commercial for the show's sponsor General Electric depicted scenes from Japan meant to evoke a culture mirroring the United States, including shots of a thriving metropolis, digital stock market boards, a fashion show on a giant video screen, a baseball game that resembled the national pastime. Eventually Japanese executives and American representatives met and bowed to one another. The accompanying song was in Japanese, with subtitles reading: "We make you pretty / We make you smile / GE / We bring good things to life."[59] A voice-over then detailed a massive international project meant to weave the world closer together: "When Tokyo Electric Power gave GE our largest export order ever, it gave Tokyo the largest, most efficient power plant of its kind in the world, which means more jobs for our people back home, and a better future for the people of Japan."

In Nashville, Tennessee, on affiliate WKRN, the slick commercial depicting a new, glitzy, interconnected world lit by the efforts and power of international corporations was followed by a series of drab and lifeless community messages. There were calls for donations of clothes and essentials, contributions to help those in dire need, and, above all, a call for volunteers to help in community centers, volunteers to help the elderly and the impoverished, volunteers to work without pay to assist suffering Americans, volunteers to keep the lights on.

CHAPTER 9

∗   ∗   ∗

The Age of Irrational Exuberance

When Democratic operative Al From paid Bill Clinton a fateful visit on April 6, 1989, Clinton was the forty-two-year-old, popular governor of Arkansas. Handsome and charismatic, not to mention a native Southerner, Clinton was already regarded as a rising star and a possible presidential contender. He had weighed a run the previous year but ultimately lent his endorsement to Massachusetts governor Michael Dukakis, who only managed to carry ten states and the District of Columbia in a landslide loss to then–vice president George H. W. Bush. That blowout worsened suspicions within the party that the electoral map had turned away from Democrats and might remain solidly in Republican favor for the foreseeable future.

Ronald Reagan had successfully cast the Democrats as unpatriotic scolds in the thrall of big labor and a coalition of minority populations, effectively portraying them as opponents of economic expansion. Reagan's campaign had so succeeded in positioning him as the embodiment of mythical America, and the nation had so embraced the earthly delights of hypercapitalism, that it seemed as if the Democratic Party might well be on its way to extinction.

Determined to avoid obsolescence, From pressed Governor Clinton to accept the chairmanship of his upstart group, the Democratic Leadership Council (DLC). "I've got a deal for you," he said, quickly getting to his point. "If you agree to become chairman of the DLC, we'll pay for your travel around the country, we'll work together on an agenda, and I think you'll be president one day and we'll both be important."[1]

From's plan to revitalize the Democratic Party had been unspooling since the electoral disaster five years earlier. Following Reagan's dominant victory over Mondale, From circulated a memo among his party brethren announcing the formation of the DLC that would, in From's words, "assume the role and the authority of the policy making, governing body of the party," mirroring how Republicans had ceded control to the Heritage Foundation and other think tanks.[2] It was a rebranding push for Democrats to abandon their identities as liberals and move right on the political spectrum, a concession that Republicans had won the messaging battle and creating what liberal historian Arthur Schlesinger Jr. termed "Reaganism with a human face."[3]

The DLC's message was that traditional liberal strategies had not only failed but would continue to fail in perpetuity: in its words, "a coalition of liberals and minorities is not the way to win national elections."[4] To regain power, From and the DLC targeted "men, whites, independents, and young voters" and planned to "attract moderates and conservatives." To do this, they would need to accept Reagan's trickle-down economics, a form of capitalism that favored the wealthy and corporations, while demonstrating to voters they were no longer the party of social justice and could be as tough on national security and crime as the Republicans. It was a refashioning of history that accepted the Republican revision that the playing field had been effectively leveled in the 1960s and '70s and that reform movements, including racial, sexual, and class struggles, would now take a backseat to supposed unity and economic competition.

This proposed shift was met with sharp criticism within the party by members who had worked to build viable coalitions among underrepresented populations in the face of continued discrimination. Chief among them was Jesse Jackson, who had organized alongside Martin Luther King Jr. before carrying the struggle of the civil rights movement into the new era. Jackson considered the DLC's plan a tragic betrayal of minorities who had constituted the Democratic base following Lyndon Johnson's Civil Rights Act and had been actively left out of Reagan's economic model and victim to his "color-blind" policies. "If we are all things to all people," Jackson warned in a rebuke of the DLC, "we become rather ill-defined, indecisive—kind of like warm spit."[5]

Though Jackson's own candidacy for the presidency proved a viable campaign could still be crafted from a coalition of minority voters, the DLC saw his brand of progressive politics as a road to electoral irrelevance. As writer Joan Didion observed, Democrats viewed Jackson as "a bomb that had to be defused," and his supporters, still voting their consciences and believing in the transformative power of politics, were regarded as "self-indulgent" and "immature."[6]

From believed this focus on minority coalition building had positioned Democrats as the "no-growth party," as they had become "so obsessed with how we carved up the pie . . . it stopped growing."[7] To assuage worries that Democrats would continue representing their diverse base of voters, including organized labor and vulnerable populations, From assured his desired base of white and independent voters, "Labor's views are important, but we're not going to labor and adopt their ideas, and go to gay, lesbian, black, Hispanic, Jewish caucuses."

Centrist Democrats were quick to sign on, but for From to assume control of the party he needed to convince others of the necessity of rebranding. To do this he relied on what he called "reality therapy," a type of psychotherapy founded by Dr. William Glasser in the 1960s that proposed mental illness was largely predicated on an individual's denial of accepted reality. This illness, Glasser asserted, was curable by a systematic dismantling of the sufferer's worldview and therapy would be "successful when they [were] able to give up denying the world and recognize that reality not only exists, but that they must fulfill their needs within its framework."[8]

The DLC overwhelmed Democrats with an abundance of polling data and focus group testing meant to convince liberals the world had changed around them. In doing so, a distorted picture emerged in which Reagan and Republicans had so defined the political debate that actual change would never be possible again. It didn't matter that the polls only tested researched rhetoric and empty phrases directed at centrists or that studies at the time unnecessarily represented white voters over minorities. This dose of reality therapy won the DLC and From the control they so desperately sought.

While liberals' desires to promote social justice, equality, and fairness within society were noble, the DLC told them these goals simply weren't compatible with the new reality. Reagan and the Republican Party, they argued, had so radically changed the conversation in America that any hint of liberal discussion would be seen as un-American and lead to more and more lopsided elections. Democrats insisting on that course, despite data that showed predictable outcomes, were essentially engaging in psychotic behavior.

To ever win the presidency again, From pressed on them, Democrats needed a drastic reinvention and to give themselves over to Reagan's mythology and economic model.

Clinton was the ideal New Democrat. In the failed counterculture revolution of the 1960s and '70s, Clinton had been an active participant, but never so much as to totally eschew the machinery of power. In 1972, he had worked for Democratic presidential candidate George McGovern, an unabashed liberal who sought to radically alter society and who lost overwhelmingly to Richard Nixon after a disastrous campaign. The defeat injured Clinton, leaving him with a sense that for Democrats to have any future success, they would need to modulate their approach by letting go of liberal policies and adopting the pragmatism and cynicism of Nixon and the Republicans.

Philosophically, Clinton was flexible. Conservative pollster Dick Morris, a Clinton confidant who secretly advised the president, to the chagrin of his administration, defined Clinton's decision making as reflecting the ideas of Georg Wilhelm Friedrich Hegel, a philosopher Clinton studied in his collegiate days. Like Hegel, Clinton would examine two extreme, opposing opinions and then combine them, synthesizing them into a new centrist idea that might appeal to both sides of the political spectrum. "In understanding the core Clinton," Morris remarked, "you can't look for ideology. You have to look for achievements."[9]

With the DLC, Clinton and From oversaw the construction of an operation to rival the Republican apparatus. They produced policy finely tuned and tested by polls to appeal to voters and built a list of corporate donors to fund and shape messaging. The party that had once prided itself on challenging the economic order and opposing big business was now in league with AT&T, Chevron, DuPont, Coca-Cola, IBM, and a number of other prominent corporations.

From made good on his promise to Clinton and established him as a contender for the presidency. In 1992, Clinton announced his candidacy and presented himself as a working-class hero who had lifted himself from poverty by his bootstraps, proving that the market worked and created opportunities for transcendence. Abandoning traditional Democratic messages of equality, he campaigned against President George H. W. Bush from the right, accusing Bush of stepping in the way of economic progress, in hopes that Democrats might wrest away the legacy of Ronald Reagan. "The change we must make," Clinton said, "isn't liberal or conservative. It's both, and it's different . . . People out here don't care about the idle rhetoric of 'left' and 'right' and 'liberal' and 'conservative.'"[10]

Clinton's speech intentionally echoed Reagan, drafting for Democrats a new reliance on religion, traditional values, and personal responsibility. "We need a new covenant to rebuild America," he said. "It's just common sense. Government's responsibility is to create more opportunity. The people's responsibility is to make the most of it." New Democrats, under Clinton, followed Republicans in limiting government, slashing social programs, and championing free-market solutions to expand the ranks of the wealthy instead of attempting to change the established economy.[11]

"Join with us," Clinton invited Americans. "I ask for your prayers, your help, your hands, and your hearts. Together we can make America great again and build a community of hope that will inspire the world."[12]

★

Despite a litany of scandals, Bill Clinton won the presidency in 1992, becoming the first Democratic executive in the White House in over a decade. He had promised a new kind of politics that moved beyond liberalism and conservatism, a third way that combined elements of free-market thinking with moderate social reform. In the months leading up to his term, he found this new philosophy came with an awful price.

Like his world-changing meeting with Al From three years before, a newly elected Clinton welcomed Alan Greenspan, the chair of the Federal Reserve, to Little Rock, Arkansas, and entertained yet another seductive proposal. An avid disciple of Ayn Rand, Greenspan believed the government had no right to interfere in the pursuits of heroic industrialists and that its only responsibility was a dutiful stewarding, a role Greenspan hoped to impress upon Clinton. Greenspan entered the meeting unsure as to what to expect. His experience with politicians had left him unimpressed, but in Clinton he found a willing conversation partner, an intelligent, hands-on president-elect unencumbered by burdensome ideology, calling him "an intellectual pragmatist."[13]

Though the Federal Reserve and the White House were to remain independent of each other, Greenspan instructed Clinton on how he might enjoy a healthy economy and, by extension, a successful presidency. Greenspan explained that his influence as chair "reached far beyond economics and had a psychological and a political dimension," essentially informing Clinton that, depending on his actions, Greenspan could either gift him success or destroy his presidency before it ever began.[14]

Economics, Greenspan explained, was a game of perception. His ability to raise or lower interest rates, and the market's tendency to fluctuate, were essentially maneuvers to deliver feedback to politicians. If legislation were presented that was deemed unhelpful to the wealthy, then the economy would suffer from poor confidence and decreased spending. That pressure then harmed the politicians responsible and held government hostage until there was a changing of course.

Greenspan informed Clinton that should he pursue social programs that might help the American people at the expense of the wealthy, he would watch the economy suffer and endure political fallout. But if Clinton chose instead to reduce the federal deficit and signal that his administration would be friendly to free markets, then Greenspan would lend his support and unleash the economy.

Clinton left the meeting believing he and Greenspan had come to an understanding, telling his vice president–elect Al Gore, "We can do business."[15] Greenspan left Little Rock confident that "a consensus was emerging" in which Democrats and Republicans might bridge their political divide and establish an accord in the economic realm.

In carrying out his end of the bargain, Clinton soon learned just how restrictive that new consensus could be. During a meeting with policy advisors who delivered the bad news that Clinton's new presidency would have to forgo most of its programs to deliver Greenspan his targeted reduction, Clinton raged, "You mean to tell me that . . . my reelection hinges on the Federal Reserve and a bunch of fucking bond traders?"[16]

That hard lesson set a new tone. The trade-off for electoral success was that the Democrats essentially ceded all control over politics to the market and its beneficiaries. Further efforts to improve society and the lives of the people would now be the responsibility of corporations and modern robber barons to handle as they saw fit, a callback to the workings of the Gilded Age and the maturation of the neoliberal mindset that Reagan had unleashed in his remaking of the economy.

Under these restrictions, Clinton approached his work much as Reagan and his Republicans had. Programs were cut, budgets leveled. In the words of Clinton's chairman of the Council of Economic Advisers Joseph Stiglitz, Clinton and his administration "succumbed to the deregulation mantra" of the Reagan era and furthered the loosening of oversight.[17] Greenspan signaled his approval and the economy went wild as investors breathed a sigh of relief. They had worried the election of a Democrat might slow their orgy of profit, but Clinton had come through on his assurances that he was a new kind of Democrat who would maintain the Noble Lie of American exceptionalism and serve as a steward for economic growth.

Almost exactly a year after his meeting with Greenspan, Clinton signed the North American Free Trade Agreement into law. NAFTA had its origins in Reagan's speech announcing his candidacy in 1979, where he declared that "the nations of North America are ready, within the context of an unswerving commitment to freedom, to see new forms of accommodation," and that partnership should allow "the people's commerce [to] flow more freely across their present borders."[18] That idea germinated within the Republican Party until

George H. W. Bush negotiated with Mexico and Canada from 1990 to late 1992. When Clinton took office he was handed the task of spearheading the drive to ratify NAFTA, a fight bolstered primarily by Republicans but helped by significant Democratic support.

Clinton spoke before signing the treaty into law and announced NAFTA as the beginning of a larger "global economic expansion" that would produce a new "economic order."[19] He heralded that new order as the dominion of the United States, replacing the struggle of the Cold War and mutually assured destruction with "the exuberant uncertainty of international economic competition."

NAFTA was indeed part of an effort toward globalization, a spreading of American economic ideals and culture that interlocked nations in a mode reminiscent of what Roosevelt, Churchill, and Stalin had proposed during World War II. Political means like the United Nations had failed and turned toothless, and taking their place was what neoliberals and conservatives alike believed was a more stable and permanent force: capitalism.

As the victors of the Cold War, Americans were able to determine for the world the tone and tenor of the new system. They guided the world into a persistent present as history paused, allowing them to micromanage events around the globe without having to fire a shot or deploy the military. The pressure of market forces was more than enough. And, in a nod to Thomas Jefferson's efforts to offload the scourge of industry in the nineteenth century, free trade meant companies could move their production to other countries, freeing Americans, in the neoliberal fantasy, to escape the toil of the factory and ascend into the middle class.

At best, it was a pipe dream, but even if it had worked as hoped, globalism only functioned if there was an inherent hierarchy that benefited world powers at the expense of other nations. Just as it had been following the world wars, the major powers took advantage of smaller, poorer countries, casting them in a system meant to exploit their natural resources while using their populations for the type of labor they saw as beneath their own people.

Globalism meant corporations could skirt US regulations, including the minimum wage, environmental protection laws, and codes and standards, and then ship their products back to America without penalty. The economic and human cost would be cast off on developing countries, where people were underpaid—or even not paid at all—for backbreaking, dangerous labor.

This global system surrendered to corporations and assisted in their hyper state of growth. They grew to become nationless states unto themselves, straddling continents as they shifted assets and jobs between banks and other countries to avoid paying American taxes. The results were disastrous. Education suffered. Infrastructure suffered. Health care suffered. The government became a subsidizer, gifting corporations tax breaks for even gesturing toward staying in America. Corporations took full advantage, paying their employees less and relying on the government to put their underpaid workers on welfare and assistance programs, and to cover their medical expenses as health insurance was either withheld or intentionally unreliable.

The nightmare of neoliberal globalism wasn't that the world was connected or interdependent, but that its structure was created by those already in power to best accelerate its own wealth and dominance, an echo of America's founding. It limited competition by allowing the traditional giants to either crush emerging challengers or swallow them up before they might mature. In many cases, it permanently ended any opportunity for organized labor to gain a foothold, as even the rumor of a union could lead to a business shutting its doors and fleeing the country for the safety of a sweatshop.

In the United States, the Randian utopia Greenspan and his fellow financiers had dreamed of came into being. Capitalism had been lifted to the status of a world religion and had all but overtaken politics. For a law to pass it needed to be approved and vetted by powerful, wealthy lobbyists in Washington. The two parties were locked in perpetual stalemate on many social issues but agreed in economic principle. The politicians themselves, because of the rising cost of campaigns, tended to be wealthy, a modern version of the aristocracy in government the Founders intended, and dedicated to furthering the interests of the market over the people.

★

For the Republican Party, it could have been a bittersweet moment. Though a Democrat had won the presidency, the GOP had succeeded in pushing their opponents so far right that the mainstream political spectrum was now decidedly conservative. Clinton and his fellow Democrats supported free markets and remade themselves as anti-welfare, tough-on-crime politicians, resulting in sweeping defunding of the social safety net and a harsh wave of new crime laws that disproportionately affected the African-American community.

If the stated principles of the GOP were its true core, then the Clinton presidency should have been a period of bipartisanship and cooperation, but neoliberalism presented a new electoral challenge. Conservative analysts worried that if Clinton was able to continue piling on victories by synthesizing the personality of the left with the perceived toughness of the right, then the new Democratic Party might be unstoppable.

This realization crystalized as Clinton waded into health care reform in 1993. Hillary Rodham Clinton, the First Lady and a longtime equal collaborator with the president, helmed the fight for modest reform and in the opening months was quite successful, her bouts of testimony in front of congressional committees notable for their "absence of serious criticism from Republicans."[20]

After that relatively smooth introduction, hard-liners within the GOP began to rankle as a symbolic victory was within reach. Republican strategists were certain that if health care reform were to pass, the Democrats would notch a major victory and gain a foothold that might last for decades. In other words, a win for the American people would be a loss for the GOP's bid for power—and its control over the American narrative.

The call to destroy health care reform began with William Kristol, the founder of *The Weekly Standard* and chairman of the Project for the Republican Future, a strategy body dedicated solely to the electoral success of the GOP at any cost. In a notorious memo penned in December 1993, Kristol acknowledged that the health care system in America was deeply flawed but advised that any attempt to improve it while Clinton was president would gift Democrats a tremendous victory. Health care reform, he wrote, was a "serious threat to the Republican Party" and therefore Republicans must "adopt an aggressive and uncompromising counter strategy designed to delegitimize the proposal and defeat its partisan purposes."[21]

For Kristol and like-minded Republicans, the game of politics was too important to compromise. If helping the people meant losing an advantage, then the people were on their own. Kristol proposed a reconfiguring of reality: Though Republicans knew there were calamitous problems within the health care system, they could simply deny that fact and create, within their political base, an alternate reality wherein American health care was fine.

The vast array of Republican think tanks and strategy houses distributed market-tested facts and figures, rhetoric to undermine the president's messaging, and an organized communication strategy that kept all Republican lawmakers operating from the same script. All public appearances and speeches were now dotted with the same language and the same assertion Senator Bob Dole made in the Republican response to Clinton's 1994 State of the Union address: There simply was no health care crisis.[22]

But to fully create this alternate reality for their voters, Republicans had to supply another explanation for Clinton's health care push. If there was no crisis, then why the reform? Republicans simply

denied the centrist reconfiguring of the Democratic Party and reignited old fears of socialism and liberal overreach. Suddenly, center-
right became dangerously far left, the Democrats now filling the
oppositional vacuum left in the wake of the collapse of the Soviet
Union and representing a threat against America. With that recon-
figuration, the political spectrum of America twisted beyond com-
prehension.

The grand conductor of this twisting was Congressman Newt
Gingrich, a megalomaniacal figure who saw himself as a man for the
ages, the kind of hero lionized in Ayn Rand's novels. Once he told a
reporter, "People like me are what stand between us and Auschwitz,"
a statement that perfectly encapsulates the earnestness of his own
grandiosity.[23] Gingrich was a new breed of politician, both pragmatic
and an idealist. He believed wholeheartedly that "the Left in America
is to blame for most of the current major diseases which have struck
this society," but also understood the game politics had become.[24] As
early as 1978, Gingrich was telling Republicans they needed to throw
away concepts of respect and forbearance as they were fighting "a
war for power."[25]

Gingrich understood better than anyone else at the time the
nature and place of media in shaping political reality and deciding
the outcome of that war: "The No. 1 fact about the news media is they
love fights. When you give them confrontations, you get attention."[26]
In the past, Congress and the minority party had mostly operated
quietly, preferring to challenge the president through lawmaking and
procedures, but Gingrich knew he could seize the moment and position himself as a foil to Clinton by continually giving the media conflicts to cover.

Under Gingrich, politics became a round-the-clock television
show. There had been moments in the past, particularly in crises
and scandals, where showdowns between the parties captivated the
people, but now every single day was a news cycle to be won or lost
by the parties. Clinton continued to push bipartisan, conservative

ideas while Gingrich excoriated him and accused him of liberal take-overs and power grabs. In the lead-up to the 1994 midterms, Gingrich traveled the country and made every district race about Clinton, a major departure from how past campaigns had functioned. He brought congressional Republican candidates under one umbrella, focusing them on researched proposals and tuning them to strategized rhetoric that demonized their opponents and Clinton. It was a restructuring reminiscent of top-down economics. No longer would the party be defined by a collection of principles held by its members, but its members would be defined by the party's principles as determined by strategy.

In the past the Heritage Foundation had scripted Republican administrations, but now they provided for the national party an identity with the "Contract with America," a promise to the voters to "restore the bonds of trust between the people and their elected representatives" and end Congress's "cycle of scandal and disgrace."[27] It was a piece of think-tank strategy with no relationship to reality, the purpose having nothing to do with governing and instead determined to, as the Heritage Foundation admitted, "draw the attention" of voters and "delineate to the general public . . . contrasting philosophies of government."[28] It was a rebranding of the political debate.

"If the American people accept this contract," Gingrich declared, hyping the product to obscene levels, "we will have begun the journey to renew American civilization."[29] Gingrich sold the campaign prop as the first step toward realizing Jefferson's assertion of inalienable rights, a bridge toward the pursuit of happiness and liberty and achieving the American dream. But that wasn't all. Again, positioning himself as savior, Gingrich couldn't help but proclaim the revolution he was leading would "help every human across the planet seek freedom, prosperity, safety and the rule of law. That is what is at stake."

Gingrich might not have pulled it off without conservative radio talk show host Rush Limbaugh. A provocateur who regularly called feminists "feminazis" and gleefully made racist comments, featured comedic updates about the AIDS epidemic, and often dropped pro-choice callers by playing an abrasive sound effect meant to mirror the sound of painful abortion, Limbaugh was the tasteless hit man of the Gingrich revolution. He was loud and intentionally contro-versial, abusive and beholden to no constituency. And, as the Reagan administration had repealed the Fairness Doctrine, the regulation that guaranteed countervailing opinions would be heard on the air-waves, Limbaugh could attack Democrats and liberals without so much as a counterargument. The more partisan and unreasonable his behavior, the more his audience swelled.

Limbaugh and Gingrich made a formidable one-two punch. Gin-grich spun a reality beneficial for Republicans but divorced from any-thing approaching shared reality, and Limbaugh continually reinforced those ideas in his broadcasts. His stories incensed his listeners, who then forced their Republican representatives to move farther right. When Gingrich experienced problems with party members, Lim-baugh was only a phone call away and more than willing to shine a white-hot spotlight of anger at a moment's notice.

Limbaugh called the '94 midterms "Operation Restore Democracy" and referred to Clinton's presidency as "the hostage crisis."[30] A contest between a centrist president and a right-wing party, both of which agreed on nearly everything save for a handful of social wedge issues, had become a battle to save the very soul of the country. Gingrich and Limbaugh prevailed as the push to nationalize congressional elections gave turnout a modest spike and Republicans took control of Congress. At Gingrich's victory party the night of the election, as controversial Atlanta radio host Sean Hannity played emcee, supporters in the crowd waved signs reading, "Rush Limbaugh for President."[31]

Later, in an orientation event for incoming Republican represen-tatives organized by the Heritage Foundation, Limbaugh was invited to speak and was gifted a pin that read, "Majority Maker." He riled the Republicans up as if they were at a pep rally, asking them in their coming electoral slaughters to "leave some liberals alive" so in the future they could "show [their] children what they were."[32]

★

The war Republicans waged against Bill Clinton was the most visible, but far from the only, war being waged. Beyond the halls of Washington a showdown between the people and the government was brewing that would leave hundreds dead and the nation fractured.

This war took place in an alternate reality rooted in Christian apocalypticism, the moral panics of the 1980s; with the dispatch of the Soviet Union, a new devil had emerged. Now the threat was internal and omnipresent. The name was taken from George H. W. Bush's proposed new world order and was alleged, by members of white identity Christianity, to be a world system of manipulation hiding the machinations of Satan himself.

The New World Order sprouted from a conspiracy theory equal parts white supremacy, Christian occultism, and paranoia originating in fear of emerging global economics. There were echoes of the Elders of Zion, the predictions of Hal Lindsey, the worldview of Ronald Reagan, elements of popular culture, and a continued fetishization of militarism and American exceptionalism. In short, it was an alternate reality that white identity Christians and opponents of globalization could inhabit and in which they could serve as heroes in the vein of the revolutionary Founding Fathers.

One of the believers of this fantasy was Randy Weaver, an army veteran and white supremacist who moved his family to Ruby Ridge, Idaho, in the 1980s to wait out the apocalypse as envisioned by his wife. As the family's religious leader, Vicki Weaver had cobbled together her own prophecies by cribbing from Hal Lindsey's *The Late, Great Planet Earth* and the Book of Revelation. The retreat to the wilderness had been predicated by Vicki's "dreams of great violence and a cabin on a mountaintop," an apocalyptic showdown she believed the family would have with an oppressive United States government in league with an international cabal of evil forces.[33]

In August of 1992, the US government attempted to arrest Randy Weaver on gun charges and initiated an eleven-day siege that would see federal agents kill Vicki Weaver; the Weavers' son, Samuel; and the family dog. It was a terrible operation with terrible results that demonstrated a lack of ability by the federal government to deal with citizens determined to draw them into militaristic showdowns.

A few months later, the government was drawn into yet another incident in Waco, Texas, where the Branch Davidian sect resisted a raid on their compound and killed agents of the Bureau of Alcohol, Tobacco, and Firearms. The leader of the Branch Davidians was a man named Vernon Howell who had come to call himself David Koresh. He believed he was the reincarnation of Jesus Christ and was destined to engage in "an apocalyptic firefight with law-enforcement officials that could be a precursor to the end of the world."[34] Frustrated by a fifty-one-day siege, the FBI escalated the situation on April 19, 1993, sending tanks equipped with tear gas that led to a fire that killed seventy-six.

The tragedies of Ruby Ridge and Waco represented a moment of crisis in the American experiment. What had been founded on individual liberty and the right of revolution had evolved into a tenuous state of authority where the government could not abide even a momentary challenge by its people, lest a revolution take hold. In both cases, the US government was guilty of incompetence, poor planning, and a reliance on aggression as a means to mask ineptitude. In Idaho and Texas, people lost in their own realities and fighting their own wars against the United States had drawn the government into their dark, violent fantasies.

Many saw ineptness while others had their paranoia confirmed. Around the country those distrustful of the government, most of them white Americans embroiled in white identity Christianity, formed militias and separatist organizations dedicated to bringing the government and the imagined organizers of the New World Order to its knees. Extremist leaders and white supremacists used the controversies to recruit and build terrorist-style cells around the country that would amass weapons and train for the coming war.

These cells were connected by a system of communication and organization that was only possible near the end of the twentieth century. They traded VHS tapes with lectures and lessons by white supremacists that portrayed the New World Order as pervasive and engaged in a racial war against white men. Radio shows and publishers peddling conspiracy theories thrived. Many members were recruited at gun shows that suddenly sprouted up around the country in alarming numbers, most located in areas devastated by loss of industry and forgotten by globalism. At these shows customers found vast armories of weapons alongside piles of propaganda, including pamphlets, magazines, literature, tapes, cassettes, advertisements for separatist groups, and instructions for wiring bombs and other weapons of mass destruction.

It came to be called the Patriot Movement, and it grew as fear of the government spread. Members were indoctrinated to believe they were Christian warriors staring down the apocalyptic march of fascism, their lives always one day away from having to wage an insurgent war against the United States government and the forces of the United Nations, their wives and children endangered like Weaver's and Koresh's families.

"This is a revolution," explained Bob Miles, a white supremacist militia leader in Michigan and a key architect in the movement's creation. "Like Johnny Appleseed, we've sowed the seeds. I told the FBI . . . It's too late, we've done the work, and you can't reverse it. And out there those seeds we know will grow into apple trees and bear fruit."[35]

With this movement, the National Rifle Association and the Republican Party saw an opportunity. NRA officials like Neal Knox stoked fears of the New World Order, asking if the chaos of the recent past, including the assassinations of the 1960s, was the creation of global forces "for the purposes of disarming the people of the free world."[36] NRA head Wayne LaPierre took full advantage, comparing Clinton's government to Stalinist Russia and likening federal officers to "Nazi storm troopers."[37] In fundraising efforts, LaPierre referred to "Nazi bucket helmets" and "black storm trooper uniforms," all of it pointing at a rising threat of fascism.[38] In 1994, he declared, "The final war has begun," and claimed he'd glimpsed documents detailing government plans "to eliminate private firearms ownership completely and forever."[39]

While the NRA assisted gun and defense manufacturers by fueling paranoia, they also helped the Republican Party make its case against Clinton by partnering in the hearings into the Waco tragedy, funding experts and providing messaging. At the time, a columnist for *The Washington Post* noted that the "GOP has allowed the NRA to fuse with it," a mutually beneficial arrangement that gave the NRA unbelievable influence in government and Republicans an ally in crafting a fear-based reality where they could still win elections.[40]

Republicans embraced this new paranoid reality and found they could signal to it while keeping their distance and maintaining respectability, just as they had with the Southern Strategy. It became readily apparent that Republicans, desperate for a winning strategy, needed to bring together evangelicals, white nationalists, and the economic elite, forming a coalition predicated on the idea that Democrats and liberals intended to overthrow the social and economic order.

This narrative succeeded, in part, because globalism was so complicated that only specialists and economists could fully grasp its workings. By design, the order of the world was complex and opaque, byzantine and abstract. In lieu of an explanation for the order that was holding Americans down, conspiracy theories filled the vacuum, and much like what had happened with fascist movements in the early twentieth century, they offered simplified explanations that told a power group, in this case white Christians, that their very lives were threatened.

Tragically, it was only a matter of time until Americans believing they were at war with their government would carry out an attack on their own country. On April 19, 1995, Timothy McVeigh detonated a truck bomb under the Alfred P. Murrah Federal Building in Oklahoma City, killing 168 and wounding nearly 700. Since returning home from the Persian Gulf War, and after watching the tragedies of Ruby Ridge and Waco with disgust, a disillusioned McVeigh had turned to the conspiratorial writing of the white supremacist Patriot Movement for direction, and found his answers in the work of neo-Nazi impresario William Pierce.

McVeigh had found Pierce's 1978 book *The Turner Diaries*, written under the pseudonym Andrew Macdonald, by way of an advertisement in a gun magazine that asked, "What are you going to do when they take your guns?"[41] The dystopic novel portrayed an America where whites had been de-armed and overwhelmed by a clandestine conspiracy that weaponized minorities, a New World Order that sought to bring an end to "God's great Experiment."[42] McVeigh read closely, took heed of the call for violent revolution, and distributed copies to his friends and family. In a letter to a newspaper in 1992, he asked forebodingly, "Do we have to shed blood to reform the current system?"[43]

The answer Pierce supplied was yes. *The Turner Diaries* served as a thinly veiled instruction manual on organizing terrorist cells and carrying out insurgent attacks. McVeigh followed the instructions and produced a bomb. He marveled later at how closely the result had resembled the explosion in the book: "A huge, gaping hole yawned in the courtyard pavement just beyond the rubble of collapsed masonry, and it was from this hole that most of the column of black smoke was ascending."[44]

Like so many others, McVeigh had lost himself in a fiction and believed he was the hero of *The Turner Diaries* come to life. Convinced he was a soldier opposing a tyrannical government, he expected the bombing to signal the beginning of a race war where white Americans would rise up and take the battle directly to the New World Order. At his trial, he laid the blame squarely on the United States by quoting the words of former Supreme Court justice Louis Brandeis, saying, "Our government is the potent, the omnipresent teacher. For good or for ill, it teaches the whole people by its example."[45]

Pierce wasn't that surprised by McVeigh's bombing, as he said "many, many Americans" considered "the U.S. government their worst enemy," particularly as it continually catered to "homosexuals," "the 'career' woman," and "the minorities."[46] *The Turner Diaries* had inspired other deadly attacks as well, but Pierce believed those incidents would only work if "sustained over a period of time."[47] Pierce, whose life's work was connecting several neo-Nazi organizations throughout America and then spreading the organizations worldwide, made contacts with far-right and white identity groups in several foreign countries, promising, "One day, there will be real, organized terrorism done according to plan."

★

The disaster in Oklahoma City was broadcast around the nation as networks showed the devastation of the Alfred P. Murrah building. Anchors spoke at length about the human suffering and the bravery of the first responders as still photos played of survivors being helped from the ruins and of dazed people caked in dust and blood who sat on sidewalks and held their heads in their hands. Any discussion of causes or relevant history was jettisoned in favor of dramatic, stunned, immobilized grief.

Americans didn't know it yet, but they were being prepared for decades of senseless tragedies, hundreds of hours of coverage documenting the madness and calamity of a country coming apart at the seams. This was the birth of tropes that defined how America would come to talk about its own disintegration, how it would come to view the collapse of empire as if it were a television show.

The age of mass-media, cable-news spectacle had begun, arguably, the year before with the fiery hell of Waco. But it fully matured with the surreal instance of Hall of Fame NFL running back–turned–double murderer O. J. Simpson leading police on a low-speed chase through Los Angeles in June 1994. The event had everything a TV producer might want—action, drama, high stakes—and was aided by a sea of helicopters armed with video cameras. It interrupted feeds across the country, including the pivotal Game 5 of the NBA Finals between the Houston Rockets and the New York Knicks.

Hours into the chase, something odd happened. People started parking their cars and standing at the edge of the highway. Some held signs encouraging Simpson. Some jumped and waved at the cameras as they passed. Later, in the wake of the chase, reporters asked Americans why they'd been so captivated. "That was the most compelling television," one person told *The New York Times.* "It was more exciting than the basketball game. It was cool, like the movie 'The Fugitive' in real life."[48]

The Simpson story gripped the nation like few single events ever had before. The verdict in late 1995 was viewed by more Americans than any event other than the moonwalk and coverage of the assassination of John F. Kennedy. Over the course of the trial, day-to-day broadcasts, including pre- and post-hearing analysis by experts and pundits, made CNN the go-to home for news over the traditional networks. It also established Court TV, a cable channel dedicated to airing trials, as a ratings powerhouse. As the drama played out, more Americans knew the name of the judge of the trial than could identify Speaker of the House Newt Gingrich.[49]

Program executives came to understand that America craved spectacle. Market segmentation dictated the imperative to capture niche audiences, but full-scale spectacles presented as Rorschach tests for every viewer to make their own judgments. The racially charged

Simpson case earned massive numbers and huge advertisement revenues for news networks. Soon, American reality was being scoured for spectacle, every crime and incident tested for potential, every celebrity feud and collapse given time in the spotlight, every scandal supercharged for super ratings. The wide-ranging consequences of the neoliberal order, the redistribution of wealth from the public to private individuals, the neglect of public services, the rise of desperation, and the ghastly suffering of the American people were being mined for profit and entertainment.

With spectacle driving audiences, cable news was booming. CNN turned into the hub for round-the-clock updates on ongoing stories like the Simpson case. NBC partnered with Microsoft to create MSNBC, a network that premiered in 1996 with a stylistic appeal to tech-savvy metropolitanism. Both, however, reported along the same lines of corporate, objective-ish news, a centrist approach that rarely troubled the new neoliberal economic consensus.

As a conscious alternative, conservative media became a billion-dollar business. Newspapers and magazines carried the conservative message while talk radio recruited new devotees every day, primarily by targeting disillusioned white men who either struggled in the new economy or felt their riches should be even more substantial. Roger Ailes, the television guru who had assisted Nixon, Reagan, George H. W. Bush, and a host of others, saw an opportunity with this group as he produced a televised version of Rush Limbaugh's radio show in the early nineties.

In 1996, Ailes partnered with Australian billionaire Rupert Murdoch to launch Fox News. Freed by deregulation, Murdoch had accumulated key media pieces throughout the world, and his accrual meant he could construct an alternate universe conservatives could populate and live inside. The plan for Fox News from the start was to deliver explicitly partisan news that could profit from segmenting the market and tilt the political scales.[50]

At the press conference announcing Fox News, Ailes stated,

"Somewhere between 56 and 82 percent of American people think news is biased, negative and boring. So let's take 60 percent as the number—it looks like a marketing niche to me."[51] Fox News appeared to target conservatives exclusively, shunning consensus appeal and building a designed market in the same way cable networks were slicing up their own audiences. By calling itself "Fair and Balanced," Fox News sought to insinuate both that its competitors were inferior and that its coverage was rooted in reality.

Like Limbaugh, Fox News functioned as a reality producer for the Republican Party. It pandered to its audience, pushed corporate-designed propaganda that questioned consensus science, attacked practically every piece of Democratic legislation as a dangerous takeover, and shined a spotlight on outlandish conservative pundits more than happy to battle in endless culture wars.[52] This pushed Republicans further right as they were forced to treat this constructed reality as if it were real. Republicans who refused were targeted in the network's coverage.

Ailes understood that Americans needed a dichotomous myth to unite them; it didn't matter who the opposition was as long as there was opposition. Ailes structured Fox News programming to convey a nightmarish world where minorities were dangerous and liberals manipulated, all of it alluding to a conspiracy that looked a lot like the New World Order. At the top of the pyramid were Bill and Hillary Clinton. Fox News and Limbaugh and their developing army of conservative personalities seemed to suggest that the pair were guilty of mass corruption on an international scale and even a slew of deaths, including longtime aide Vince Foster in 1993 and Democratic National Committee employee Seth Rich in 2016.

In January 1998, the Monica Lewinsky scandal broke and Fox News seized the opportunity to hammer Clinton for improprieties. Goaded by Fox News's allegations of bias and their desperation for spectacle, members of the mainstream media overcompensated by hitting Clinton harder in an attempt to prove their impartiality. It didn't help that the scandal constituted another ratings-catching spectacle. An analysis later showed that for the first three months of the scandal, outlets dedicated 46 percent of all their time and coverage to the affair.[53]

The outrage manufactured by Fox News and the conservative universe of pundits led to Clinton being only the second president ever impeached in the history of the United States, despite an overwhelming understanding that the impeachment was both futile and erroneous. Support in the public was severely lacking as most Americans regarded it as political maneuvering. Republican congressman Christopher Shays likened it to the opening of Pandora's box, saying, "It feels like it's out of control. Everything's set in motion and I don't know how you put it back in the box."[54] Republicans were performing and acting against the wishes of their constituents, pushed by narrative makers in their media base.

Clinton survived his impeachment and continued gaining support. Republicans had been forced to try the president in what a majority of Americans believed was a sham exercise, a television show for their supporters watching at home. And, like most television shows, viewers had a choice whether to change the channel. As evidenced by declining voter turnout in elections and participation within the system, Americans were tiring of the spectacle and phoniness of politics. The vote to acquit Clinton was only watched by 2.2 million on CNN, a number eclipsed by the 4.4 million who, earlier that week, tuned in to TNT, another Time Warner property, to watch a program they considered as unreal as the impeachment spectacle: World Championship Wrestling.[55]

★

Three years before his impeachment, Clinton had signed the Telecommunications Act of 1996 surrounded by Republicans and corporate executives. The bill was the essence of neoliberalism, deregulating the media and opening the field for hyper-competition between the wealthiest companies in the country. It was yet another moment of bipartisanship as the parties put aside their showy disputes to free the market.

"Today," Clinton said to mark the occasion, equating corporate freedom with the concept of revolutionary liberty, "the Information Revolution is spreading light, the light [Thomas] Jefferson spoke about, all across our land and all across the world."[56]

The grandiose rhetoric was appropriate considering it was generally accepted before the turn of the millennium that computers and the internet would transform society and help create a better future. For half a century it had been the goal and dream of technologists who believed there was no problem that could not be answered by the spread of personal computing.

That dream stretched as far back as 1945, when *The Atlantic* published an article by Vannevar Bush, the head of the military's Office of Scientific Research and Development during World War II. Mere months after the surrender of Nazi Germany, Bush imagined a future where humankind might transcend war and embrace knowledge. "Science," he reasoned, had enabled humans "to throw masses of people against one another with cruel weapons"; why then couldn't it invent a machine that might give them instant access to the breadth of human knowledge, helping them "to grow in . . . wisdom"?[57]

Scientists worked for decades on realizing Bush's vision to create a symbiotic relationship between humans and machines that might facilitate learning, communication, and a safer, more peaceful world. The military, however, bankrolled much of the internet's development, and cared little about the interpersonal benefits and more about its utility. It was seen as a means for continuing communication in the case of a nuclear attack, and by default it became another of the inventions co-opted for the purposes of maintaining power and militaristic domination.

This designation was challenged by counterculture figures, including Stewart Brand, who played an oversized role in the commune movement of the 1960s. The child of an advertising man, Brand used his marketing acumen to create *The Whole Earth Catalog*, a semi-regular list of products, books, and necessary information for any self-respecting hippie looking to leave corrupt society behind and create their own self-sufficient world. *The Whole Earth Catalog* premiered in 1968 with the words "We *are* as gods and might as well get used to it." With the advent of personal computing, Brand turned his communal idealism toward creating utopia through technology.

This odd cross-section of ideas formed the basis for modern tech. Brand and others like him, including John Perry Barlow, a lyricist for the Grateful Dead, saw computers and the internet as weapons designed for oppression that could, with the right effort, be used as "tools of liberation." By the dawning of the cyber age, Brand had grown weary of the counterculture's means of challenging the system, saying, "Power to the people was a romantic lie. Computers did more than politics did to change society."[58] Like Bill Clinton, his contemporaries in the counterculture grew weary of the fight and began accepting the oppressive strategies and technologies of the previous generation to ascend to power.

Barlow envisioned cyberspace as a brand-new world removed entirely from the corrupted terrestrial plane, writing in a manifesto that governments should leave it alone, calling them "weary giants of flesh and steel," and declaring, in a voice borrowed from Jefferson, that online pioneers would marshal the liberty and freedom to "create a civilization of the Mind" that would be "more humane and fair than the world your governments have made before."[59]

That idealism was short-lived. The internet and its ability to transcend borders proved an ideal tool to spread neoliberalism and support burgeoning world markets. Like the unspooling of telegraph wire and the laying of railroad tracks in the nineteenth century, the internet relied on government mobilization and private financing, and like the barons that grew from the developing infrastructure in the wake of the Civil War, a new class of oligarchs gained their fortunes. Politicians like Newt Gingrich, who spearheaded the conservative think tank the Progress & Freedom Foundation and stocked it with Ayn Rand devotees, saw the monetary potential and focused on efforts to further "dynamic competition in every aspect of the cyberspace market," drafting the death warrant of the utopian internet before it ever had a chance to form.[60]

By the time the Telecommunications Act was signed, it was already obvious that the trajectory and philosophy of the internet needed reconsidering. The first generation of online businesses had rocketed in value, only for their worth to plummet as the tech bubble popped in spectacular fashion. The innovation had fueled a mania on Wall Street that overvalued public offerings and nearly destroyed the economy. Alan Greenspan was caught by surprise when it became clear the economy wasn't as prescient or self-regulating as once believed. In typical Greenspan fashion, he muted the massive blow in a public speech by nodding knowingly toward the president and asking a simple rhetorical question: "But how do we know when irrational exuberance has unduly escalated asset values . . . ?"[61]

That was enough to send investors into a frenzy and change the paradigm. The Age of Clinton, with all its razzle-dazzle, all its spectacle, all its pomp and circumstance and promise, had been built on the foundation of a reality that had never existed in the first place. The great hope for the future needed to be reconfigured, reset, and retested, the old economy and the old reality discarded and new ones engineered.

★

Weeks after Bill Clinton's acquittal and eight months before the dawning of the new millennium, Warner Bros. released *The Matrix*, a cyberpunk, science-fiction flick about a character named Neo, played by Keanu Reeves, who discovers the world he lives in is merely a simulation of the twentieth century designed by intelligent computers to freeze time and end history. Hiding behind the veneer of normalcy, the authentic, real world is a dystopic nightmare where humans are being farmed as renewable energy. Armed with this knowledge, Neo is able to reenter the simulation and bend the laws of nature, allowing him to become a living god.

Due in part to its cutting-edge special effects and its novel premise, *The Matrix* was a surprising blockbuster. It was the right movie at the right time as Americans, having consumed decades of misinformation and spectacle, were becoming increasingly skeptical of the authenticity of their daily lives. The idea of existing in a computer simulation didn't seem like such a stretch in a world that felt increasingly artificial.

It was also based largely on alternative philosophy that worked outside of America's preconceived notions. Screenwriters the Wachowski sisters married elements of Eastern thought, Buddhist teachings, and parts of Christianity to form a wholly new mythology. One of the biggest influences was the writings of a French philosopher named Jean Baudrillard, whose book *Simulacra and Simulation* appeared briefly in the first act of the film.

Simulacra and Simulation was an influential postmodern text first published in the early 1980s that explained how much of culture had come to mean nothing. Baudrillard argued that society relied primarily on symbols and that over time, these symbols had become so ubiquitous that even the illusion of meaning had been lost. People began "substituting the signs of the real for the real,"[62] which resulted in a "hyperreal" society based on "models of a real without origin or reality."[63]

Baudrillard criticized *The Matrix* for what he claimed was a base misunderstanding of his work. His treatise described the world in which we lived, often at the behest of a population desperate for spectacle and its accompanying trappings. Civilization, Baudrillard held, had become so enraptured by its own fantasies, so lost in a hall of mirrors constructed by marketing appeals, mass consumerism, political propaganda, and the illusion of personal identity, that extricating reality from myth was next to impossible.

In its clumsy way, with its emphases on artifice and power through influence—not to mention the transference of existence through phone lines and digital circuits—*The Matrix* explored how humans had come to use their own tools to dominate themselves. It was a harbinger of the future: Neo's ability to thrive in the simulated arena foretold a new era where anyone who recognized that reality was pliable might bend laws and customs to their will and rule as gods. Everyone else would fuel the machine.

Already in 1994, as the internet was still gaining steam, an early adopter calling herself "humdog" had begun sounding an alarm that something wasn't right. She noticed cyberspace was far from the more humane world that had been promised: It had a tendency to function as a black hole and reduce its users to commodities. Her expression of herself and her feelings had become a product to be bought and sold. "i sold my soul like a tennis shoe," she wrote, "and i derived no profit from the sale of my soul."[64]

The Matrix wasn't prophesizing just any high-tech apocalypse. It was predicting how the internet would come to threaten the very concept of reality, and with it the basis for shared society, politics, and the Enlightenment itself.

CHAPTER 10

* * *

The Kingdom of
the Crooked Mirrors

As the twentieth century ticked into the new millennium, Russian president Boris Yeltsin appeared on television to announce his resignation. Since being elected in 1991, Yeltsin had presided over de-Sovietization with mixed results. He had rolled back much of the governmental control that had plagued Russian life, but his efforts to privatize industry had given rise to a dominant new oligarchy that towered over the people not unlike the vanquished ruling party had.

Once the embodiment of reform, Yeltsin had succumbed to this corruption and was surrounded by "the Family," a government that functioned more like organized crime than a representative body. Yeltsin had all but collapsed after years of leading Russia through unimaginable transition. He drank too much, he faced prosecution, and with the dream of transforming Russia into a free and prosperous society in tatters, it was time to step aside.

"Russia must enter the new millennium with new politicians, with new faces, with new, smart, strong, energetic people," he reasoned in his New Year's Eve address. His handpicked successor was Vladimir Putin, whom Yeltsin described as "a strong man who is worthy of being president and with whom practically every Russian today ties his hopes for the future."[1]

Only most Russians had no idea who Vladimir Putin was. He had risen from relative obscurity to the presidency of Russia, a nondescript man who seemed to manifest one day on their television only to be declared their future.

"It's very difficult to say who he is," one Russian political analyst remarked as Putin assumed power. "He's just a nicely wrapped package."[2]

A former KGB agent, Putin had been chosen as Yeltsin's successor in part because of his nondescriptness and sobriety. He was an intentional departure from Yeltsin and a means for the ruling party to maintain control of the office. Once the decision was made, Putin's anonymity gave way to an extensive public relations campaign that sought to mold him into a character worthy of the role. To do this, they looked to a 1973 miniseries called *Seventeen Moments of Spring*, one of Russia's most beloved cultural artifacts.

A propaganda tool of Yuri Andropov, the head of the KGB who wanted to redeem the agency's post-Stalin reputation, *Seventeen Moments of Spring* followed a Russian secret agent named Otto von Stierlitz as he infiltrated Nazi Germany and worked to undermine a secret deal between the Third Reich and the United States. The series changed the narrative of World War II to a victory of Russia against the rest of the world and solidified the idea that national security hinged on the KGB's trademark subterfuge and secrecy.

It was a phenomenon. Tens of millions tuned in, during both its initial run and its annual re-airings. According to journalist Hedrick Smith, who toured Russia and studied its people, "ordinary Russians" not only overwhelmingly loved *Seventeen Moments* but accepted it as "historic truth."[3]

Putin had been so inspired that he clothed himself in Stierlitz's persona and joined the KGB. Later, as a counsellor to the Leningrad City Council's chairman, Putin was approached by a documentarian who asked him to re-create a scene in which Stierlitz drives his iconic GAZ Volga back to Berlin. As the telltale music swelled, a young Putin played the role for everything it was worth, narrating as he and his hero fused into one: "We all think—and even I think it sometimes—that if we bring order with an iron fist, life will be easier, more comfortable and safer. But in reality . . . the iron fist will soon strangle us all."[4]

Now, to ensure his political success, Russia's technologists sought to make Putin the living embodiment of Stierlitz. He was shown next to powerful men in every broadcast, his public persona supplemented with macho acts that showcased the diminutive Putin as strong and athletic. Infamous photo ops had him riding shirtless on horseback, or diving into the sea and discovering planted ancient relics one moment and then taking to the air and piloting colossal bombers the next. On television, news anchors and pundits never missed a chance to compare him to Stierlitz and shower him with ubiquitous praise.

The celebration was not to last. In May 2000, a document leaked that described an insidious plan to remake the Russian government in the wake of Yeltsin's tenure. Called "Reform of the Administration of the President of the Russian Federation," it detailed a new means of governing that recalled the Soviet past and used "open" and "closed functions" to engineer an intentional shadow government that would "*tangibly* and *concretely* influence all political processes that are occurring in society."[5] To "ensure social order and stability," Putin's government intended to "not only be able to forecast and create 'necessary' political situations in Russia, but really be able to manage social and political processes."[6]

This task was largely the undertaking of a young propagandist named Vladislav Surkov. An avid postmodernist with a background in theater, Surkov understood that reality was not only malleable but controllable, and with the assistance of Russia's oligarchs he transformed the nation's politics into an experimental performance. Out of thin air he created events and controversies that aided Putin's agenda. He also built opposition parties and opposition candidates that gave the illusion of holding Putin accountable and the appearance of a real democracy, only for Putin to prevail in the end. While dissidents, journalists, and critics were murdered, intimidated, bribed, and imprisoned, Surkov authored reality day-to-day in Russia like a director improvising a play.

The result: an innovative, postmillennial, new-media-powered form of government combining totalitarian rule with the façade of liberal democracy. This artificial world benefited from the citizens' expectations of both choice and spectacle, but also from the conquering of the citizenry. Over time, it didn't matter if Russians understood the government was lying to them, that events like terrorist bombings were being manufactured. The apathy of Soviet powerlessness reemerged as Putin appealed to the past glories of the Soviet Union and linked his rule to the Christian church, positioning himself as a religious warrior on their behalf.

Referring to a 1963 children's film where a fantasy world is controlled by a secret cabal using reality-distorting mirrors to subdue its subjects, one Muscovite lamented to journalist Damon Tabor, "Russia is like the Kingdom of the Crooked Mirrors."[7]

Surkov calls this new form of government "the ideology of the future," and Putin and his conspirators are dedicated to spreading it throughout the world.[8] Much of the work has been done on the back of a doctrine called Neo-Eurasianism, a concept advocated by Russian philosopher Alexander Dugin. Like Surkov, Dugin believes reality is pliable and that manipulating it is the perfect means for fighting American hegemony; undermining the neoliberal, globalist system; and manufacturing a new world order infected with Putinism and subject to covert Russian influence.

To Dugin, Neo-Eurasianism represents "a fundamental revision of the political, ideological, ethnic, and religious history of mankind," which is no small feat considering the deep entrenchment of the American version of history and culture and the achievements of the Enlightenment.[9] To unseat the United States, Dugin believes it is imperative "to reject classical political theories, both winners and losers, strain our imaginations, seize the reality of the new world, correctly decipher the challenges of postmodernity, and create something new."[10]

In practice, this "something new" is actually an amalgam of the past, a sloppy combination of the tenets of socialism, fascism, Nazism, communism, capitalism, and nationalism into a system meant to be all things at all times to all people. For an origin, Dugin provides a new interpretation of world history, beginning, like Ronald Reagan's guru Manly P. Hall, with mythical Atlantis and its supposed rival Hyperborea, which Dugin claims as the philosophical ancestor of Russia and Putinism. Much like evangelicals and radical Islam are locked in fictional battles over a shared End Times war, Dugin seeks to engage the United States in a totally separate and peculiar fictional duel.

Nonsensical but adaptable to any population, it is a new myth that can be distributed throughout the world and appeal to disparate populations by reigniting the national visions and previously held myths troubled by globalism and American rule. In essence, it is a veneer that can stream across borders and the disguise that will hide the authoritarian control of Putinism and oligarchical kleptocracy.

Dugin's ideas are bizarre, but they have found purchase in Putinist Russia, a country desperate for even a hint of ideology to undergird its ruthless plundering and rampant corruption. His books are widely read and distributed to its political and military elites and his ideas seen as a blueprint for future domination. It is believed that America's stumbles—the flagrant power grab of unnecessary wars, the cruelty of globalism, the straining of its ideals and loss of moral and ethical leadership—have left it vulnerable to attack and defeat.

Modernity, Dugin holds, is at its "terminal point," meaning it is now possible to kill liberalism "once and for all."[11] His plans call for the spreading of Neo-Eurasianism, the gospel of mingled nationalism and inherent racism, to infiltrate the countries of Europe via propaganda and intelligence operations that create controllable, artificial parties and movements just as Surkov has done within Russia. The plan includes manipulating Great Britain into willingly isolating itself from the European Union. It also includes stoking American divisions with misinformation and psychological operations until the nation tears itself apart based on social, political, and economic differences. Both steps successfully manufactured destabilization and a loss of standing in the eyes of the world, presenting an opportunity that Russia had longed for since the USSR slipped away in the quiet of a New Year's Eve night.

★

America's first presidential election of the new millennium was a hint of the political chaos to follow. Texas governor and son of a former president Republican George W. Bush narrowly captured the White House over Democrat Vice President Al Gore in a scrum that bloomed into a constitutional crisis.

The disputed results famously hinged on Florida, whose governor was Bush's brother Jeb and whose elections were overseen by the Bush campaign's state cochair. After a brutal slog that saw Republican and Democratic operatives swarm courthouses and polling locations throughout the state, Bush's lawyers filed a complaint claiming the continued counting of legal ballots, the recognition of the rights of voters, threatened "irreparable" harm on Bush by "casting a cloud on . . . the legitimacy of his election."[12] The conservative judges on the US Supreme Court agreed, and ruled 5–4 on strictly partisan lines to end the recount and gift the election to Bush.

All signs were there that something had gone wrong in American politics. Only 56 percent of eligible voters had even bothered to cast a ballot. Bush won the presidency due to the Electoral College but lost the popular vote, or at least the vote that was counted that year; a later study found that four to six million votes in the 2000 election had gone unrecognized due to systemic errors.[13]

Bush had run as a "compassionate conservative" to counter the Democratic Party's poaching of conservative policy stances, and presented himself as a less rigid standard-bearer than his father. Despite being born in Connecticut, graduating from Yale, and having been the beneficiary of enormous wealth and privilege his entire life, Bush followed the advice of his public relations managers and distanced himself from the persona of an East Coast elite wimp that had undone his father. Instead, Bush crafted a persona closer to the idealized everyman conquerors of America's past. He played the role of a self-made, rough-and-tumble Texan who spent his time in front of the cameras clearing brush and playing a pretend roughneck at his ranch in Crawford.

The branding worked, but there didn't seem to be much motivating Bush to seek higher office beyond a desire to follow in his father's footsteps. In 1997, he had confided in Bandar bin Sultan, Saudi Arabia's ambassador and close friend of the Bush family, that he didn't "have the foggiest idea" what he thought about foreign policy.[14] Like the unprepared Harry Truman, Bush's ignorance created a vacuum quickly and happily filled by hard-liners looking to win influence.

Members of a group calling themselves the Project for the New American Century, a neoconservative think tank founded by William Kristol and Robert Kagan, happily supplemented Bush's sparse knowledge. According to the Project, in the wake of Reagan and H. W. Bush, American conservatives had been "adrift" in the realm of foreign policy and should increase defense spending and activity abroad to maintain the United States' "benevolent global hegemony" in the wake of the Cold War.[15] This concept was first presented in a 1992 post–Cold War plan drawn up by then–secretary of defense Dick Cheney's Pentagon that stated America's "first objective is to prevent the re-emergence of a new rival . . . to prevent any hostile power from dominating a region whose resources would, under consolidated control, be sufficient to generate global power," including, as the report specifically notes, "access to vital raw materials, primarily Persian Gulf oil."[16]

These neoconservatives were believers in Madisonian control and disciples of philosopher Leo Strauss, an avid proponent of Plato's concept of the Noble Lie who believed the best-constructed societies were managed by a group of ruling elites wielding powerful myths to unite their subservient populations. "The good city," he wrote, citing *The Republic*, "is not possible then without a fundamental falsehood."[17] Following in the tradition of Plato and Alexander Hamilton's reasoning in *The Federalist Papers*, Strauss stressed the ultimate Noble Lie was the possession of the narrative of history, a dominance of the story of humanity, its past, its present, and, by extension, its future. Strauss and his neoconservative devotees maintained that America prospered when presented as a mythical hero of freedom in the face of an existential threat. If necessary, that existential threat could be easily manufactured. What truly mattered was the crusade and its results.

Neoconservatives and members of the Project for the New American Century stocked the Bush administration, including Vice President Dick Cheney, Secretary of Defense Donald Rumsfeld, and Deputy Secretary of Defense Paul Wolfowitz. Though Bush didn't have the foggiest idea what he wanted from foreign policy, the Project lent him their constructed vision of the United States as a benevolent protector of the rights of man.

Perhaps the Bush administration was looking too far ahead in its plans to remake the world, because it missed glaring signs that a small band of terrorists calling themselves al-Qaeda might carry out an audacious terror attack in the fall of 2001. Osama bin Laden, one of the founders of al-Qaeda, had proclaimed a fatwa in 1996 against America's "crusader armies," making no distinction between military and civilian targets.[18] Despite this very public declaration, terrorism was fundamentally "considered a dead issue" according to Winston Wiley, the deputy chief of the Counterterrorism Center for the CIA.[19]

By the summer of 2001, the Bush administration had received numerous warnings from the intelligence community. CIA director George Tenet recalled "the system was blinking red," but calls for preparation went largely unacknowledged.[20] On August 6, a month before nineteen hijackers killed nearly three thousand Americans, the CIA delivered a briefing to the administration titled "Bin Ladin Determined to Strike in US" that laid out, in no ambiguous terms, that members of al-Qaeda had "resided in or traveled to the US for years" and might be planning to "hijack a US aircraft."[21] Another urgent briefing followed on September 6, but did little good.

The tragedies of the terrorist attacks of September 11 were many. The thousands who died and the millions who felt intense mourning, trauma, and insecurity. Those around the globe who suffered from the resulting endless wars and societal and political upheaval, and the generations who would follow and bear the brunt of economic mismanagement from years of wasting money on unwinnable wars and neglecting the basic needs of people. It might have been avoided had the Bush administration heeded the warnings of its intelligence community and acted to thwart attacks that were, by all accounts, predictable.

Video of the tragedy itself was rebroadcast round the clock on networks trying to grasp the loss while also keeping viewers glued to their television screens. Al-Qaeda took advantage of our media to amplify the attack and deliver a shock, both literal and metaphorical, to Americans, who, in the six decades following Pearl Harbor, had come to believe the homeland was beyond the reach of war. As they watched the World Trade Center towers crumble on live television, that illusion crumbled as well and gave way to a primal and violent insecurity.

Al-Qaeda and bin Laden made a wager that an isolated attack on the symbols of America's economic, military, and political power would provoke the United States to "lose consciousness and act chaotically against those who attacked it."[22] According to this plan, America would overcompensate militarily; launch multiple, costly wars; and lose the support of the international community, while al-Qaeda would grow in numbers with every passing day. Depressingly, just as American citizens had drawn the government into their apocalyptic fantasies in the 1990s, al-Qaeda, a death cult starving for destruction, successfully forced the United States to play its preferred role.

Instead of accepting their responsibility for missing the warning signs, the Bush administration overcorrected and built al-Qaeda into a worldwide threat. At the time, the terrorist group had less than a hundred members, but to convince Bush's constituents that they had concocted a complete surprise attack, they had to be portrayed as an existential enemy on a level equal to America. Ever ready for cowboy posturing, Bush told his administration he wanted to rid the world completely of terrorists. When advised any operation on that scale would include military intervention in at least sixty countries, he replied with his usual effortless, incurious certainty: "Let's pick them off one at a time."[23]

In declaring a "War on Terror," the Bush administration invented a worldwide campaign that cost, over the next seventeen years, $5.9 trillion, killed nearly half a million human beings, laid waste to civilian lives and infrastructure, undermined America's principles, and resulted in military and intelligence operations in seventy-six countries.[24] Al-Qaeda and affiliated Islamic extremists grew as the United States gifted them notoriety and disrupted the political order in the Middle East. In America, the war effort damned thousands of soldiers to arduous, traumatic, pointless combat while ensuring the economic prosperity harnessed in the 1990s would go toward military operations instead of domestic needs, including education, health care, and infrastructure.

Feverish patriotism following the attacks curdled into a noxious sense of insecurity as Americans willingly sacrificed their liberties and needs in exchange for symbolic protections. The Bush administration adopted extreme surveillance measures, impinged on civil liberties, and betrayed America's espoused principles by implementing horrific interrogation strategies, including physical and psychological torture. To justify these measures, lawyers played semantic games with reality, twisting and torquing it until it threatened to snap. In a series of memos that legalized torture, lawyers termed al-Qaeda members "illegal combatants" instead of prisoners of war, arguing they were not protected under the Geneva Conventions.[25] In an insidious piece of reasoning, the administration argued that the reality of whether an act constituted torture relied on the "mental state" of the torturer instead of the tortured.[26]

In the wake of September 11, the United States had received the near-universal support and sympathy of the world, but the Bush administration squandered that goodwill by acting unilaterally and cruelly in its pursuit of the War on Terror. Borrowing from the reality-bending concepts of global capitalism and international sidestepping of labor laws, they outsourced prisoners to countries with less stringent rules about torture. At these CIA "black sites," prisoners were beaten, humiliated, sexually molested, and subjected to psychological torture, and, in the reemergence of the "water cure" technique from the subjugation of the Philippines, prisoners suffered agonizing simulated drowning. As one CIA operative involved remarked, "If you don't violate someone's human rights some of the time, you probably aren't doing your job."[27]

After invading Afghanistan to unseat the al-Qaeda–linked Taliban, the Bush administration began working on fulfilling the Project for the New American Century's foremost goal of regime change in Iraq. They believed an invasion could establish a foothold in the Middle East and control over oil and, possibly, set off a series of revolutions. Cheney, Rumsfeld, and Wolfowitz relentlessly pushed the concept and held constant meetings with intelligence officials who warned them there was no proof that Iraq had participated in 9/11 or had weapons of mass destruction. Desperate for the war, the Bush administration pushed against those warnings and sought out intelligence, no matter how flawed, that proved their desired assertion.

What they found was intelligence largely provided by Ahmed Chalabi, an Iraqi politician—intelligence that would seem questionable even to a casual observer. Chalabi had spent millions of American dollars on fancy homes, luxury cars, and a comfortable life as he and the Iraqi National Congress, an exiled anti-Hussein group, provided America with constant accusations against Hussein in an attempt to create a war that might advantage them. In a move that echoed the lobbying efforts that led to the Persian Gulf War in the early nineties, they hired Black, Kelly, Scruggs & Healey, a public relations firm, to build their case against Hussein. After it became clear Chalabi and his colleagues had misled the United States and that Iraq had never possessed weapons of mass destruction and had no ties to al-Qaeda, Chalabi proclaimed, "We are heroes in error," and maintained, "As far as we're concerned we've been entirely successful. That tyrant Saddam is gone and Americans are in Baghdad. What was said before is not important."[28]

Despite obviously flawed intelligence and a misinformation campaign aimed at creating an unnecessary, illegal war, Bush and Cheney earned the support of Congress in October 2002 in a largely bipartisan vote. As the opposition, the Democratic Party was responsible for holding the president in check, but following 9/11 they had acquiesced to nearly every request, no matter how troubling, unconstitutional, or dangerous, out of fear they might appear unpatriotic or weak on national security. By March 2003, the stage was set for America to invade a country and make war against a sovereign nation without provocation.

The myth of America was coming unraveled by the day. What had long survived and prospered under the auspices of benevolence, under the appearance of the United States as a force for good and justice, was quickly expiring. "Around the globe," said West Virginia Democratic senator Robert Byrd on the day the Iraq War launched, "our friends mistrust us, our word is disputed, our intentions are questioned."

That truth was mostly absent on America's airwaves as networks portrayed the Iraq War as just and an exhibition of the United States' righteousness. Behind the scenes, Roger Ailes advised the Bush administration on how to win support for the war. He also directed Fox News to prepare a jingoistic, prepackaged broadcast they code-named "Operation Rolling Thunder" that sought to market the conflict and engage audiences in a reality-TV war replete with twenty-four hours a day of graphics and patriotic symbols.[29] As Fox News enjoyed rising ratings from an American public enraptured by televised war and revenge, other networks attempted to re-create the spectacle. Soon American media was saturated with glitzy broadcasts of an illegal war that refused to discuss the context of the hostilities or question the official message of an administration openly lying to the public. By the time actual hostilities commenced, more than 70 percent of Americans supported war, with 69 percent erroneously believing that Saddam Hussein had been involved in the September 11 attacks.[30]

It hardly mattered. The networks had a spectacle that transcended demographics and segmentation. They treated it like a television show, calling it a "soap opera in the center of Baghdad," and referred to "plotlines" and "storylines," continually remarking the war was "going as scripted."[31] It was all marketed as the crusade the Bush administration had craved, an apocalyptic showdown between good and evil.

The Iraq War reached its televised climax on April 9, 2003, as US troops rolled through Baghdad and into Firdos Square, where a minuscule band of Iraqis was attempting to topple a statue of Saddam Hussein. American troops assisted, as they were advised the statue was a "target of opportunity" for psychological operations to produce a lasting symbol that might build a favorable narrative of the war.[32] As they brought the statue down, American networks gushed over the spectacle, a CNN anchor likening it to "seminal moments in a nation's history" and comparing it to the fall of the Berlin Wall.[33]

Bizarrely, journalists on the ground at Firdos Square were seeing something else. As they looked around, they noted only a smattering of people and a largely unremarkable affair. It was essentially a non-story. Their editors at home, watching the grand scene unfold all over their television screens, told their reporters to look again. Surely, they were missing a moment of historic importance occurring before their very eyes.

In a press briefing, Secretary of Defense Donald Rumsfeld followed the CNN anchor's lead, comparing the event to the defeat of Hitler, Stalin, and Lenin, saying, "Watching them, one cannot help but think of the fall of the Berlin Wall and the collapse of the Iron Curtain."[34]

On May 1, the Bush administration tried another piece of myth-making. Riding in a Lockheed S-3 Viking jet, the president landed on the USS *Abraham Lincoln* off the coast of San Diego. Dressed like a fighter pilot fresh from the war front, Bush, who had avoided combat in the Vietnam War, strutted across the aircraft carrier in a flight suit, shaking hands and greeting the crew. Later, in front of a banner reading "Mission Accomplished," Bush declared victory, saying, "In the battle of Iraq, the United States and our allies have prevailed."[35]

That brought to an end the televised Iraq War, but combat was far from over. Even after Saddam Hussein was captured and executed, even after the United States declared victory, the tragic and costly war continued for another eight years. Insurgents waged a bloody and costly battle with US troops as a new terror group calling itself ISIS seized territory, established a caliphate, executed non-believers, kidnapped women and sold them into slavery, and collected new recruits dedicated to an apocalyptic war with American crusaders. Not only had the war been waged based on a lie, but the consequences were unimaginable in their scope and cost. The myth-making was revealed, piece by piece, as a willful lie and manipulation, and the United States, just as al-Qaeda had planned, lost the trust and respect of the world.

What had started on a bright Tuesday morning in September had reverberated through the years. A small group of terrorists had managed a feat even the Soviet Union never could: exposing the con-tradictory construction of American reality.

★

Like a record on repeat, the American economy crashed as trusting bankers and corporations to police themselves backfired as it always does. The sad truth was that the loss and the destruction were as predictable as the turning of seasons, but in two centuries, American leaders had yet to see the pattern and take necessary precautions.

On October 23, 2008, as the economy faltered, the usually steadfast Alan Greenspan appeared before a House committee and admitted he had discovered "a flaw," saying, "I don't know how significant or permanent it is. But I have been very distressed by that fact." Asked if the flaw was his belief that self-regulation worked, Greenspan re-lented: "Absolutely, precisely."[36]

Two years later, Greenspan presented a report to the Brookings Institution nicknamed "The Crisis Paper." In this report, Greenspan, a Randian economist who had perpetually cursed regulation of any kind, admitted the economy was inherently unstable, that his decades of belief that the market was self-sufficient and, above all, always right might have been in vain. The infallibility of the market, the defining tenet of the neoliberal order and the new world, had been a myth all of its own.

"Unless there is a societal choice to abandon dynamic markets and leverage for some form of central planning," Greenspan said, "I fear that preventing bubbles will in the end turn out to be infeasible. Assuaging their aftermath seems the best we can hope for."[37]

What had shaken Greenspan to his core?

A market that had grown so huge and independent of oversight and regulation that it had cannibalized itself as banks sought more and more profit and cast aside even the appearance of good faith. Years of irresponsible lending, of preying on overleveraged consumers who desired homes beyond their means, of selling the illusion of transcending class on the backs of reckless loans, and of creating new concepts like derivatives, a trading chip that even seasoned economists barely understood, had created a house of cards destined to collapse. Even those who worshipped the market as if it were a deity had to admit that the world was tied to an unstable and mercurial system.

One expert called it a "circular Ponzi scheme."[38]

Another "the biggest floating craps game of all time."[39]

But, as with any Ponzi scheme or game of craps, there was always going to be a loser, some schmuck destined to roll snake eyes. Banks and investment houses passed the toxic assets back and forth, hoping whenever the bill came due it would be somebody else's to pay.

Naturally, the sucker was the American people.

The financial crisis of 2008 cost trillions of dollars and millions of jobs. It wiped out one generation's retirement and doomed another to lessened expectations and diminished opportunities. The effects would last for decades to come. And, because the banks and investment houses had grown so fat off an economy designed specifically for them; because they had become so integrated in the daily function of the economy; because they had profited so wildly off a system that allowed them to destroy it, they were deemed too large to fail and gifted a $400 billion bailout funded by the American public, $1.6 billion of which went to the executives who caused the crisis and nearly $20 billion of which paid the bonuses of the architects.[40] There were raises, lavish trips to exotic locales, private jets that allowed the wealthy to soar above the wreckage they'd left behind.

As the economy melted down, Americans yearned for a new direction. A young senator from Illinois named Barack Obama offered a fresh vision of the American Myth tailored to stabilizing a volatile world. Back in 2004, Obama had captured the national imagination in a speech to the Democratic National Convention in Boston that pushed against the notion that America had divided into two separate nations, saying, "There's not a liberal America and a conservative America."[41] He leveled his criticism at pundits and partisans who "like to slice-and-dice our country into Red States and Blue States," rejecting the conventional wisdom that politics had to be trench warfare, an exhibition of zero-sum game theory. "We are one people," he said, promising that with the right imagination and right intentions, America could transcend its differences and unite in the common good.

For all of his soaring rhetoric, Obama functioned as a pragmatic politician who straddled the divide between left and right much as Bill Clinton had. In his acceptance of the Democratic Party's nomination in 2008, he spoke of "individual responsibility and mutual responsibility," a bridging of liberal and conservative ideology that nodded toward cooperation within a neoliberal system.[42] The united America Obama spoke of was still predicated on a free market that operated the way Ronald Reagan had envisioned.

Despite his advocating traditional policies mixed with uniting rhetoric, Obama was continually harangued by a conservative media that seemed obsessed with the fact that he was an African-American man and, strangely enough, convinced the center-left Obama was somehow a closeted socialist.

Regardless, he won an easy victory in 2008 over Republican John McCain, and in subsequent meetings with congressional Republicans it became very obvious very quickly that Obama had actually meant what he said about wanting to govern the country in a bipartisan, healing fashion. For once, a leader who had crafted an ideal America genuinely tried to bring it to life. He communicated with Republicans, heard their thoughts and concerns, and was willing to compromise.

Instead of accepting his gestures of good faith, Republicans were terrified. While such a president might be good for the United States of America, particularly following the disaster of the Bush presidency, such a unifying Democratic president would be terrible for the Republican Party.

As one Republican staffer remarked after a particularly inspiring meeting with Obama, "If he governs like that, we are all fucked."[43]

And so, instead of working with Obama to create a better future for the people, Republicans responded as they had with Clinton. They chose to confront a fictional version of Obama the conservative media had built during the 2008 campaign. The decision was aided by a recognition of the movement that had swept Obama into office. Instead of relying on appealing to white voters and independents, as Clinton, Gore, and John Kerry in 2004 had tried to do, Obama created a broad coalition, including working-class whites, women, African Americans, the LGBT community, and Hispanic-Latinx citizens. It was clear that if Obama and the Democratic Party were to hold on to this coalition, especially as demographics continued to shift, they could dominate politics for a generation, if not longer.

Conservative media doubled down on their portrayal of an America divided by race and ethnicity, perpetuating a sense of grievance among the Republicans' white base. The narrative was that in the post-recession struggle, minorities were being favored by a Democratic Party desperate for votes. They believed Obama was obsessed with redistributing wealth and proof of a dangerous, racial shift in power.

This manipulation was most prominent on Fox News, where Roger Ailes continued his career of stoking racial resentment. Coverage spotlighted crimes by minorities and depicted an America where whites were under constant threat from a protected and pre-ferred group. It was a realization of every fear that had percolated in the conservative consciousness since the civil rights movement and the uprisings of the 1960s. Every second of Fox News sounded the alarm that the radicals had taken over.

In February 2009, on the financial channel CNBC, former hedge-fund executive and on-air personality Rick Santelli reported live from the floor of the Chicago Board of Trade and quickly flew into in an impassioned rant. Angered by the bailout, Santelli asked the assembled traders, "How many of you people want to pay for your neighbor's mortgage, that has an extra bathroom, and can't pay their bills? Raise their hand." Amid a chorus of boos, Santelli asked President Obama if he was listening and uttered a sentence that changed the political landscape: "We're thinking about having a Chicago Tea Party . . ."[44]

Santelli's bluster quickly went viral as it embodied much of the population's anger at the economic crisis while transferring the blame from the financial sector, which had caused the meltdown, to Obama, who had only taken the oath of office a month prior. The call to action hit home with livid white Americans who felt both injured financially and threatened by the political sea change of Obama's election.

Almost overnight, several groups adopting the Tea Party moniker materialized across the country. The name carried power as it har-kened back to the revolutionary bluster that had founded the country and articulated the level of fury and panic felt by white conservatives. True to branding, the Tea Partiers believed they were inheritors of the name and in opposing Obama were carrying on the proud tra-dition that began with revolutionaries opposing King George III.

Their meetings were marked with baseless paranoia. They were afraid of Muslims' invading and forcing Sharia law on sleepy American towns. They were afraid of African Americans killing them and abusing the welfare system. They were afraid that Obama, a center-left president, might be planning on imprisoning and slaughtering them. After years of consuming conservative media and being warned that one day they might lose their country to dangerous minorities and lawless liberals, they truly believed it was time for a new revolution.

What united the Tea Party was bigoted, abject fear; there was little in the way of actual or consistent ideology. They claimed to want limited government only to starve the Obama presidency and undermine his programs. What they opposed wasn't government spending, it was government spending in helping *others*. Decades of Republican trench warfare and zero-sum politics had created an overtly self-seeking base whose principles were situational and decidedly tribal.

Such a base was ripe for plundering, so wealthy conservatives looking to undermine Obama's presidency and further tilt the political landscape to their favor bankrolled the new project, most notably brothers Charles and David Koch, who shared an almost religious devotion to extreme libertarianism and the virtual demolition of government. They inherited that ideology from their father, Fred C. Koch, a businessman who cofounded the paranoid fringe group the John Birch Society in 1958 and spent his later years warning that the United States government had been infiltrated and subverted by communist spies.

Rather than promote their ideas openly, the Kochs manipulated politics through surreptitious means. In this way, the Tea Party was incredibly attractive to them. As a former advisor told journalist Jane Mayer, "This right-wing, redneck stuff works for them. They see this as a way to get things done without getting dirty themselves."[45] Determined to push libertarian ideals and solidify control of the Republican Party, to which the brothers had gifted enormous sums, the Kochs floated the Tea Party and lent it the support of their group Americans for Prosperity, which organized events, trained Tea Party personalities, and served as a communications wing for the nascent uprising.

With this help, the Tea Party grew in scope until it threatened to replace the Republican Party entirely. Republicans were quickly becoming victims of their own successes as their gerrymandering and disenfranchising of minority voters had created seats around the country they were never in serious danger of being lost to Democrats, but created perilous primary battles wherein established Republicans faced more and more extreme challengers. A ruling by the Supreme Court in 2010 in the case of *Citizens United* freed corporations and wealthy donors to pour money into elections, but the resulting super PACs meant more funds were going to outside groups that targeted Republicans who compromised or failed to toe the conservative line.

Meanwhile, the reach of conservative media continued to expand. The alternate reality that had been birthed in the 1990s and ensured that conservative viewers and listeners remained in their own bubbles matured, and those listeners and viewers began to wonder why Republican lawmakers didn't seem to live in the same world. While they were more than happy to appear on Fox News and give lip service to the terrifying reality being sold to the audience, their actions in government told a different story. After years of lurking mistrust, this conservative base began to reject mainstream Republicans and move toward the Tea Party, a political body headquartered explicitly in this alternate reality.

In another instance of history repeating itself, the Republican Party recognized an opportunity when the Democratic president made a push to reform health care. This time Obama proposed a plan with roots in the conservative world, a plan that had been more or less proposed by the Heritage Foundation in 1989.[46] Republican governor Mitt Romney, who eventually challenged Obama in 2012, had actually passed a version of the plan in Massachusetts.

The Affordable Care Act was a practical, commonsense, moderate reform of the health care system crafted with input from hundreds of health groups and corporations, but the Republican Party pounced anyway. Borrowing a page out of Newt Gingrich's playbook, they called the reform a socialist plot and accused Obama of tyrannical ambitions. They replayed their past strategies, declaring there was no health care crisis in America and sacrificing the betterment of Americans' lives for political gain.

Conservative media and pundits embraced the paranoia of the Tea Party. The Affordable Care Act was depicted as a piece of dictatorial legislation dooming Americans to certain death and the beginnings of Obama's despotic takeover. At a Tea Party rally, a Fox Business anchor asked the crowd, "Guys, when are we going to wake up and start fighting the fascism that seems to be permeating this country?"[47] Sean Hannity, the Atlanta radio pundit who emceed Gingrich's election-night party in 1996, had become a megastar on Fox News in part because of his willingness to label Obama's every action an existential threat against the United States. Hannity warned of "a government rationing body that tells women with breast cancer, 'You're dead.'"[48] In a particularly infamous post online, former vice presidential candidate Sarah Palin told her followers the bill would lead to Nazi-like "death panels" that would decide whether people lived or died based on their "level of productivity in society."[49]

The paranoia only increased in intensity and absurdity. Billionaire mogul and reality television star Donald Trump appeared regularly on Fox News to stoke the conspiracy theory of birtherism, constantly demanding Obama produce a birth certificate to prove he was born in America. He recklessly speculated that Obama had been born in Africa, or that the birth certificate might have something "very bad for him," saying he had heard "where it says religion, it might have Muslim."[50]

Birtherism was a poisonous conspiracy theory that played upon white anxiety and the racist belief that America was a country by, for, and of white people, and that people of color were not truly American, a belief that had plagued debates about citizenship and immigration for centuries. By questioning whether Obama was even from the United States, or if he was secretly a Muslim, birtherism recalled the white supremacy that had been woven into the system with the drafting of the Constitution.

What's more, the question Trump was raising fueled the New World Order conspiracies that had emerged during the Clinton administration. To Americans steeped in evangelical, white identity Christianity, and the still-fervent members of the Cult of the Shining City, Obama represented a fulfillment of long-held, anxious prophecies. His ascent to the presidency was a symbol of the perilousness of white America, and if he wasn't from the United States, the question was begged: How was he capable of forging a new identity and becoming president? Was he a puppet of the New World Order?

Or something worse?

In the eyes of many Americans, almost all of them steeped in the myth of the Shining City, Obama was a prime candidate for the prophesied antichrist, the ultimate satanic villain who would rise up, deceive the world, deliver it unto the Devil himself, and then plunge civilization into an apocalyptic battle. Again, many turned to Hal Lindsey's *The Late, Great Planet Earth,* which had created the idea of the antichrist in the popular mind, describing the great villain as a man of "magnetism" who would be a "completely godless, diabolically evil 'future fuehrer.'"[51] Throughout Obama's tenure, e-mail inboxes were clogged with misspelled and frantic forwards overflowing with bastardized scripture that seemed to predict Obama's meteoric rise.

This type of madness found its way onto Fox News as a new personality named Glenn Beck hosted a daily fever-dream conspiracy hour. Beck scribbled furiously on blackboards featuring photos of Obama among portraits of Stalin, Pol Pot, and Adolf Hitler. He hinted at covert plans and diabolical conspiracies, many of which seemed to point toward Obama becoming the "future fuehrer" Lindsey had predicted. According to Beck, Obama had a "deep-seated hatred for white people" and was determined to "settle old racial scores."[52] In Beck's America, Obama's administration was hidden in shadows, planning a new Holocaust and putting into motion plans for "forcing abortions and putting sterilants in the drinking water to control population."[53] He suggested that the progressive billionaire George Soros controlled the operation—an alarmingly overt invocation of international Jewish conspiracy theories.

Beck represented a turning point as Fox News sank deeper into conspiracy theory and fearmongering. The network became a nightmare machine, churning out delusional programming intended to keep its audience afraid and angry, ensuring they retreated to their alternate reality. There, everyone understood that the opposition was dead set on stealing their money and indoctrinating and abusing their children, and always on the cusp of shredding the Constitution and plunging the country into a Book of Revelation–style horror. The network's commercials profited off these fears, selling its viewers doomsday prepping supplies and gold coins that would come in handy when society collapsed.

This shift occurred at least in part because the man in charge had started believing his own propaganda. In 2014, Republican Speaker of the House John Boehner went to discuss Republican messaging with Roger Ailes only to discover to his terror that the Fox News chief "had black helicopters flying all around his head" and "believed in all this crazy stuff."[54] Since 9/11, Ailes had lost his grasp of reality and grown increasingly paranoid, believing he was under constant surveillance and subject to nonexistent threats. He paid exorbitant fees to have a safe room built in his house stocked with weapons and state-of-the-art security, believing Obama was not only a secret Muslim, but a secret Muslim out to destroy Ailes and the country he so loved.

Inevitably, the paranoia manifested in violent action. On July 18, 2010, a man named Byron Williams was pulled over by Oakland, California, police before opening fire on them. After his arrest, it was discovered that Williams was speeding toward San Francisco, where he planned to attack the offices of the American Civil Liberties Union and an organization helmed by George Soros. He hoped to "start a revolution" and strike a mortal blow against what he believed was an international conspiracy.[55] Williams's mother described him as "angry at the federal government. And the shadow government that operates behind the scenes, manipulating things," an idea fostered by Williams's dedication to Fox News.[56] In custody, Williams told a reporter that Glenn Beck and his daily deluge of conspiracy theories "blew [his] mind."

A new crisis gripped the nation as men like Williams picked up weapons and waded into public places to fight an invisible war. In the seven years from 2012 to 2019, there were over a hundred mass shootings with over seven hundred victims, most killed by semiautomatic rifles purchased by legal means. Many of the killers were frustrated white men indoctrinated by paranoid media and possessed of wild-eyed conspiracy theories, including Dylann Roof, a twenty-two-year-old South Carolina man who killed nine parishioners of the Emanuel African Methodist Episcopal Church in Charleston. Roof engrossed himself in radical readings and websites that told the story of a racial crisis. He reasoned, "Well, I had to do it because somebody had to do something, because, you know, black people are killing white people every day . . . They rape white women, 100 white women a day."[57]

The digital world radicalized killers like Roof through misinformation and propaganda, a phenomenon that had reared its head in 2011, when a twenty-three-year-old named Jared Lee Loughner opened fire at a political event outside a grocery store in Tucson, Arizona, killing six and injuring thirteen, including Representative Gabby Giffords, who survived a gunshot to the head. Loughner's motivations were inexplicable, his stated ideology indecipherable. What could be gathered was that he had been deeply affected by conspiracy theories and repeated viewings of the independent documentaries *Zeitgeist* and *Loose Change*, which charged that all political reality was an intentional hoax, including the September 11 attacks, which were supposedly staged by the government.

One of the producers of *Loose Change* was Alex Jones, a Texas conspiracy theory mogul who built an empire out of irrational and outrageous claims about the coming New World Order, including allegations that Democratic leaders like Obama were agents of super-natural, satanic evil. Jones told a reporter he doubted the official story behind the shooting in Tucson, saying, "My gut tells me this was a staged mind-control operation. The government employs geo-metric psychological-warfare experts . . . They implanted the idea in [Loughner's] head."[58]

One year later, when twenty-year-old Adam Lanza killed twenty-seven people, most of them schoolchildren, at Sandy Hook Elemen-tary in Newtown, Connecticut, Jones took to the airwaves to again cast doubt on the legitimacy of the events, accusing New World Order goons of having orchestrated a fake massacre to undermine gun rights and civil liberties. "Sandy Hook is a synthetic, completely fake [*sic*] with actors in my view, manufactured," Jones said. "I knew they had actors there, clearly, but I thought they killed some real kids. And it just shows how bold they are, that they clearly used actors."[59]

With Fox News covering a nightmarish alternate reality and Republicans like Sarah Palin using social media to stoke unrea-sonable fears, the environment was primed for someone like Jones to gain influence. Based on his irrational and irresponsible claims, Jones built a lucrative business and substantial following for himself, primarily with the help of the dark corners of the internet, a dan-gerous and unsettling place where Lanza had spent time before his crime. Following the tragedy, it was discovered Lanza had been a member of several online communities obsessed with mass shootings, the members trading graphic pictures from past massacres and dis-cussing strategies and fantasies of perpetrating their own. Inves-tigations revealed this "negative micro-society" furthered Lanza's radicalization.[60]

Lanza's mass-shooting forums were only part of a growing, disturbing trend online. What had begun as a brave new world ripe with potential and honorable purpose had descended into anarchical bedlam that exposed and promoted humanity's darkest impulses. On an internet forum called 4chan, users were treated to overwhelming doses of "Weird pornography, in-jokes, nerdish argot, gory images, suicidal, murderous and incestuous thoughts, racism and misogyny" that numbed and radicalized them.[61] Some argued it was harmless, the inevitable consequence of free speech and free thought, but those claims grew more difficult to support as more mass shooters frequented the forum and its successor 8chan.

Maybe it should have been obvious that reality and the unreality of the internet, and perhaps the culture altogether, were merging with disastrous results. That it was becoming an existential crisis might have been apparent in 2014 when a user named David Michael Kalac posted pictures on the forum of what appeared to be a murdered woman. "Turns out," he wrote, moments after killing his girlfriend, "it's way harder to strangle someone to death than it looks on the movies."[62]

★

4chan wasn't the only part of the online world that took a dark turn in these years; much more mainstream sites and tech subverted Americans' rights and opened the country up to foreign interference, all while creating an isolating, brand-driven social environment.

After the tech bust of the 1990s, internet companies had seen their avenues to profit disappear as commerce was revealed as insufficient for their operations and necessary growth. But now they recognized their ability to monetize data and sell their unparalleled access to the behavior of their users. This information was virtually priceless to businesses looking for more efficient and effective means of selling products to consumers.

Behind their computer screens, at their keyboards, and operating the touchscreens of their smartphones, consumers gave the tech giants unbridled admission to the thoughts, interests, insecurities, and passions they hid from the world. Over time, the companies used artificial intelligence to decipher pathways to find patterns that even the users themselves might not have recognized. They sold this information to companies for exorbitant prices.

Much of the business was generated by the need for users to express themselves and supplement their doubts, anxieties, and fears by adopting personas, the basis of consumerism since Edward Bernays had used his uncle Sigmund Freud's theories in the early twentieth century. As Mark Zuckerberg, the founder of Facebook, admitted, the users of his platform were engaged in "building an image and identity for themselves, which in a sense is their brand."[63] Facebook and the other social media platforms played an incredible trick on users, asking them to provide their likes, interests, and opinions, all of them framed as markers of identity for their own private brand, essentially goading them to present to Facebook their marketing preferences, both conscious and unconscious.

All of this turned into what social psychologist Shoshana Zuboff termed "surveillance capitalism," a system where internet users are "tracked, parsed, mined, and modified."[64] The strategy is complicated, but it produces unbelievable profits and creates political and social control for the tech companies.

The architects of this system of commerce and control are, almost to a person, followers of a Randian-like worldview that opposes governmental interference and democratic hurdles, and sees its users as a natural resource to be exploited. Unconcerned with concepts like civil liberties or inalienable rights, tech leaders have shown an eagerness to partner with authoritarian dictatorships, including China, where Facebook "quietly developed software to suppress posts from appearing in people's news feeds," a creation necessary to "help Facebook get into China."[65] Meanwhile, China has established a futuristic technocratic dictatorship that stifles personal expression and has led to dangerous protests where citizens are forced to arm themselves with surveillance-fighting equipment and don face-recognition-software-combating disguises lest they be targeted for reprisal. Almost to a person, tech leaders show a predilection for a post-political world where democracy is discarded and representative government serves only as a support body for their grandiose designs.

As the tech giants pilot the business of government, they continue to pursue post-human goals. Google is determined to create an artificial intelligence superior to humans and uses every query into its search engine, as well as a scanning of nearly every publication in history and a thorough mapping of the world through its Google Earth program, to create a machine that transcends understanding and could change the course of history in ways even the tech gods can only guess at. With billionaires Jeff Bezos and Elon Musk, the dream is to fund private forays into space with the eventual goal of colonizing other planets. Most of these obscenely powerful and wealthy men fund programs that are designed to either erase the threat of death or push technology to the point where people and machines are merged in a post-human future.

Compared to these auspicious goals, Mark Zuckerberg and Facebook seem positively mundane, but what they have unleashed has been significant and deeply damaging in the present and possibly damning for the future. By linking users together and fundamentally positioning Facebook as the lens through which they see the world and human connections, Zuckerberg has seemingly created a reality at the mercy of his whims and algorithms. Using artificial intelligence and harnessing data, it is as if he seeks to control the functions of society.

The first time users were made aware of these designs was possibly in 2014, when a study was published regarding a test two years prior that Facebook had undertaken. In this study, 689,003 users were targeted and their newsfeeds altered to be either more positive or more negative "to see what effect the changes had on the tone of the posts the recipients then wrote."[66] Facebook found through this unregulated testing on humans that their tinkering set off a "contagious" effect that radically changed their users' reality and dispositions. That power, however, was not necessarily benevolent, considering tech's willingness to eschew ethics in favor of profit.

Russian intelligence services recognized the potential of using social media to undermine reality and infiltrate the political affairs of its rivals. In Great Britain, Russian misinformation spurred the Brexit referendum that would force the country's exit from the European Union, isolating one of Vladimir Putin's rivals and weakening its stature. Ahead of the 2016 presidential election in America, Putin "ordered an influence campaign . . . to undermine public faith in the U.S. democratic process."[67] State-sponsored and -funded operations in Russia harnessed troll farms and armies of social media bots that could influence news within the United States and alter users' sense of reality. To accomplish this, Russia targeted "social divisions in America by stoking disagreement and division around a plethora of controversial topics," a plan that saw "hundreds of millions of interactions" with US citizens and voters.[68]

Though Zuckerberg called the idea that Facebook and its deluge of fake news had influenced the 2016 election "a pretty crazy idea," it was immediately obvious the site deserved a large share of the blame.[69] Fake news stories promoting Republican nominee Donald Trump, the candidate favored by Putin and the Russian machine, outperformed legitimate news organizations because Facebook users were linked into a system of perpetuating their views and opinions as the site marketed their ideas back to them, creating a feedback loop that undeniably affected voting decisions.

If that wasn't enough, a bizarre incident in May 2016 provided much fodder for consideration when a Facebook group catering to Texans in favor of secession staged a protest in Houston. Across the street were "United Muslims of America," another Facebook group that had scheduled a protest in the exact same location, on the same day, at the same time. Unbeknownst to the members, both groups had been created by troll farms in Russia tasked with manipulating and pitting Americans against one another. For $200, they had placed ads on Facebook that gathered significant crowds determined to tear one another apart.[70] The Texans for secession had even been prompted to bring guns to the confrontation by a troll farm in St. Petersburg, but luckily, despite hot tempers and a slew of confrontations, cooler heads prevailed and no one was killed.[71]

Putin's mysterious technologist Vladislav Surkov does not often comment to the press but was positively euphoric in March of 2019 when asked about Russia's efforts to manipulate global affairs. "Foreign politicians complain that Russia is meddling in elections and referendums around the world," he said. "It's much more serious than that. Russia is meddling in their brains, changing their consciousness, and they have no idea what to do about it."[72]

★

For Donald Trump to become president of the United States of America in 2016, there had to be a complete failure in the system envisioned in 1787. Generations had to pass, each one making its own cataclysmic mistakes. Those errors and missteps had to promote a prejudiced, rigged capitalistic order that held down entire groups of people in favor of economic minorities. All of it had to be centered around and supported by invalid myths that enabled America to build an empire that encompassed the globe while spreading its unrealities to every corner of the Earth.

For such a thing to happen, American politics had to be so corrupted by special interests and its politicians so obsessed with their own empowerment that governance was reduced to a meaningless game—a game that wasn't won by whoever helped the people but by those who managed to prevent their enemies from helping the people.

By 2015, when Trump announced his decision to run for the office by vilifying Mexican immigrants as murderers and rapists, two centuries of bigoted, xenophobic white supremacy had to have unfurled and infected the financial, judicial, and political institutions, leading to a deadly democratic disease of which Trump was merely a glaring symptom.

Born the son of a wealthy real-estate tycoon, Trump was gifted the wealth and privilege necessary to begin his own operations but lacked the acumen and talent to succeed. Over the course of his career, he lost unbelievable amounts of money and his corporation declared bankruptcy multiple times as his mishandling of buildings, casinos, hotels, resorts, and airlines revealed a stunning ineptitude. In fact, at times Trump lost more money than any other taxpayer in America, setting an inglorious standard for personal futility.[73]

Trump did have one talent, which was his understanding of how American media operated and fed off the myth of wealth and meritocracy. Beginning early in his career, he worked harder to promote himself as a success in newspapers, magazines, and television than he did to prosper in business. Because of his adeptness at managing his image, his lenders and debtors in bankruptcy judged his fictional persona as a successful businessman was worth more than the trouble of stripping him of his veneer, deciding "they were better off with Trump's" name on his devastated properties "than they were without it."[74]

Pushed forward by a system of privilege and perception, Trump continued to fail upward. The media's portrayal of him as the epitome of American success netted him numerous cameos in popular culture that kept his fictional persona aloft until he landed a starring role on the reality television show *The Apprentice*. The brainchild of producer Mark Burnett, who created the neoliberalism-in-action dog-eat-dog contest *Survivor*, *The Apprentice* portrayed Trump and his failed business as the television embodiment of high-stakes corporate intrigue, a program only possible in the postmodern, hyper-capitalistic era. Over its run, Trump was seen as a presidential figure who picked the winners from the losers and signified the visible-invisible hand of the market.

Even in this, Trump's persona was a fraud, as he regularly made inexplicable choices and forced hurried post-production efforts to "reverse engineer" and "assemble an artificial version of history in which Trump's shoot-from-the-hip decision made sense."[75] As the new myth was being authored, members of *The Apprentice*'s production team noted that Trump's was a "crumbling empire" marked with "chipped furniture" and a tarnished finish they were entrusted with giving an artificial luster.

That façade held considerable clout, though, as the neoliberal system maintained that anyone of wealth and power surely must have earned it if the idea of a meritocracy were to be believed. In this sense, Trump's character of a wildly successful, golden-touched tycoon became a reality because he was continually presented as such in mass media, lending him credibility and expertise when he was neither credible nor an expert.

His understanding of, and personal obsession with, the media paid unbelievable dividends. Speaking to Republican voters in the primaries with a voice directly lifted from Fox News, he destroyed any distance between himself and the propaganda machine, becoming the standard-bearer of the alternate reality where the complicated trouble of globalism was replaced with a simplistic conspiracy that shifted blame to vulnerable minorities. With mainstream sources, Trump ensnared them in a cycle of perpetual coverage that earned him upwards of $5 billion in free coverage as the networks and newspapers relied on him for record ratings and traffic that bolstered their profits.[76]

The frenzied disaster that was the Donald Trump campaign and the rise of white supremacist, fascist populism held the nation in an anxious, stunned captivation, creating what CNN head Jeff Zucker called "the biggest story we could ever imagine."[77] Describing the benefit for media at the expense of the country and its people, CBS president Les Moonves infamously admitted Trump's campaign "may not be good for America, but it's damn good for CBS," adding, "The money's rolling in and this is fun."[78]

Like the user humdog had so feared, new media had evolved to take the people's anxieties, in this case the fear of an authoritarian president and a growing fascistic movement, and spin them into profit models.

Trump gave the networks and publications the spectacle they so desperately wanted. For those who supported him, he delivered a rebuke of politics and diversity, voicing their anger and frustration every single day. For those who hated him, he fueled and inspired overwhelming anxiety that addicted voters to their newsfeeds and headlines to keep an eye on a rising threat. Like mass spectacles of the past, a consensus of opinion wasn't necessary as everyone was tuning in and clicking articles, even if it was for wholly different reasons. In this way, Donald Trump, a C-list celebrity and an abject failure for decades, had transformed into an integral fixture in the American imagination.

By targeting disaffected, angry white voters and embattled culture warriors in the evangelical community, promising to "Make America Great Again" and to return the country to some mythical, ill-defined, nonexistent past, and piecing together libertarian and businesses-minded voters on the right, not to mention by employing a war of disinformation and propaganda that was, at the very least, parallel to the efforts by Russian intelligence, Trump won the presidency in November of 2016. The win was thanks in large part to the Electoral College; his opponent Hillary Clinton, long the target of conspiracy theories and derision on the right, took the popular vote by 2.8 million, but the Electoral College, engineered by the Founders to advantage slaveholding states against fears of majority rule in the eighteenth century, gave Trump the election.[79]

Trump was the ideal candidate of the time. His inherent understanding of malleable reality and its dependence on perception prepared him to win in the twenty-first century. In a deposition in 2007, he had admitted to a long-rumored charge that his hard-to-nail-down net worth fluctuated, in his own words, "with attitudes and with feelings, even my own feelings," laying out an incredible definition of reality as perception and modeling the concept of relativism.[80]

This flexible worldview lent itself to a nonexistent relationship with the truth and perhaps rendered the very concept extinct and passé. In speeches, press conferences, and internet missives, Trump lied at an alarming pace, often contradicting himself in the space of seconds. Everything became supple and virtually meaningless. This spread through his administration, leading advisor Kellyanne Conway to invent the term *alternative facts* in place of *lies*, and confidant Rudy Giuliani to tell a disbelieving television host, "Truth isn't truth."[81] In an incredibly Orwellian moment that encapsulated a new state of being in which spin and outright lies threatened to destroy the very concept of objective reality forever, Trump himself told one crowd, "Just remember: What you're seeing and what you're reading is not what's happening."[82]

What was happening in America in 2016 was eerily reminiscent of what had taken place in Putin's Russia at the beginning of the century. Just as technologists in Moscow had learned anything was possible when objective reality was obliterated, Trump and his team found that consistent lying and a perpetual attack on the truth took a toll on the American consciousness. Like Putin, candidate Trump was free to commit any crime and trample any norm as he enjoyed the benefit of a manufactured reality suited to his tastes and advantage, all of it supported by a right-wing media ecosystem that functioned as state-run propaganda. At all times, he maintained a rabid cult dedicated to authoritarianism in the name of recreating past glories and battling ascending populations that might threaten their power.

As he literally hugged and kissed the flag, Trump claimed the role of ambassador of the American Myth, promising white Americans the reality they had lived in their entire lives; the history and narrative that crowned them as champions of the world was once again saved from a rising tide of multiculturalism and swiftly changing demographics. But the patriotism was a veneer as he operated with a corporate mindset devoid of duty and was concerned only with personal enrichment and empowerment.

His lies and failures mattered little, however, as no scandal or misstep could challenge his sway over his base. The product of Jerry Falwell's hijacking of Christianity and Ronald Reagan's hypercapitalism, the Cult of the Shining City, a nationalistic, white-identity, evangelical movement with conspiracy-minded, occult beliefs, raised Trump on high like a faulty messiah, and as they lauded him with titles like "chosen one," his blasphemous word became living gospel. Trump's opponents, whether liberals or diplomats or members of the Republican Party, were summarily placed within the paradigm of "the Deep State," the newest iteration of the New World Order conspiracy theory, and branded as evil criminals determined to destroy the Shining City.

As it became clear that Trump could win the Republican primary, Fox News realized its destiny and embraced him, seeming to audition to be a propaganda organ for a future Trump administration. Its producers and pundits warped reality at a moment's notice when Trump contradicted himself, discarding long-held Republican principles and positions to maintain ever-tenuous cohesion. Any pretense of objectivity or respectability disappeared as Democratic and Republican critics of Trump were presented as sinister actors at the helm of a feverish, paranoid conspiracy.

Republican politicians, realizing their party had been taken over by the fringe Tea Partiers and now authoritarian Trumpists, did the mental math and reasoned that enabling and empowering Trump would gain them political advantage, room to further their economic reconfiguring, dominance over the nation's judiciary, and an opportunity to maintain electoral viability despite diminishing popularity.

As they did so, the system designed by James Madison, a system that required people to work in the interest of the nation and with competition between branches of the government instead of overt cooperation, began to fray in alarming and obvious ways.

What had begun as a great experiment with self-governance and a society grounded in reason, the philosophies that had birthed the American nation, had devolved into a mismanaged system of control and profit fortified by myths designed to undermine the power of the people. The question of whether the people would ever fully recognize that power, if they would ever be allowed to self-govern or determine their own destinies, had been in doubt since the moment concepts like government and politics and power had first been invented. But now, with the very notions of truth and reality troubled to the point of extinction, the question hangs precariously in the balance.

★   ★   ★

Epilogue

On a miserable, drizzly morning in January of 2017, Donald Trump was inaugurated before a disappointing throng of supporters who huddled against one another and, like the crowd witnessing the inauguration of Confederate president Jefferson Davis, hailed the birth of a new country where minorities would be put in their place and their version of reality would reign supreme. Trump's inaugural speech matched the day's dreariness. He offered little inspiration and not much in the way of unity, his speech less an inspiring vision and more a declaration of victory in a hard-fought war. The America he addressed was destroyed, an impoverished state suffering from poor education, rampant crime, drug addiction, and chronic unemployment. To a smattering of applause, he bellowed, "This American carnage stops right here and stops right now."[1]

This carnage, Trump offered, had been wrought by presidents and politicians who had given America the short end of the economic stick and instead represented the wealthy and the powerful. Though

Trump said this with an eye toward a conspiracy of the elite and the Deep State, offshoots of the irrational New World Order conspiracy theory, what he said wasn't completely inaccurate. The betrayal hadn't been forged in a conspiracy hatched in smoky rooms, however, but had been carried out by generations of self-interest that favored the destructive pragmatism of Madison over the principles of Jefferson and the Enlightenment.

As dangerous and corrupt as Trump was, his embodiment of the nation's disease constituted an opportunity to see the problems for what they are. Over and over again in his slipshod presidency, Trump's inarticulate manner and incompetence have exposed the shallowness of politics. When he defended Saudi Arabia following the brutal murder of journalist Jamal Khashoggi, shrugging at people's concern and freely admitting it was a matter of money, he laid bare the cravenness of American foreign policy. For years the United States had pretended to be universally in favor of human rights and freedom only to conveniently look the other way on abuses and atrocities when it served its economic interests. Now Trump wasn't going to even bother hiding the hypocrisy.

Though the Republican Party prided itself on its values and unchanging principles, Trump's rampant disrespect and cruelty, not to mention his garishness, extramarital pursuits, and chronic sexual abuse, destroyed any notion of piety. Their flag-waving patriotic façade crumbled as Trump offended troops, generals, and veterans, all while seeking relationships with brutal dictators and sacrificing military advantage. In governance, he was an authoritarian who lusted after broad powers and ran up the deficit, putting the final nail in the coffin of the perception of Republicans as small-government minded or fiscally conservative. It became glaringly obvious their principles weren't just flexible but altogether nonexistent.

Trump's personal foibles—his obvious incompetence, his unabashed racism, and his unfailing insecurity—created a moment of reckoning for many of America's most firmly held myths and beliefs that had long gone untested. Watching Trump falter, it became commonplace to wonder how such a blundering, untalented man had ever risen to such a high stature, much less won the presidency.

The only possible answer was that something was wrong. That the political, social, and economic structures were wired incorrectly. That the prejudice that had echoed throughout the centuries in the form of economic privilege, racial privilege, and gender privilege was not only real but a pervasive, existential threat.

Meanwhile, as politics had been co-opted as a means for the wealthy to become wealthier and the powerful to become more powerful, the people suffered terribly. Globalism had taken a great toll, wiping out entire industries and leveraging the world's populations against one another so as to advantage the employers over the employees. Rampant automation left many out of work. Wages were stagnant. The wealth gap grew to staggering proportions as the top 400 Americans were worth more than the bottom 150 million combined.[2]

While billionaires plotted a future among the stars, the people toiled in the dirt.

Corporations and the wealthy continued to duck their taxes and starved the coffers of government. In states throughout the Union, teachers were underpaid and overworked, their schools run-down, their students recipients of an education that failed to prepare them for the critical thinking the era demanded. It was a self-destructive cycle that hampered invention and all but closed the door on America's leading in innovation. The lessons Americans learned were shaped and edited by political battles, and as a result, Americans found themselves unprepared to understand the increasingly complicated world and sort actual information from misinformation, making them vulnerable to interference by malicious actors.

At the college level, anger and trepidation caused by the failed revolution of the 1960s and '70s made universities the target of ire from conservatives. In retaliation, academics were maligned and isolated, their work that might explain and possibly better society quarantined from the public and subject to spiteful underfunding. Higher education transformed from a preparation for a well-balanced, thoughtful life to job training, and the corporate ethos of neoliberalism quietly turned it into a profit center, damning a generation of students to irresponsible and unthinkable levels of debt. By 2019, the student debt crisis reached a ghastly $1.6 trillion, ensuring that graduates spent most of their lives chained to a burden and unable to properly get ahead or contribute to the economy.[3]

Just as disturbing, the US health care system continued to lag behind those of other industrialized nations. America's bills piled up as costs grew more and more exorbitant. To add insult to injury, Republicans continually tried to repeal the Affordable Care Act. It became commonplace for citizens to resort to crowdfunding online for cancer treatments and other lifesaving procedures, their survival predicated on their ability to perform for the online space and often dependent on whether they could go viral on social media. Always desperate to profit off misery, American pharmaceutical corporations flooded markets with opioids that managed pain rather than treated it, knowingly addicting millions and annually killing more people than guns or car accidents.[4]

Infrastructure decayed.

For many, clean water became a luxury.

Global climate change, perhaps the greatest existential crisis in the history of humankind, loomed over the horizon as the people damned themselves by falling prey to misinformation campaigns waged by conservatives and corporations, battling over whether to even accept obvious reality instead of taking necessary and drastic action to curb the inevitable disaster.

The rights of the people were trampled with great regularity.

A pandemic forced society into hibernation, exposing the fatal instability of the market and the decay of the health care system, the preference of business over human lives, and the impotence of the government in addressing existential threats.

For political advantage, the Republican Party intentionally disenfranchised minority voters, tinkered with polling places, and trafficked misinformation meant to confuse and obstruct.

The policing system became an antagonistic force at constant war with the population, often killing innocent African Americans whose only crime was being in the wrong place at the wrong time. America's prisons bloated with minority populations failed by the system, their incarceration turned into a ghastly profit source.

Women were subjugated, abused, and discriminated against, their right to control their bodies continually troubled, with each new piece of infringing legislation greeted as another win in the culture wars. Their constitutional right to safe and legal abortions was chiseled away in red states until that right was virtually nonexistent.

LGBTQ+ Americans were hunted down in the streets and subject to exhausting abuses, harassment, and discrimination.

Immigrants and refugees seeking a better home in the fabled American tradition were dehumanized, scapegoated for the nation's problems, and locked in cages. Many would die or suffer intolerable cruelties in cold, dark captivity, their fates merely blips on the evening news.

Mass shootings, mostly by disaffected white men radicalized in the same manner as ISIS members, became depressingly commonplace as conspiracy theories continued to fuel murderous sprees by white men believing they were soldiers in an invisible war, including a massacre in 2019 carried out by a twenty-one-year-old named Patrick Crusius who killed twenty-two in an El Paso Walmart, explaining he was attempting to thwart a "Hispanic invasion of Texas" and repeating conservative rhetoric that "white people were being replaced by foreigners."[5]

Any action against the epidemic of mass shooting was steadfastly stalled by the Republican Party and an NRA determined to never budge an inch lest they lose funding or support, even while the building danger threatened to eradicate the very concept of a free and open society.

The internet, which had been heralded as a shining new tool that might promote learning, democracy, individuality, and invention, turned into a dystopia, a destroyer of agency, an agent of conformity, and just another tool to sell people things they didn't need for reasons they didn't understand.

Politics became a means to an end and representatives spent more time raising money for their next campaign than they did serving their constituencies. The representative body envisioned by the Founders grew into a clearinghouse where corporations and the wealthy jockeyed to see whose interests would be served, the chambers of government used as a means to outsource solutions to problems created by the reckless and inhuman pursuit of profit.

Predictably, this perverted government drew the attention of people like Donald Trump. It was now a side grift, a stepping stone to wealth, a means to an end. These people were decidedly post-political and aspired to move beyond the deliberation of the people's business as it hampered the speed at which they might profit and progress toward a frictionless future where capital and currency might flow between the countries of the world, bypass the people altogether, and disappear into clandestine coffers.

With this post-political mindset came the resurgence of fascism. The American Myth had long hidden fascistic currents and shielded them from public scrutiny. American history had provided a story in which fascism had been a distinctly European phenomenon, an anomaly that had manifested in Germany and Italy before being dispatched and eradicated from the world stage. But fascism was an inherent human folly, a mindset that transcended borders and nationality—as the march of modern Nazis on Charlottesville in 2017 proved in a sobering reminder. The constant human struggle was between the better angels of our nature, the voice and will of a reasoned, humane people, and the merciless, inhuman tug of ugly tyranny.

The true history of America isn't the sanitized story appearing in children's books or the tidy narrative sold on television, but a struggle between the powerful and the people at their mercy to control the machine and the fire of the Revolution. And, in times like these, when the powerful hoard the power for themselves, the infection of fascism predictably grows in the shadows.

The question now is not even distinctly American. The world is on the precipice of a new age, something beyond the Enlightenment. The struggle is to determine whether the species will make good on promises long held in theory, or if it will retreat back to the Dark Ages. In this age, though, America has influenced global politics, culture, thought, and reality, and the hegemony America has created means it and its people have not just a stake in protecting the concept of democracy but a responsibility to ensure its survival.

As the self-appointed trustees of the Revolution, Americans must undertake a great reckoning and simultaneously work through the past as they plot the future. The long-held myths must be dispelled, scrutinized, and reinterpreted to develop an accurate understanding of where we have been, what we have done, what our mistakes have amounted to, and how we have come to this fateful moment. We must unspool our idea of objective reality and acknowledge that it was never objective at all: It was a story told in support of white supremacy meant to disadvantage others and construct a world and social model beneficial to maintaining power and profit. We must reject that myth out of hand.

It is a matter of soul-searching, of redefining who we are as individuals, as a nation, and as a people, to find something resembling actual, objective reality that takes into consideration the plurality of existences and perceptions and finds something real and human and good, creating a new, consistent ideology that is better and actually, faithfully real.

Failure to do so will be cataclysmic. The world wars of the twentieth century revealed that military strength had less and less to do with control of the world and its destiny. The real battle was over possession of reality and what the possessor meant to do once they held it in their sway. Unfortunately, the ruling elite fashioned tools and theories to get inside our heads and author our experiences, leaving us ensconced in make-believe worlds while they furthered their control.

It does not have to be like this. Politics should not be a spectacle to watch on our televisions and subject to passive comments and shrugs of exhaustion. Representatives do not have to function like characters on the newest network drama, their arduous passion plays carried out for the omnipresent camera and parsed on cable news by pundits dissecting strategies like sports analysts reviewing winning plays. It is this illusion that convinces people the game is rigged and therefore not worth playing.

But it's not a game, and the people lose every time when they acquiesce and leave politics to the elite class.

Americans must reassert their democratic right to free and fair elections and shake off the rust of apathy. Blatant corruption must not breed more blatant corruption. Citizens must organize to reject this post-political mindset and hold politicians who engage in overt falsehoods and calculated misinformation accountable, both in the voting booth and in the public sphere. We must not reject politics as too toxic to participate in and leave the business of deciding to those willing to drown in the cesspool.

We must turn our back on the business of spectacle until corporate media sees no financial advantage in portraying our political process as a television show replete with fictionalized characters and dramatic story lines. We must move past the tired and false narratives of American exceptionalism and easy, cliché explanations in order to grasp our true history, understand our mistakes, and chart a new and successful path.

To do this, we need a new appreciation for experts, for education, for human experiences that go beyond the pursuit of profit and power and instead emphasize humanity in all of its pluralistic forms. We must do better than simply paying rhetorical respect to the people and institutions we claim to cherish and hold dear and shift our priorities from militarism and corporate dominion to investing in a mutually beneficial future.

And Americans must take a firm and nonnegotiable stand for fair representation and democratic values, understanding that electoral wins and losses need not be apocalyptic scenarios; grasp that divisive politics have been used as a weapon against the people from the very beginning; and recognize that communal good can far outweigh the visceral and toxic appeals of prejudice and tribalism.

The myth of American exceptionalism tells us that greatness and talent reside naturally within us, that our achievements are expected and dully ordinary, but by casting aside this myth, this product of superficial politicking and opportunistic branding, what we find is that normal people have been excelling and achieving greatness in spite of America. Once this is clear, it becomes obvious that the march on Selma, the Stonewall uprising, Frederick Douglass's fearless turn as America's conscience, the perpetual struggle by women and vulnerable minorities to seek equality, and even the ability of people to continue striving, dreaming, and just surviving in a system designed to hinder them at every turn, are just as inspiring as a band of eighteenth-century revolutionaries defeating Great Britain, the world's foremost empire.

By changing our perspective; by moving past the intentional dividing of people as envisioned by Madison; by rejecting the top-down model of politics and economics that defines our modern world; and by resurrecting the concept of a system by, for, and of the people, we can rediscover the fire that lit the way out of the darkness. We can protect it from those who might seek to snuff it out, and ensure it might burn brighter and truer than ever before.

ACKNOWLEDGMENTS

This book would have never been possible without the logistical support of the Zach S. Henderson Library and Dr. Russell Willerton, chair of the department of Writing and Linguistics at Georgia Southern University. Thank you to Marya Pasciuto for the leap of faith in diving down this rabbit hole and for the invaluable direction along the way. To Ross Harris, my agent, who came along at exactly the right time and never stops fighting. And, most of all, thank you to my loved ones, friends, colleagues, and students who took this journey with me and offered their boundless love, inspiration, and encouragement.

NOTES

CHAPTER 1

1. Thomas Hobbes, *Leviathan* (Indianapolis, IN: The Bobbs-Merrill Company, 1958), 106.

2. John Locke, *Two Treatises of Government* (Cambridge, UK: Cambridge University Press, 1963), 474.

3. George Bancroft, *History of the United States, from the Discovery of the American Continent*, vol. 7 (Boston: Little, Brown and Company, 1873), 21.

4. Thomas Jefferson, "From Thomas Jefferson to William Stephens Smith, 13 November 1787," National Archives, founders.archives.gov/documents /Jefferson/01-12-02-0348.

5. "Jefferson's 'Original Rough Draught' of the Declaration of Independence," Papers of Thomas Jefferson, Princeton University, jeffersonpapers.princeton .edu/selected-documents/jefferson%E2%80%99s-%E2%80%9Coriginal -rough-draught%E2%80%9D-declaration-independence.

6. Benjamin Rush, "An Address to the People of the United States," *American Museum*, January 1787.

7. Thomas Jefferson, "Thomas Jefferson to James Madison, Sept 6, 1789," Papers of Thomas Jefferson, Princeton University, jeffersonpapers.princeton .edu/selected-documents/thomas-jefferson-james-madison.

8. Robert A. Gross, "The Uninvited Guest," in *In Debt to Shays: The Bicentennial of an Agrarian Rebellion*, ed. Robert A. Gross (Charlottesville, VA: University Press of Virginia, 1995), 1.

9. George Washington, "From George Washington to Henry Knox, 25 February 1787," National Archives, founders.archives.gov/documents /Washington/04-05-02-0048.

10. John W. Burgess, *Political Science and Comparative Constitutional Law: Vol. 1, Sovereignty and Liberty* (Boston: Ginn & Company, 1890), 104–5.

11. James Madison, *The Constitutional Convention: A Narrative History from the Notes of James Madison*, eds. Edward J. Larson and Michael P. Winship (New York: The Modern Library, 2005), 17–18.

12. Ibid., 18.

13. Ibid., 35.

14. Ibid., 32–33.

15. Ibid., 109–10.

16. Ibid., 110.

17. Ibid., 65.

18. Ibid., 69.

19. Ibid., 70.

20. Ibid., 134.

21. Ibid., 152.

22. Ibid., 154.

23. Pauline Maier, *Ratification: The People Debate the Constitution, 1787–1788* (New York: Simon & Schuster, 2010), 70.

24. Ibid., 71.

25. Ibid., 331.

26. Ibid., 41.

27. Ibid., 6.

28. Plato, *The Republic*, trans. Allan Bloom (New York: Basic Books, 1968), 93.

29. Alexander Hamilton, James Madison, and John Jay, *The Federalist Papers*, ed. Clinton Rossiter (New York: Mentor Books, 1999), 7.

30. Ibid., 234.

31. Ibid., 222.

CHAPTER 2

1. Thomas Jefferson, "From Thomas Jefferson to William John, 12 June 1823," National Archives, founders.archives.gov/documents/Jefferson/98-01-02 -3562.

2. Charles A. Beard, *Economic Origins of Jeffersonian Democracy* (New York: Dover Publications, 2017), 402.

3. John Rutledge Junior, "To Alexander Hamilton from John Rutledge, Junior, 10 January 1801," National Archives, https://founders.archives.gov /documents/Hamilton/01-25-02-0162.

Notes

4. Daniel Walker Howe, *What Hath God Wrought: The Transformation of America 1815–1848* (New York: Oxford University Press, 2007), 141.

5. Robert D. Richardson, *Emerson: The Mind on Fire* (Berkeley: University of California Press, 1995), 152.

6. Alexander Hamilton, "From Alexander Hamilton to James A. Bayard, 16 January 1801," National Archives, founders.archives.gov/documents /Hamilton/01-25-02-0169.

7. Thomas Jefferson, "From Thomas Jefferson to Pierre Samuel du Pont de Nemours, 18 January 1802," National Archives, founders.archives.gov /documents/Jefferson/01-36-02-0242.

8. Thomas Jefferson, *Notes on the State of Virginia* (Richmond, VA: J. W. Randolph, 1853), 176–77.

9. Bernard DeVoto, ed., *The Journals of Lewis and Clark* (Boston: Mariner Books, 1997), 203.

10. Stephen E. Ambrose, *Undaunted Courage: Meriwether Lewis, Thomas Jefferson, and the Opening of the American West* (New York, Simon & Schuster, 1996), 154.

11. Andrew Carroll, ed., *Letters of a Nation: A Collection of Extraordinary American Letters* (New York: Broadway Books, 1997), 15.

12. Ibid., 16.

13. DeVoto, *Journals of Lewis and Clark*, 438.

14. Ibid., 439.

15. Ibid., 440.

16. Parson Weems, *A History of the Life and Death, Virtues and Exploits of General George Washington* (New York: Grosset & Dunlap, 1927), 13.

17. John Reid and John Henry Eaton, *The Life of Andrew Jackson*, ed. Frank L Owsley Jr. (Tuscaloosa, AL: University of Alabama Press, 1974), 379.

18. John Henry Eaton, *The Life of General Andrew Jackson* (Philadelphia: McCarty & Davis, 1830), 424.

19. Gabriel L. Lowe Jr., "John H. Eaton, Jackson's Campaign Manager," *Tennessee Historical Quarterly* 11, no. 2: 104.

20. Ibid., 134.

21. Sam Haselby, *The Origins of American Religious Nationalism* (New York: Oxford University Press, 2015), 305.

22. Ibid., 306.

23. James D. Richardson, ed., *A Compilation of the Messages and Papers of the Presidents, 1789–1897* (United States Congress, 1900), 457–58.

Notes

24. James Wilson, *The Earth Shall Weep: A History of Native America* (New York: Grove Press, 1998), 270.

25. Richardson, *A Compilation of the Messages*, 519–20.

26. Ibid., 522.

27. Andrew Jackson, "December 3, 1833: Fifth Annual Address to Congress," UVA Miller Center, millercenter.org/the-presidency/presidential-speeches /december-3-1833-fifth-annual-message-congress.

28. Wilson, *The Earth Shall Weep*, 278.

29. Robert Silverberg, *Mound Builders* (Columbus, OH: Ohio University Press, 1986), 48.

30. Richardson, *A Compilation of the Messages*, 521.

31. William Cullen Bryant, "The Prairies," Poetry Foundation, www .poetryfoundation.org/poems/55341/the-prairies.

32. Sam W. Haynes, *James K. Polk and the Expansionist Impulse* (New York: Longman, 1997), 102.

33. Reginald Horsman, *Race and Manifest Destiny: The Origins of American Racial Anglo-Saxonism* (Cambridge, MA: Harvard University Press, 1981), 90.

34. Robert C. Byrd, ed., *The Senate, 1789–1989: Classic Speeches, 1830–1993* (Washington, DC: Government Printing Office, 1994), 219.

35. Robert Sampson, *John L. O'Sullivan and His Times* (Kent, OH: Kent State University Press, 2003), 229–30.

36. John O'Sullivan, "Annexation," *United States Magazine and Democratic Review* 17, no. 1 (July–August 1845): 8.

37. Ibid., 9.

38. Ibid., 9–10.

39. "Mexico," *Democratic Review* 18 (June 1846): 434.

40. Haynes, *James K. Polk*, 25; Amy S. Greenberg, *A Wicked War: Polk, Clay, Lincoln, and the 1846 U.S. Invasion of Mexico* (New York: Vintage Books, 2012), 95–96; Haynes, *James K. Polk*, 71.

41. Walter R. Borneman, *Polk: The Man Who Transformed the Presidency and America* (New York: Random House, 2008), 150.

42. Ray Allen Billington, *Westward Expansion: A History of the American Frontier* (New York: The Macmillan Company, 1960), 575.

43. Borneman, *Polk*, 191.

44. Ibid., 200.

45. Billington, *Westward Expansion*, 579.

46. Borneman, *Polk*, 205.

47. Charles A. McCoy, *Polk and the Presidency* (Austin: University of Texas Press, 1960), 188.

48. Ibid., 191.

49. Robert W. Johannsen, *To the Halls of Montezuma: The Mexican War in the American Imagination* (New York: Oxford University Press, 1985), 221.

50. Ibid., 222.

51. Greenberg, *A Wicked War*, 171.

52. Ibid., 172.

53. Reginald Horsman, *Race and Manifest Destiny: The Origins of American Racial Anglo-Saxonism* (Cambridge, MA: Harvard University Press, 1981), 241.

54. Frederick Merk, *Manifest Destiny and Mission in American History* (Cambridge, MA: Harvard University Press, 1995), 162.

CHAPTER 3

1. James M. McPherson, *Battle Cry of Freedom: The Civil War Era* (New York: Oxford University Press, 1988), 120.

2. Phillip S. Paludan, *A Covenant with Death* (Urbana, IL: University of Illinois Press, 1975), 3.

3. David M. Potter, *The Impending Crisis: 1848–1861* (New York: Harper & Row, 1976), 43.

4. Joanne B. Freeman, *The Field of Blood: Violence in Congress and the Road to Civil War* (New York: Farrar, Straus and Giroux, 2018), 68.

5. Ibid., 236.

6. Ibid., 27.

7. Evan Carton, *Patriotic Treason: John Brown and the Soul of America* (New York: Free Press, 2006), 86.

8. Tony Horwitz, *Midnight Rising: John Brown and the Raid That Sparked the Civil War* (New York: Henry Holt and Company, 2011), 212–13.

9. Potter, *The Impending Crisis*, 378.

10. John J. McDonald, "Emerson and John Brown," *New England Quarterly* 44, no. 3 (September 1971): 386.

11. James Redpath, *Echoes of Harper's Ferry* (Boston: Thayer and Eldridge, 1860), 19.

12. Ibid., 309.

Notes

13. Thomas B. Reed, ed., *Political Oratory* (Philadelphia: Doria and Company, 1903), 1065–66.

14. Ibid., 1066.

15. David S. Heidler, *Pulling the Temple Down: The Fire-Eaters and the Destruction of the Union* (Mechanicsburg, PA: Stackpole Books, 1994), 163.

16. Paul Finkelman, *An Imperfect Union: Slavery, Federalism, and Comity* (Chapel Hill: University of North Carolina Press, 1981), 20.

17. David Goldfield, *America Aflame: How the Civil War Created a Nation* (New York: Bloomsbury, 2011), 186.

18. Jefferson Davis, "Jefferson Davis' First Inaugural Address," Papers of Jefferson Davis, Rice University, jeffersondavis.rice.edu/archives/documents /jefferson-davis-first-inaugural-address.

19. Jefferson Davis, "Jefferson Davis' Second Inaugural Address," Papers of Jefferson Davis, Rice University, jeffersondavis.rice.edu/archives/documents /jefferson-davis-second-inaugural-address.

20. Anne Sarah Rubin, *A Shattered Nation: The Rise and Fall of the Confederacy, 1861–1868* (Chapel Hill: University of North Carolina Press, 2005), 14–15.

21. Ibid., 20.

22. Goldfield, *America Aflame*, 184.

23. Allen C. Guelzo, *Fateful Lightning: A New History of the Civil War and Reconstruction* (New York: Oxford University Press, 2012), 87.

24. George C. Rable, "Despair, Hope, and Delusion," in *The Collapse of the Confederacy*, eds. Mark Grimsley and Brooks D. Simpson (Lincoln: University of Nebraska Press, 2001), 150.

25. McPherson, *Battle Cry of Freedom*, 243.

26. Guelzo, *Fateful Lightning*, 39.

27. Rubin, *A Shattered Nation*, 32.

28. Harold Holzer, Edna Greene Medford, and Frank J. Williams, *The Emancipation Proclamation: Three Views* (Baton Rouge: Louisiana State University Press, 2006), 10.

29. Heather Cox Richardson, *The Death of Reconstruction: Race, Labor, and Politics in the Post–Civil War North, 1865–1901* (Cambridge, MA: Harvard University Press, 2001), 9, 12.

30. Abraham Lincoln, *Collected Works of Abraham Lincoln, Vol. 4* (Ann Arbor: University of Michigan Digital Library, 2001).

31. Edwin C. Rozwenc, ed., *The Causes of the American Civil War* (Boston: D. C. Heath and Company, 1961), 45.

Notes

32. Frederick Douglass, *The Portable Frederick Douglass*, eds. John Staffner and Henry Louis Gates Jr. (New York: Penguin, 2016), 458, 460.

33. Michael P. Johnson, ed., *Abraham Lincoln, Slavery, and the Civil War* (Boston: Bedford/St. Martin's, 2010), 45–46.

34. *Political Debates Between Abraham Lincoln and Stephen A. Douglas* (Cleveland: Burrows Brothers, 1894), 164.

35. Allen C. Guelzo, *Lincoln's Emancipation Proclamation: The End of Slavery in America* (New York: Simon & Schuster, 2004), 5; Goldfield, *America Aflame*, 261.

36. *New York Times*, August 24, 1862, 1.

37. Abraham Lincoln, "The Emancipation Proclamation," National Archives, www.archives.gov/exhibits/featured-documents/emancipation -proclamation.

38. W. E. B. DuBois, *Black Reconstruction in America, 1860–1880* (New York: Free Press, 1998), 84.

39. Guelzo, *Lincoln's Emancipation Proclamation*, 121.

40. DuBois, *Black Reconstruction*, 149.

41. Eric Foner, *The Fiery Trial: Abraham Lincoln and American Slavery* (New York: W. W. Norton and Company, 2010), 186.

42. Guelzo, *Lincoln's Emancipation Proclamation*, 142.

43. Potter, *The Impending Crisis*, 36.

44. Phillip W. Magness and Sebastian N. Page, *Colonization After Emancipation: Lincoln and the Movement for Black Resettlement* (Columbia, MO: University of Missouri Press, 2011), vii.

45. Martha Hodes, *Mourning Lincoln* (New Haven: Yale University Press, 2015), 97–98.

46. Frederick Douglass, *Life and Times of Frederick Douglass* (Hartford, CT: Park Publishing, 1882), 587.

47. Ibid., 588–89.

48. Mourner, "Is President Lincoln a Martyr?" *New York Times*, April 26, 1865, www.nytimes.com/1865/04/26/archives/is-president-lincoln-a -martyr.html.

49. Andrew Johnson, *The Papers of Andrew Johnson, Vol. 13, September 1867– March 1868*, ed. Paul H. Bergeron (Knoxville: University of Tennessee Press, 1996), 286.

50. Eric Foner, *Reconstruction: America's Unfinished Revolution, 1863–1877* (New York: Harper & Row, 1988), 180.

Notes

51. Mark Wahlgren Summers, *The Ordeal of the Reunion: A New History of Reconstruction* (Chapel Hill: University of North Carolina Press, 2014), 69.

52. Richard Wormser, *The Rise and Fall of Jim Crow* (New York: St. Martin's Press, 2003), 7.

53. DuBois, *Black Reconstruction*, 219.

54. Wormser, *Jim Crow*, 8.

55. Douglas R. Egerton, *The Wars of Reconstruction: The Brief, Violent History of America's Most Progressive Era* (New York: Bloomsbury, 2014), 178.

56. John David Smith, *An Old Creed for the New South: Proslavery Ideology and Historiography, 1865–1918* (Carbondale, IL: Southern Illinois University Press, 1985), 28.

57. Allen W. Trelease, *White Terror: The Ku Klux Klan Conspiracy and Southern Reconstruction* (New York: Harper and Row, 1971), 10.

58. Foner, *Reconstruction*, 567.

59. Lloyd Robinson, *The Stolen Election: Hayes Versus Tilden—1876* (New York: Forge Books, 2001), 109.

60. Paul Starr, *The Creation of the Media: Political Origins of Modern Communications* (New York: Basic Books, 2004), 186.

61. Tim Wu, *The Master Switch: The Rise and Fall of Information Empires* (New York: Knopf, 2010), 23; Starr, *The Creation of the Media*, 187.

62. Robinson, *The Stolen Election*, 124.

63. Roy Morris Jr., *Fraud of the Century: Rutherford B. Hayes, Samuel Tilden, and the Stolen Election of 1876* (New York: Simon & Schuster, 2003), 15.

64. Rutherford B. Hayes, *Diary and Letters of Rutherford Birchard Hayes, Vol. III, 1865–1881* (New York: Kraus, 1974), 377.

65. William H. Rehnquist, *Centennial Crisis: The Disputed Election of 1876* (New York: Knopf, 2004), 178.

66. Isabel C. Barrows, ed., *First Mohonk Conference on the Negro Question* (Boston: Geo. H. Ellis, Printer, 1890), 8.

67. Ibid., 9.

68. Ibid., 13.

69. Ibid., 83.

70. Ibid., 18.

71. Ibid., 137.

Notes

CHAPTER 4

1. Jack Beatty, *Age of Betrayal: The Triumph of Money in America, 1865–1900* (New York: Knopf, 2007), 168.

2. Adam Winkler, *We the Corporations: How American Businesses Won Their Civil Rights* (New York: Liveright Publishing, 2018), 113.

3. Ibid., xiii.

4. Adam Winkler, "'Corporations Are People' Is Built on a 19th-Century Lie," *Atlantic*, March 5, 2018, www.theatlantic.com/business/archive/2018/03 /corporations-people-adam-winkler/554852/.

5. H. W. Brands, *American Colossus: The Triumph of Capitalism, 1865–1900* (New York: Anchor Books, 2010), 96–97.

6. William Graham Sumner, *What Social Classes Owe to Each Other* (New York: Harper & Brothers, 1883), 20.

7. Andrew Carnegie, "Wealth," *North American Review* 148, no. 391 (June 1889): 653.

8. Ibid., 663, 655.

9. Winkler, *We the Corporations*, 123.

10. Nell Irvin Painter, *Standing at Armageddon: A Grassroots History of the Progressive Era* (New York: W. W. Norton & Company, 2008), 136.

11. Winkler, *We the Corporations*, 201.

12. Painter, *Standing at Armageddon*, 99.

13. H. D. Lloyd, "The Story of a Great Monopoly," *Atlantic*, March 1881, www.theatlantic.com/magazine/archive/1881/03/the-story-of-a-great -monopoly/306019/.

14. Painter, *Standing at Armageddon*, 33.

15. Paul T. McCartney, *Power and Progress: American National Identity, the War of 1898, and the Rise of American Imperialism* (Baton Rouge: Louisiana State University Press, 2006), 91.

16. Evan Thomas, *The War Lovers: Roosevelt, Lodge, Hearst, and the Rush to Empire, 1898* (New York: Little, Brown and Company, 2010), 269.

17. McCartney, *Power and Progress*, 103.

18. Stephen Kinzer, *The True Flag: Theodore Roosevelt, Mark Twain, and the Birth of American Empire* (New York: Henry Holt and Company, 2017), 37.

19. McCartney, *Power and Progress*, 162.

20. Thomas, *The War Lovers*, 271.

21. Ibid., 345.

22. Ibid., 362.

23. Theodore Roosevelt, *The Rough Riders* (New York: P. F. Collier & Son, 1899), 108.

24. Ibid., 110–11.

25. McCartney, *Power and Progress*, 162.

26. Stephen Kinzer, "McKinley's Dream of a Global Empire," *Boston Globe*, March 23, 2018, www.bostonglobe.com/ideas/2018/03/23/mckinley -dream-global-empire/w9PUBZWJZEQmICtPqJwZHO/story.html.

27. Robert Torricelli and Andrew Carroll, *In Our Own Words: Extraordinary Speeches of the American Century* (New York: Washington Square Press, 1999), 5.

28. *Congressional Record*, 55th Congress, 2nd Session, 6532.

29. Julian Go and Anne L. Foster, eds., *The American Colonial State in the Philippines: Global Perspectives* (Durham, NC: Duke University Press, 2003), 8.

30. Dylan Rodriguez, *Suspended Apocalypse: White Supremacy, Genocide, and the Filipino Condition* (Minneapolis: University of Minnesota Press, 2010), 124.

31. Ibid., 126.

32. Gregg Jones, *Honor in the Dust: Theodore Roosevelt, War in the Philippines, and the Rise and Fall of America's Imperial Dream* (New York: New American Library, 2012), 209–10.

33. Ibid., 213.

34. Frank Hindman Golay, *Face of Empire: United States–Philippine Relations, 1898–1946* (Madison: University of Wisconsin–Madison Center for Southeast Asia Studies, 1998), 83.

35. Stuart Creighton Miller, *Benevolent Assimilation: The American Conquest of the Philippines, 1899–1903* (New Haven: Yale University Press, 1982), 220.

36. A. G. Hopkins, *American Empire* (Princeton, NJ: Princeton University Press, 2018), 415.

37. Theodore Roosevelt, *The Messages and Speeches of Theodore Roosevelt, 1901–1905*, ed. Alfred Hewey Lewis (Washington, DC: Bureau of National Literature and Art, 1906), 31.

38. Gretchen Murphy, *Hemispheric Imaginings: The Monroe Doctrine and Narratives of U.S. Empire* (Durham, NC: Duke University Press, 2005), vii.

39. H. W. Brands, *American Colossus: The Triumph of Capitalism, 1865–1900* (New York: Anchor Books, 2010), 124.

40. Painter, *Standing at Armageddon*, 16.

Notes

41. Michael McGerr, *A Fierce Discontent: The Rise and Fall of the Progressive Movement in America, 1870–1920* (New York: Free Press, 2003), 119.

42. Jack Beatty, *Age of Betrayal: The Triumph of Money in America, 1865–1900* (New York: Knopf, 2007), 349.

43. Page Smith, *The Rise of Industrial America: A People's History of the Post-Reconstruction Era* (New York: McGraw-Hill, 1984), 218.

44. Ibid., 134; Maureen A. Flanagan, *America Reformed: Progressives and Progressivisms, 1890s–1920s* (New York: Oxford University Press, 2007), 22.

45. Theodore Roosevelt, "1901 State of the Union," *Courier-Journal Almanac for 1902*, vol. 5 (Louisville, KY: Courier-Journal Company, 1902), 365–66.

46. Gary Gerstle, *American Crucible: Race and Nation in the Twentieth Century* (Princeton, NJ: Princeton University Press, 2001), 23–24.

47. Thomas C. Leonard, *Illiberal Reformers: Race, Eugenics and American Economics in the Progressive Era* (Princeton, NJ: Princeton University Press, 2016), 110.

48. Theodore Roosevelt, *Theodore Roosevelt: Letters and Speeches*, ed. Louis Auchincloss (New York: Library of America, 2004), 802.

49. Sidney M. Milkis, *Theodore Roosevelt, the Progressive Party, and the Transformation of American Democracy* (Lawrence: University Press of Kansas, 2009), 186.

50. Theodore Roosevelt, *Selected Speeches and Writings of Theodore Roosevelt*, ed. Gordon Hutner (New York: Vintage Books, 2013), 162.

51. Woodrow Wilson, *A History of the American People*, vol. 4, *Critical Changes and Civil War* (New York: Harper and Brothers, 1901), 196.

52. Ibid., 250.

53. Ibid., 50.

54. Wilson, *A History of the American People*, vol. 5, 59.

55. Ibid., 99.

56. Niels Aage Thorsen, *The Political Thought of Woodrow Wilson, 1875–1910* (Princeton, NJ: Princeton University Press, 1988), 62.

CHAPTER 5

1. Dick Lehr, *The Birth of a Nation: How a Legendary Filmmaker and a Crusading Editor Reignited America's Civil War* (New York: Public Affairs, 2014), 123.

Notes

2. A. Scott Berg, *Wilson* (New York, G. P. Putnam's Sons, 2013), 348.

3. Lehr, *Birth of a Nation*, 156.

4. Karen L. Cox, "The Confederacy's 'Living Monuments,'" *New York Times*, October 6, 2017, www.nytimes.com/2017/10/06/opinion/the-confederacys -living-monuments.html.

5. John Dos Passos, *Mr. Wilson's War* (Garden City, NY: Doubleday, 1962), 300.

6. Ibid., 4.

7. Statutes at Large, United States Congress, vol. 40, 65th Congress, 1917–1919, 553.

8. Carl R. Weinberg, *Labor, Loyalty, and Rebellion: Southwestern Illinois Coal Miners and World War I* (Carbondale, IL: Southern Illinois University Press, 2005), 127.

9. David M. Kennedy, *Over Here: The First World War and American Society* (New York: Oxford University Press, 1980), 68.

10. Berg, *Wilson*, 452.

11. Gene Smith, *When the Cheering Stopped: The Last Years of Woodrow Wilson* (New York: William Morrow and Co., 1964), 38.

12. Ibid., 39.

13. Ibid., 43.

14. Sidney Bell, *Woodrow Wilson and the Evolution of the New Diplomacy* (Port Washington, NY: Kennikat Press, 1972), 192.

15. Patricia O'Toole, *The Moralist: Woodrow Wilson and the World He Made* (New York: Simon & Schuster, 2018), 372.

16. Edward Bernays, *Propaganda* (New York: IG Publishing, 1928, 2005), 37–38, 48, 57.

17. Stuart Ewan, *PR!: A Social History of Spin* (New York: Basic Books, 1996), 148.

18. Walter Lippmann, *Public Opinion* (New York: Free Press, 1922), 17, 73.

19. Ibid., 131.

20. Ewan, *PR!*, 224.

21. Robert K. Murray, *Red Scare: A Study in National Hysteria, 1919–1920* (Minneapolis: University of Minnesota Press, 1955), *61*.

22. David J. Goldberg, *Discontented America: The United States in the 1920s* (Baltimore: Johns Hopkins University Press, 1999), 42.

23. Murray, *Red Scare*, 77.

24. "Reds Try to Stir Negroes to Revolt," *New York Times*, July 28, 1919, 4.

25. Jerrold M. Packard, *American Nightmare: The History of Jim Crow* (New York: St. Martin's Press, 2002), 130.

26. Ibid., 63.

27. Winfield Jones, *Story of the Ku Klux Klan* (Washington, DC: American Newspaper Syndicate, 1921), 82.

28. Daniel J. Kevles, *In the Name of Eugenics: Genetics and the Uses of Human Heredity* (Cambridge, MA: Harvard University Press, 1995), 97.

29. Harry H. Laughlin, *Immigration and Conquest* (New York: The Special Committee on Immigration and Naturalization of the Chamber of Commerce of the State of New York, 1939), 9.

30. Thomas C. Leonard, *Illiberal Reformers: Race, Eugenics and American Economics in the Progressive Era* (Princeton, NJ: Princeton University Press, 2016), 109.

31. Harry Laughlin, *The Legal Status of Eugenical Sterilization* (Chicago: Annual Report of the Municipal Court of Chicago, 1929), 65.

CHAPTER 6

1. Winston Churchill, *The Great Republic: A History of America* (New York: Random House, 2001), 274.

2. Ibid., 277.

3. Robert Sobel, *Panic on Wall Street: A History of America's Financial Disasters* (New York: Beard Books, 1999), 366.

4. David M. Kennedy, *Freedom from Fear: The American People in Depression and War, 1929–1945* (New York: Oxford University Press, 1999), 39.

5. Lothrop Stoddard, *The Rising Tide of Color Against White World-Supremacy* (New York: Scribner, 1920), vi, 198.

6. Madison Grant, *The Passing of the Great Race; or, The Racial Bias of European History* (New York: Scribner, 1923), 48.

7. Max Wallace, *The American Axis: Henry Ford, Charles Lindbergh, and the Rise of the Third Reich* (New York: St. Martin's Press, 2003), 46.

8. John Grafton, ed., *Great Speeches: Franklin Delano Roosevelt* (Mineola, NY: Dover Publications, 1999), 17.

9. Ibid., 30.

10. Charles Higham, *American Swastika* (Garden City, NY: Doubleday, 1985), 5.

11. Sarah Churchwell, *Behold, America: The Entangled History of "America First" and "the American Dream"* (New York: Basic Books, 2018), 226.

Notes

12. Michael Kazin, *The Populist Persuasion: An American History* (Ithaca, NY: Cornell University Press, 2017), 131.

13. Wallace, *American Axis*, 118.

14. Charles Lindbergh, "Des Moines Speech," CharlesLindbergh.com, www .charleslindbergh.com/americanfirst/speech.asp.

15. Wallace, *American Axis*, 281.

16. Johnpeter Horst Grill and Robert L. Jenkins, "The Nazis and the American South in the 1930s: A Mirror Image?" *Journal of Southern History* 58, no. 4 (1992): 671.

17. James Q. Whitman, *Hitler's American Model: The United States and the Making of Nazi Race Law* (Princeton, NJ: Princeton University Press, 2017), 27.

18. Ibid., 56.

19. Ibid., 62.

20. Theodore S. Hamerow, *Why We Watched: Europe, America, and the Holocaust* (New York: W. W. Norton & Company, 2008), 131.

21. Ibid., 50.

22. Rafael Medoff, "American Jewish Responses to Nazism and the Holocaust," in *Columbia History of Jews and Judaism in America*, eds. Marc Lee and Rafael Medoff (New York: Columbia University Press, 2008), 297.

23. David Okrent, *The Guarded Gate: Bigotry, Eugenics and the Law That Kept Two Generations of Jews, Italians, and Other European Immigrants Out of America* (New York: Scribner, 2019), 374.

24. "Atlantic Charter," Avalon Project, Yale Law School, avalon.law.yale.edu /wwii/atlantic.asp.

25. "War Situation," vol. 374, British Parliament, Commons Sitting, September 9, 1941, https://api.parliament.uk/historic-hansard/commons/1941/sep/09 /war-situation.

26. Rober Beitzell, ed., *Tehran, Yalta, Potsdam: The Soviet Protocols* (Hattiesburg, MS: Academic International, 1970), 79.

27. Michael Dobbs, *Six Months in 1945: From World War to Cold War* (New York: Knopf, 2012), 37.

28. James F. Byrnes, "Yalta—High Tide of Big Three Unity," in *The Yalta Conference*, ed. Richard F. Fenno (Washington, DC: Heath and Company, 1955), 10.

29. Lawrence E. Davies, "Nation After Nation Sees Era of Peace in Signing Charter," *New York Times*, June 27, 1945, 1.

Notes

30. E. Bartlett Kerr, *Flames over Tokyo: The U.S. Army Air Forces' Incendiary Campaign Against Japan, 1944–1945* (New York: Donald I. Fine Inc., 1991), 197, 202.

31. Max Hastings, *Inferno: The World at War, 1939–1945* (New York: Knopf, 2011), 617.

32. John Toland, *The Rising Sun: The Decline and Fall of the Japanese Empire, 1936–1945* (New York: Random House, 1970), 839.

33. Commission on Wartime Relocation and Internment of Civilians, *Personal Justice Denied: Report of the Commission on Wartime Relocation and Internment of Civilians* (Seattle, WA: Civil Liberties Public Education Fund, University of Washington Press, 1997), 66.

34. Turner Catledge, "Our Policy Stated," *New York Times*, June 24, 1941, 7.

35. Michael Neiberg, *Potsdam: The End of World War II and the Remaking of Europe* (New York: Basic Books, 2015), 244; Dobbs, *Six Months in 1945*, 329.

36. Robert P. Newman, *Truman and the Hiroshima Cult* (East Lansing, MI: Michigan State University Press, 1995), 80–81.

37. Peter Wyden, *Day One: Before Hiroshima and After* (New York: Simon & Schuster, 1984), 167.

38. Ibid., 166–67.

39. Leslie R. Groves, *Now It Can Be Told: The Story of the Manhattan Project* (New York: Harper & Row, 1962), 266.

40. Ibid., 267.

41. Dan Listwa, "Hiroshima and Nagasaki: The Long Term Health Effects," Columbia University K=1 Project, August 9, 2012, k1project.columbia.edu /news/hiroshima-and-nagasaki.

42. Neiberg, *Potsdam*, 256.

43. Albert Resis, ed., *Molotov Remembers: Inside Kremlin Politics* (Chicago: Ivan R. Dee Inc., 1993), 58.

44. Jussi M. Hanhimäki and Odd Arne Westad, eds., *The Cold War: A History in Documents and Eyewitness Accounts* (Oxford: Oxford University Press, 2004), 116–17.

45. Christopher Simpson, *Blowback: America's Recruitment of Nazis and Its Effects on the Cold War* (New York: Weidenfeld & Nicolson, 1988), 159.

46. "Telegram, George Kennan to George Marshall ['Long Telegram']," February 22, 1946, Harry S. Truman Administration File, Elsey Papers, Truman Library, https://www.trumanlibrary.gov/library/research-files /telegram-george-kennan-james-byrnes-long-telegram.

CHAPTER 7

1. Peter Gardella, *American Civil Religion: What Americans Hold Sacred* (New York: Oxford University Press, 2014), 290.

2. "1955 Disneyland Opening Day [Complete ABC Broadcast]," Marcio Disney, YouTube, July 17, 2011, 1 hour, 13 minutes, www.youtube.com /watch?v=JuzrZET-3Ew&t=943s.

3. Alex Abella, *Soldiers of Reason: The RAND Corporation and the Rise of the American Empire* (Orlando, FL: Harcourt Inc., 2008), 18.

4. John von Neumann and Oskar Morgenstern, *Theory of Games and Economic Behavior* (Princeton, NJ: Princeton University Press, 2004), 1.

5. Paul Erickson, *The World the Game Theorists Made* (Chicago: University of Chicago Press, 2015), 110.

6. Thomas C. Schelling, *The Strategy of Conflict* (Cambridge, MA: Harvard University Press, 1980), 200.

7. Herman Kahn, *The Nature and Feasibility of War and Deterrence* (Santa Monica, CA: RAND Corporation, 1960), 40.

8. Ibid., 6.

9. Herman Kahn, *On Thermonuclear War* (Princeton, NJ: Princeton University Press, 1961), 21.

10. Sharon Ghamari-Tabrizi, *The Worlds of Herman Kahn: The Intuitive Science of Thermonuclear War* (Cambridge, MA: Harvard University Press, 2005), 43.

11. "Text of Eisenhower's Farewell Address," *New York Times,* January 18, 1961, 22.

12. James Ledbetter, *Unwarranted Influence: Dwight D. Eisenhower and the Military Industrial Complex* (New Haven: Yale University Press, 2011), 97.

13. C. Wright Mills, *The Power Elite* (Cambridge, UK: Oxford University Press, 1956), 184, 200.

14. Dwight D. Eisenhower, "Scientific and Technological Resources as Military Assets," National Security Agency, April 30, 1946, https://www .nsa.gov/Portals/70/documents/news-features/declassified-documents /friedman-documents/reports-research/FOLDER_065/4170130907 4063.pdf.

15. Alex Roland, "The Military Industrial Complex: Lobby and Trope," in *The Long War: A New History of U.S. National Security Policy Since World War II,* ed. Andrew J. Bacevich (New York: Columbia University Press, 2007), 340.

Notes

16. David Talbot, *The Devil's Chessboard: Allen Dulles, the CIA, and the Rise of America's Secret Government* (New York: Harper Collins, 2015), 287.

17. United States Congress Select Committee on Intelligence, *Project MK Ultra: The CIA's Program of Research in Behavioral Modification* (Washington, DC: Government Printing Office, 1977), 2.

18. Talbot, *The Devil's Chessboard*, 379.

19. Norman Friedman, *The Fifty-Year War: Conflict and Strategy in the Cold War* (Annapolis, MD: Naval Institute Press, 2000), 365.

20. Alice L. George, *The Cuban Missile Crisis: The Threshold of Nuclear War* (New York: Routledge, 2013), 65.

21. Ibid., 55.

22. Dino A. Brugioni, "The Invasion of Cuba," in *The Cold War: A Military History*, ed. Robert Crowley (New York: Random House, 2006), 222.

23. Jonathan M. House, *A Military History of the Cold War, 1944–1962* (Norman: University of Oklahoma Press, 2012), 438.

24. Laurence Chang and Peter Kornbluh, eds., *The Cuban Missile Crisis, 1962: A National Security Archive Documents Reader* (New York: The New Press, 1992), 161.

25. John Higham, "The Cult of the 'American Consensus,'" *Commentary*, February 1959, www.commentarymagazine.com/articles/the-cult-of -the-american-consensushomogenizing-our-history/.

26. Landon R. Y. Storrs, *The Second Red Scare and the Unmaking of the New Deal Left* (Princeton, NJ: Princeton University Press, 2013), 86.

27. James Kirkpatrick Davis, *Assault on the Left: The FBI and the Sixties Antiwar Movement* (Westport, CT: Praeger, 1997), 2.

28. Tim Weiner, *Enemies: A History of the FBI* (New York: Random House, 2012), 160.

29. Ayn Rand, "Screen Guide for Americans," Motion Picture Alliance for the Preservation of American Ideals, 1947, 2.

30. Sid Bedingfield, *Newspaper Wars: Civil Rights and White Resistance in South Carolina, 1935–1965* (Urbana, IL: University of Illinois Press, 2017), 73.

31. Lawrence O'Donnell, *Playing with Fire: The 1968 Election and the Transformation of American Politics* (New York: Penguin Books, 2018), 192.

32. Elizabeth Jacoway, "Jim Johnson of Arkansas: Segregationist Prototype," in *The Role of Ideas in the Civil Rights South*, ed. Ted Ownby (Jackson: University Press of Mississippi, 2002), 142.

Notes

33. Ho Chi Minh, "Letter from Ho Chi Minh to President Harry S. Truman," National Archives, catalog.archives.gov/id/305263.

34. Marilyn B. Young, *The Vietnam Wars, 1945–1990* (New York: Harper Perennial, 1991), 11.

35. David Halberstam, *The Best and the Brightest* (New York: Random House, 1972), 37; George C. Herring, *LBJ and Vietnam: A Different Kind of War* (Austin: University of Texas Press, 1994), 130.

36. Halberstam, *The Best and the Brightest*, 523.

37. Charles Mohr, "McNamara on Record, Reluctantly, on Vietnam," *New York Times*, May 16, 1984, 24.

38. Jean-Paul Sartre, *Essays in Existentialism* (New York: Citadel Press, 1993), 41.

39. Charles A. Reich, *The Greening of America* (New York: Bantam Books, 1972), 3.

40. Ibid., 12, 17–18.

41. Ward Churchill and Jim Vander Wall, *The COINTELPRO Papers: Documents from the FBI'S Secret Wars Against Dissent in the United States* (Brooklyn, NY: South End Press, 2002), 50.

42. James Kirkpatrick Davis, *Assault on the Left: The FBI and the Sixties Antiwar Movement* (Westport, CT: Praeger, 1997), 30, 78.

43. Thomas Frank, *The Conquest of Cool: Business Culture, Counterculture, and the Rise of Hip Consumerism* (Chicago: University of Chicago Press, 1997), 4.

44. Lizabeth Cohen, *A Consumer's Republic: The Politics of Mass Consumption in Postwar America* (New York: Vintage Books, 2004), 295, 298.

45. Rick Perlstein, *Nixonland: The Rise of the President and the Fracturing of America* (New York: Scribner, 2009), 42.

46. William Safire, "The Cold War's Hot Kitchen," *New York Times*, July 23, 2009, www.nytimes.com/2009/07/24/opinion/24safire.html.

47. Barry Goldwater, *Conscience of a Conservative* (Shepherdsville, KY: Victor Publishing Company, 1960), 13.

48. Granville Hicks, "A Parable of Buried Talents," *New York Times*, October 13, 1957, 266; Gary Weiss, *Ayn Rand Nation: The Hidden Struggle for America's Soul* (New York: St. Martin's Press, 2012), 214.

49. Risa Lauren Goluboff, *Vagrant Nation: Police Power, Constitutional Change, and the Making of the 1960s* (New York: Oxford University Press, 2016), 283.

50. Ellen Schrecker, *The Lost Soul of Higher Education: Corporatization, the Assault on Academic Freedom, and the End of the American University* (New York: The New Press, 2010), 93.

51. Kiron K. Skinner, Annelise Anderson, and Martin Anderson, *A Life in Letters* (New York: Free Press, 2003), 190.

52. Scott M. Cutlip, *The Unseen Power: Public Relations, A History* (Hillsdale, NJ: Lawrence Erlbaum Associates, 1994), 628.

53. Joe McGinniss, *The Selling of the President, 1968* (New York: Trident Books, 1969), 65.

54. Peter Baker, "Nixon Tried to Spoil Johnson's Vietnam Peace Talks in '68, Notes Show," *New York Times*, January 2, 2017, www.nytimes.com/2017 /01/02/us/politics/nixon-tried-to-spoil-johnsons-vietnam-peace-talks -in-68-notes-show.html.

55. Bruce J. Schulman, *The Seventies: The Great Shift in American Culture, Society, and Politics* (New York: Free Press, 2001), 38, 41.

56. "Transcripts of Acceptance Speeches by Nixon and Agnew to the G.O.P. Convention," *New York Times*, August 9, 1968, 20.

57. Richard M. Scammon and Ben J. Wattenberg, *The Real Majority* (New York: Coward-McCann Inc., 1970), 70–71.

58. *Public Papers of the Presidents of the United States: Richard M. Nixon, 1969* (Washington, DC: Government Printing Office, 1970), 750.

59. Victor Li, *Nixon in New York: How Wall Street Helped Richard Nixon Win the White House* (Lanham, MD: Rowman & Littlefield, 2018), 275.

60. Dan T. Carter, *The Politics of Rage: George Wallace, the Origins of the New Conservatism, and the Transformation of American Politics* (New York: Simon & Schuster, 1995), 409.

61. American Archive of Public Broadcasting, "'Gavel to Gavel': The Watergate Scandal and Public Television," americanarchive.org/exhibits /watergate.

62. Mitchell K. Hall, *Crossroads: American Popular Culture and the Vietnam Generation* (Lanham, MD: Rowman & Littlefield, 2005), 152.

63. Garrett M. Graff, "The Madman and the Bomb," Politico, August 11, 2017, www.politico.com/magazine/story/2017/08/11/donald-trump-nuclear -weapons-richard-nixon-215478.

CHAPTER 8

1. Ronald Reagan, "Remarks at the National Conference of the Building and Construction Trades Department, AFL-CIO," March 30, 1981, Ronald Reagan Presidential Library and Museum, www.reaganlibrary.gov /research/speeches/33081c.

Notes

2. Peter W. Low, John Calvin Jeffries Jr., and Richard J. Bonnie, *The Trial of John W. Hinckley, Jr.: A Case Study in the Insanity Defense* (Mineola, NY: Foundation Press, 1986), 27.

3. Ibid., 30.

4. Ibid., 24.

5. *Taxi Driver*, dir. Martin Scorsese, Columbia Pictures, 1976.

6. Kim Phillips-Fein, *New York's Fiscal Crisis and the Rise of Austerity Politics* (New York: Metropolitan Books, 2017), 164.

7. Steven F. Hayward, *The Age of Reagan: The Conservative Counterrevolution, 1980–1989* (New York: Three Rivers Press, 2009), 149.

8. Alexander Lamis, *The Two-Party South* (New York: Oxford University Press, 1984), 26.

9. "Transcript of Ronald Reagan's 1980 Neshoba County Fair Speech," *Neshoba Democrat*, November 15, 2007, neshobademocrat.com/Content/NEWS /News/Article/Transcript-of-Ronald-Reagan-s-1980-Neshoba-County -Fair-speech/2/297/15599.

10. Francis A. Schaeffer, *How Should We Then Live?: The Rise and Decline of Western Thought and Culture* (Old Tappan, NJ: Fleming H. Revell Company, 1976), 29.

11. Jeffrey K. Hadden, "The Rise and Fall of American Televangelism," *Annals of the American Academy of Political and Social Science* 527 (May 1993): 120.

12. Frances Fitzgerald, *The Evangelicals: The Struggle to Shape America* (New York: Simon & Schuster, 2017), 285.

13. Norman Vincent Peale, *The Power of Positive Thinking* (Uttar Pradesh, India: Om Books, 2016), 14–15.

14. Carol V. R. George, *God's Salesman: Norman Vincent Peale and the Power of Positive Thinking* (New York: Oxford University Press, 1993), 237.

15. Ronald Reagan, "Remarks at the Presentation Ceremony for the Presidential Medal of Freedom," March 26, 1984, Reagan Library, www.reaganlibrary .gov/research/speeches/32684a.

16. Jimmy Carter, "Energy and National Goals Address to the Nation," July 15, 1979, Jimmy Carter Presidential Library and Museum, www .jimmycarterlibrary.gov/assets/documents/speeches/energy-crisis .phtml.

17. Ronald Reagan, "Election Eve Address a Vision for America," November 3, 1980, Ronald Reagan Library, www.reaganlibrary.gov/11-3-80.

Notes

18. Benjamin T. Lynerd, *Republican Theology: The Civil Religion of American Evangelicals* (New York: Oxford University Press, 2014), 189.

19. Kevin M. Kruse, *One Nation Under God: How Corporate America Invented Christian America* (New York: Basic Books, 2016), 279.

20. Donald T. Regan, *For the Record: From Wall Street to Washington* (New York: Harcourt, 1988), 74, 4.

21. Ronald Reagan, "America the Beautiful," *Echoes from the Woods*, William Woods College, June 1952, 9.

22. Ibid., 10.

23. Matt Schlap, ed., *Reagan at CPAC: The Words That Continue to Inspire a Revolution* (Washington, DC: Regnery Publishing, 2019), 16.

24. Ibid., 16–17.

25. Manly P. Hall, *The Secret Teachings of All Ages: An Encyclopedic Outline of Masonic, Hermetic, Qabbalistic and Rosicrucian Symbolical Philosophy* (New York: Dover Publications, 2010), xxxvii.

26. Manly P. Hall, *The Secret Destiny of America* (Arkosh Publishing, 2017), 6.

27. *The Late, Great Planet Earth*, dir. Robert Amram and Rolf Forsberg, Amram, 1979.

28. Hal Lindsey, *The Late, Great Planet Earth* (Grand Rapids, MI: Zondervan Publishing House, 1970), 71.

29. Joanne Omang, "The Heritage Report: Getting the Government Right with Reagan," *Washington Post*, November 16, 1980, www.washingtonpost.com /archive/politics/1980/11/16/the-heritage-report-getting-the-government -right-with-reagan/ebea1b98-1501-4de0-b599-6b92950e61cf/.

30. Amy Willentz, "On the Intellectual Ramparts," *Time*, September 1986, 77.

31. William Taubman, *Gorbachev: His Life and Times* (New York: W. W. Norton & Company, 2017), 227.

32. William E. Pemberton, *Exit with Honor: The Life and Presidency of Ronald Reagan* (London: Routledge, 1998), 111.

33. Will Bunch, *Tear Down This Myth: The Right-Wing Distortion of the Reagan Legacy* (New York: Free Press, 2010), 27.

34. Steven R. Weisman, "The President and the Press," *New York Times Magazine*, October 14, 1984, 513.

35. Mark Hertsgaard, *On Bended Knee: The Press and the Reagan Presidency* (New York: Farrar, Straus and Giroux, 1988), 66.

36. Daniel T. Rodgers, *Age of Fracture* (Cambridge, MA: The Belknap Press of Harvard University Press, 2011), 33–34.

Notes

37. Peggy Noonan, "Confessions of a White House Speechwriter," *New York Times Magazine*, October 15, 1989, www.nytimes.com/1989/10/15 /magazine/confessions-of-a-white-house-speechwriter.html.

38. "Reagan's Remarks on Presenting the Medal of Honor to Roy P. Benavidez, 2/24/81," Reagan Foundation, YouTube, May 5, 2015, www.youtube.com /watch?v=w5yJKzEzX54&t=302s.

39. Robert J. Cole, "Murdoch to Buy 7 TV Stations; Cost $2 Billion," *New York Times*, May 7, 1985, 1.

40. "President Reagan's Economic Recovery Tax Act of 1981," YAFTV, YouTube, February 6, 2014, www.youtube.com/watch?v=8k5Mq15u6d Y&t=21s.

41. Ronald Reagan, "January 20, 1981, Reagan Quotes and Speeches, Inaugural Address," Ronald Reagan Presidential Foundation and Institute, www .reaganfoundation.org/ronald-reagan/reagan-quotes -speeches/inaugural-address-1/.

42. David A. Stockman, *The Triumph of Politics: How the Reagan Revolution Failed* (New York: Harper & Row Publishers, 1986), 13.

43. Haynes Johnson, *Sleepwalking Through History: America in the Reagan Years* (New York: Anchor Books, 1992), 177.

44. Michael Isikoff and Art Harris, "PTL's Missing Millions," *Washington Post*, June 21, 1987, www.washingtonpost.com/archive/opinions/1987/06/21 /ptls-missing-millions/553aa246-42b9-49bd-954e-0c3b85349514 /?noredirect=on.

45. Walter H. Capps, *The New Religious Right: Piety, Patriotism, and Politics* (Columbia, SC: University of South Carolina Press, 1990), 137.

46. Scott Poole, *Satan in America: The Devil We Know* (Lanham, MD: Rowman & Littlefield, 2009), 174.

47. Clifford Krauss, "How U.S. Actions Helped Hide Salvador Human Rights Abuses," *New York Times*, March 21, 1993, 10.

48. Bunch, *Tear Down This Myth*, 87.

49. David B. Ottoway, "U.S. Decries Iraqi Use of Chemical Weapons," *Washington Post*, March 24, 1988, www.washingtonpost.com/archive /politics/1988/03/24/us-decries-iraqi-use-of-chemical-weapons /4421ebe8-df59-477d-882b-7d381f3a1868/.

50. Central Intelligence Agency, "Iraq: Use of Nerve Agent," March 23, 1984, https://www.cia.gov/library/readingroom/docs/DOC_0001229102.pdf.

51. Rick Atkinson, *Crusade: The Untold Story of the Persian Gulf War* (Boston: Houghton Mifflin Company, 1993), 4.

52. Tom Raum, "Bush Says Saddam Even Worse Than Hitler," Associated Press, November 1, 1990, www.apnews.com/c456d72625fba6c742d17 f1699b18a16.

53. "Bush 'Out of These Troubled Times . . . a New World Order,'" *Washington Post*, September 12, 1990, www.washingtonpost.com /archive/politics/1990/09/12/bush-out-of-these-troubled-times-a-new -world-order/b93b5cf1-e389-4e6a-84b0-85f71bf1c946/.

54. Mark Harris, "The Best Gulf War Coverage," *Entertainment Weekly*, February 1, 1991, ew.com/article/1991/02/01/best-gulf-war-coverage/.

55. Philip Taubman, "Gorbachev Assails Crimes of Stalin, Lauds Khrushchev," *New York Times*, November 3, 1987, 1.

56. Ibid., 496.

57. Serge Schmemann, "The Soviet State, Born of a Dream, Dies," *New York Times*, December 26, 1991, 1.

58. "End of the Soviet Union; Text of Bush's Address to the Nation on Gorbachev's Resignation," *New York Times*, December 26, 1991, 16.

59. "Mikhail Gorbachev's Resignation and Dissolution of the Soviet Union— Dec. 25, 1991—ABC Nightline," Shatner Method, YouTube, January 9, 2019, www.youtube.com/watch?v=zlieWAng4w8&t=740s.

CHAPTER 9

1. Al From, "Recruiting Bill Clinton," *Atlantic*, December 3, 2013, www .theatlantic.com/politics/archive/2013/12/recruiting-bill-clinton/281946/.

2. Al From, *The New Democrats and the Return to Power* (New York: Palgrave Macmillan, 2013), 52.

3. Arthur Schlesinger, "For Democrats, Me-Too Reaganism Will Spell Disaster," *New York Times*, July 6, 1986, Section 4, 13.

4. From, *The New Democrats*, 50.

5. Thomas B. Edsall, "Jackson, Robb Tussle over Democratic Strategy," *Washington Post*, March 11, 1989, www.washingtonpost.com/archive /politics/1989/03/11/jackson-robb-tussle-over-democratic-strategy /c1b3d81e-d773-4f04-9db7-b603394c6b11/.

6. Joan Didion, *Political Fictions* (New York: Vintage Books, 2001), 54–55.

7. Jane Seaberry, "Conservative Democrats Set New Agenda," *Washington Post*, November 9, 1986, www.washingtonpost.com/archive/business/1986/11/09 /conservative-democrats-set-new-agenda/6365918e-2ebb-44e3-8c85 -cd95fff88d8a/.

Notes

8. William Glasser, *Reality Therapy: A New Approach to Psychiatry* (New York: Harper & Row, 1965), 6.

9. Chris Bury, "Interview with Dick Morris," *Frontline*, June 2000, www.pbs .org/wgbh/pages/frontline/shows/clinton/interviews/morris2.html.

10. Stephen A. Smith, ed., *Preface to the Presidency: Selected Speeches of Bill Clinton, 1974–1992* (Fayetteville, AR: University of Arkansas Press, 1996), 82.

11. Ibid., 85.

12. Ibid., 86.

13. Bob Woodward, "President and the Fed Forge a New Relationship," *Washington Post*, June 6, 1994, 1.

14. Bob Woodward, *The Agenda: Inside the Clinton White House* (New York: Simon & Schuster, 1994), 68.

15. Woodward, "President and the Fed."

16. Woodward, *The Agenda*, 84.

17. Joseph E. Stiglitz, *The Roaring Nineties: A New History of the World's Most Prosperous Decade* (New York: W. W. Norton & Company, 2003), 112.

18. National Review, *Tear Down This Wall: The Reagan Revolution—a National Review History* (New York: Continuum, 2004), 15–16.

19. "Signing of NAFTA (1993)," clintonlibrary42, YouTube, September 3, 2013, www.youtube.com/watch?v=MDDuMUgt-og&t=1106s.

20. Adam Clymer, "The Clinton Health Plan Is Alive on Arrival," *New York Times*, October 3, 1993, Section 4, 3.

21. Richard M. Pious, *Why Presidents Fail* (Lanham, MD: Rowman & Littlefield, 2008), 196.

22. Adam Clymer, "In G.O.P. Response to Clinton, Dole Denies There Is 'Crisis' in Health Care," *New York Times*, January 26, 1994, 15.

23. George F. Will, "Gingrich, the Anti-Conservative," *Washington Post*, December 4, 2011, www.washingtonpost.com/opinions/gingrich-the -anti-conservative/2011/12/20/gIQALq8CAP_story.html.

24. Colman McCarthy, "The War on Poverty Hangs On," *Washington Post*, September 24, 1989, www.washingtonpost.com/archive/lifestyle/1989 /09/24/the-war-on-poverty-hangs-on/752161b5-6f44-45a8-bb10 -0ac7f79b9a36/.

25. "A 1978 Speech by Gingrich," PBS, www.pbs.org/wgbh/pages/frontline /newt/newt78speech.html.

Notes

26. McKay Coppins, "The Man Who Broke Politics," *Atlantic,* November 2018, www.theatlantic.com/magazine/archive/2018/11/newt-gingrich-says-youre -welcome/570832/.

27. "Republican Contract with America," McClatchy, media.mcclatchydc.com /static/pdf/1994-contract-with-america.pdf.

28. Jeffrey Gayner, "The Contract with America: Implementing New Ideas in the U.S.," *Heritage Foundation,* October 12, 1995, www.heritage.org /political-process/report/the-contract-america-implementing-new -ideas-the-us.

29. David E. Rosenbaum, "Republicans Offer Voters a Deal for Takeover of House," *New York Times,* September 28, 1994, 16.

30. Robin Toner, "Election Jitters in Limbaughland," *New York Times,* November 3, 1994, 29.

31. Maureen Dowd, "Vengeful Glee (and Sweetness) at Gingrich's Victory Party," *New York Times,* November 9, 1994, 2.

32. Katharine Q. Sealye, "Republicans Get a Pep Talk from Rush Limbaugh," *New York Times,* December 12, 1994, 16.

33. Jess Walter, *Every Knee Shall Bow: The Truth and Tragedy of Ruby Ridge and the Randy Weaver Family* (New York: Harper Collins, 1995), 40.

34. Sam H. Verhovek, "Scores Die as Cult Compound Is Set Afire After FBI Sends in Tanks with Tear Gas," *New York Times,* April 20, 1993, 20.

35. James Ridgeway, *Blood in the Face: The Ku Klux Klan, Aryan Nations, Nazi Skinheads, and the Rise of a New White Culture* (New York: Thunder's Mouth Press, 1995), 42.

36. Michael Waldman, *The Second Amendment: A Biography* (New York: Simon & Schuster, 2014), 90.

37. Wayne R. LaPierre, *Guns, Crime, and Freedom* (Washington, DC: Regnery Publishing, 1994), 191.

38. Guy Gugliotta, "NRA, Backers Have Focused Ire on ATF," *Washington Post,* April 26, 1995, www.washingtonpost.com/archive/politics/1995/04/26 /nra-backers-have-focused-ire-on-atf/1069869e-0bb1-4b27-ad62 -77794ab8cc9d/.

39. Fox Butterfield, "Rifle Association Has Long Practice in Railing Against Federal Agents," *New York Times,* May 8, 1995, 17.

40. Richard Cohen, "How Did Waco Become a Partisan Issue?" *Washington Post,* July 27, 1995, www.washingtonpost.com/archive/opinions/1995/07/27 /how-did-waco-become-a-partisan-issue/41c75f99-506e-445d-8915 -c5944b0e91e0/.

Notes

41. Brandon M. Stickney, *All-American Monster: The Unauthorized Biography of Timothy McVeigh* (Amherst, NY: Prometheus Books, 1996), 96.

42. Andrew Macdonald, *The Turner Diaries* (Fort Lee, NJ: Barricade Books, 1996), 35.

43. Stickney, *All-American Monster*, 137.

44. Ibid., 39.

45. Tamara Roleff, ed., *The Oklahoma City Bombing* (San Diego: Greenhaven Press, 2004), 113.

46. Kenneth S. Stern, *A Force upon the Plain: The American Militia Movement and the Politics of Hate* (New York: Simon & Schuster, 1996), 206.

47. Marc Fisher and Phil McCombs, "The Book of Hate," *Washington Post*, April 25, 1995, www.washingtonpost.com/archive/lifestyle/1995/04/25/the-book -of-hate/eb6d5812-0adf-4757-80f8-e5d9e8ccb5c0/.

48. Raymond Hernandez, "A Spectacle Gripping and Bizarre," *New York Times*, June 18, 1994, 11.

49. Gil Troy, *The Age of Clinton: America in the 1990s* (New York: Thomas Dunne Books, 2015), 135.

50. Tim Dickinson, "How Roger Ailes Built the Fox News Factory," *Rolling Stone*, May 25, 2011, https://www.rollingstone.com/politics/politics-news /how-roger-ailes-built-the-fox-news-fear-factory-244652/.

51. Gabriel Sherman, *The Loudest Voice in the Room: How the Brilliant, Bombastic Roger Ailes Built Fox News and Divided a Country* (New York: Random House, 2014), 197.

52. Ted MacDonald, "The 15 Most Ridiculous Things Media Said About Climate Change in 2019," *Media Matters for America*, December 29, 2019, https: //www.mediamatters.org/fox-news/15-most-ridiculous-things-media -said-about-climate-change-2019.

53. Kate M. Kemski, "The Framing of Network News Coverage During the First Three Months of the Clinton-Lewinsky Scandal," in *Images, Scandal, and Communication Strategies of the Clinton Presidency*, eds. Robert E. Denton Jr. and Rachel L. Holloway (Westport, CT: Praeger, 2003), 253.

54. Alison Mitchell, "The Uncertainty of 'This Excursion,'" *New York Times*, October 9, 1998, 1.

55. Michael Gartner, "How the Monica Story Played in Mid-America," *Columbia Journalism Review*, May/June 1999, 34.

56. "President Clinton Signing Telecommunications Act of 1996," clintonlibrary42, YouTube, November 19, 2013, www.youtube.com /watch?v=z1EfL8xQ5Ok.

57. Vannevar Bush, "As We May Think," *The Atlantic*, July 1945.

Notes

58. Walter Isaacson, *The Innovators: How a Group of Hackers, Geniuses, and Geeks Created the Digital Revolution* (New York: Simon & Schuster, 2014), 269.

59. John Perry Barlow, "A Declaration of the Independence of Cyberspace," February 8, 1996, Electric Frontier Foundation, EFF.org/cyberspace -independence.

60. Esther Dyson, George Gilder, George Keyworth, and Alvin Toffler, "Cyberspace and the American Dream: A Magna Carta for the Knowledge Age," Progress & Freedom Foundation, August 1994, www.pff.org/issues -pubs/futureinsights/fi1.2magnacarta.html.

61. "Remarks by Chairman Alan Greenspan," Federal Reserve Board, December 5, 1996, www.federalreserve.gov/boarddocs/speeches/1996/19961205.htm.

62. Jean Baudrillard, *Simulacra and Simulation*, trans. Sheila Faria Glaser (Ann Arbor: The University of Michigan Press, 1994), 2.

63. Ibid., 1.

64. humdog, "pandora's vox," in *High Noon on the Electronic Frontier: Conceptual Issues in Cyberspace*, ed. Peter Ludlow (Cambridge, MA: Massachusetts Institute of Technology, 1996), 439.

CHAPTER 10

1. "YELTSIN RESIGNS; In Boris Yeltsin's Words: 'I Have Made a Decision,'" *New York Times*, January 1, 2000, 19.

2. Michael Wines, "YELTSIN RESIGNS: MAN IN THE NEWS; On Top, Still a Mystery: Vladimir Vladimirovich Putin," *New York Times*, January 1, 2000, 11.

3. Erick Jens, "Cold War Spy Fiction in Russian Popular Culture: From Suspicion to Acceptance Via Seventeen Moments in Spring," *Studies in Intelligence* 61, no. 2 (2017): 35.

4. "Was the Soviet James Bond Vladimir Putin's Role Model?" BBC News, May 10, 2017, www.bbc.com/news/magazine-39862225.

5. Karen Dawisha, *Putin's Kleptocracy: Who Owns Russia?* (New York: Simon & Schuster, 2014), 253.

6. Ibid., 252–53.

7. Damon Tabor, "Putin's Angels," *Rolling Stone*, October 8, 2015, www .rollingstone.com/culture/culture-news/putins-angels-inside-russias -most-infamous-motorcycle-club-56360/.

8. Oliver Carroll, "Russia Is 'Playing with the West's Minds,' Says Putin Advisor," *Independent*, February 12, 2019, www.independent.co.uk/news

Notes

/world/europe/putin-russia-kremlin-vladislav-surkov-grey-cardinal
-moscow-a8773661.html.

9. Alexander Dugin, *Eurasian Mission: An Introduction to Neo-Eurasianism* (London: Arktos, 2014), 41.

10. Alexander Dugin, *The Fourth Political Theory* (London: Arktos, 2012), 12.

11. Alexander Dugin, *Putin vs. Putin: Vladimir Putin Viewed from the Right* (London: Arktos, 2014), 304.

12. "Supreme Court, Split 5-4, Halts Florida Count in Blow to Gore," *New York Times,* December 10, 2000, www.nytimes.com/2000/12/10/politics/supreme-court-split-54-halts-florida-count-in-blow-to-gore.html.

13. Katharine Q. Seelye, "Study Says 2000 Election Missed Millions of Votes," *New York Times,* July 17, 2001, 15.

14. Bob Woodward, *State of Denial* (New York: Simon & Schuster, 2006), 3.

15. William Kristol and Robert Kagan, "Toward a Neo-Reaganite Foreign Policy," *Foreign Affairs,* July/August 1996, www.foreignaffairs.com/articles/1996-07-01/toward-neo-reaganite-foreign-policy.

16. "Excerpts from Pentagon's Plan: 'Prevent the Re-Emergence of a New Rival,'" *New York Times,* March 8, 1992, 14.

17. Leo Strauss, *The City and Man* (Chicago: University of Chicago Press, 1964), 102.

18. "World Islamic Front Statement," Federation of American Scientists, fas.org/irp/world/para/docs/980223-fatwa.htm.

19. Timothy Naftali, *Blind Spot: The Secret History of American Counterterrorism* (New York: Basic Books, 2005), 228.

20. Ibid., 305.

21. "Bin Ladin Determined to Strike in US," National Security Archive, April 10, 2004, nsarchive2.gwu.edu/NSAEBB/NSAEBB116/.

22. Lawrence Wright, "The Master Plan," *New Yorker,* September 3, 2006, www.newyorker.com/magazine/2006/09/11/the-master-plan.

23. Bob Woodward, *Bush at War* (New York: Simon & Schuster, 2002), 33.

24. Tom O'Connor, "U.S. Has Spent Six Trillion Dollars on Wars That Killed Half a Million People Since 9/11, Report Says," *Newsweek,* November 14, 2018, www.newsweek.com/us-spent-six-trillion-wars-killed-half-million-1215588.

25. John Yoo, "Letter to Alberto R. Gonzales," August 1, 2002, https://www.justice.gov/sites/default/files/olc/legacy/2010/08/05/memo-gonzales-aug1.pdf.

26. Jay Bybee, "Memo to Alberto R. Gonzales, Office of Counsel to the President," August 1, 2002, National Security Archive, https://nsarchive2.gwu.edu/NSAEBB/NSAEBB127/02.08.01.pdf.

Notes

27. Dana Priest and Burton Gellman, "U.S. Decries Abuse but Defends Interrogations," *Washington Post*, December 26, 2002, www.washingtonpost.com/archive/politics/2002/12/26/us-decries-abuse-but-defends-interrogations/737a4096-2cf0-40b9-8a9f-7b22099d733d/.

28. Jack Fairweather and Anton La Guardia, "Chalabi Stands by Faulty Intelligence That Toppled Saddam's Regime," *Telegraph*, February 19, 2004, www.telegraph.co.uk/news/worldnews/northamerica/usa/1454831/Chalabi-stands-by-faulty-intelligence-that-toppled-Saddams-regime.html.

29. Gabriel Sherman, *The Loudest Voice in the Room: How the Brilliant, Bombastic Roger Ailes Built Fox News and Divided a Country* (New York: Random House, 2014), 273.

30. Amy Gershkoff and Shana Kushner, "Shaping Public Opinion: The 9/11–Iraq Connection in the Bush Administration's Rhetoric," *Perspectives on Politics* 3, no. 3 (September 2005): 525; "U.S. Public Thinks Saddam Had Role in 9/11," *Guardian*, September 6, 2003, www.theguardian.com/world/2003/sep/07/usa.theobserver.

31. Deborah L. Jaramillo, *Ugly War, Pretty Package: How CNN and Fox News Made the Invasion of Iraq High Concept* (Bloomington: Indiana University Press, 2009), 52.

32. David Zucchino, "Army Stage-Managed Fall of Hussein Statue," *Los Angeles Times*, July 3, 2004, www.latimes.com/archives/la-xpm-2004-jul-03-na-statue3-story.html.

33. Peter Maass, "The Toppling: How the Media Inflated the Fall of Saddam's Statue in Firdos Square," ProPublica, January 3, 2011, www.propublica.org/article/the-toppling-saddam-statue-firdos-square-baghdad.

34. "At the Pentagon: 'A Good Day for the Iraqi People,'" *New York Times*, April 10, 2003, www.nytimes.com/2003/04/10/world/a-nation-at-war-at-the-pentagon-a-good-day-for-the-iraqi-people.html.

35. David E. Sanger, "President Says Military Phase in Iraq Has Ended," *New York Times*, May 2, 2003, www.nytimes.com/2003/05/02/international/worldspecial/president-says-military-phase-in-iraq-has-ended.html.

36. Paul Mason, *Meltdown: The End of the Age of Greed* (London: Verso Books, 2010), 118.

37. Sewell Chan, "Greenspan Concedes That the Fed Failed to Gauge the Bubble," *New York Times*, March 18, 2010, www.nytimes.com/2010/03/19/business/economy/19fed.html.

38. Michael Lewis, *The Big Shot: Inside the Doomsday Machine* (New York: W. W. Norton & Company, 2010), 232.

39. Bethany McLean and Joe Nocera, *All the Devils Are Here: The Hidden History of the Financial Crisis* (New York: Portfolio, 2010), 5.

40. "$1.6 Billion of Bank Bailout Went to Execs," CBS News, December 21, 2008, www.cbsnews.com/news/16b-of-bank-bailout-went-to-execs/; Louise Story and Eric Dash, "Bankers Reaped Lavish Bonuses During Bailouts," *New York Times,* July 30, 2009, https://www.nytimes.com/2009/07/31 /business/31pay.html.

41. "Barack Obama's Keynote Address at the 2004 Democratic National Convention," *PBS NewsHour,* July 27, 2004, www.pbs.org/newshour /show/barack-obamas-keynote-address-at-the-2004-democratic-national -convention.

42. "Transcript: Barack Obama's Acceptance Speech," NPR, August 28, 2008, www.npr.org/templates/story/story.php?storyId=94087570.

43. Tim Alberta, *American Carnage: On the Front Lines of the Republican Civil War and the Rise of President Trump* (New York: Harper, 2019), 44.

44. "CNBC's Rick Santelli's Chicago Tea Party," Heritage Foundation, YouTube, February 19, 2009, www.youtube.com/watch?v=zp-Jw-5Kx8k.

45. Jane Mayer, "Covert Operations," *New Yorker,* August 23, 2010, www .newyorker.com/magazine/2010/08/30/covert-operations.

46. Stuart M. Butler, "Assuring Affordable Health Care for All Americans," Heritage Foundation, October 7, 1989, www.heritage.org/social-security /report/assuring-affordable-health-care-all-americans.

47. David Brock, Ari Rabin-Havt, and Media Matters for America, *The Fox Effect: How Roger Ailes Turned a Network into a Propaganda Machine* (New York: Anchor Books, 2012), 111.

48. Ibid., 116.

49. Ibid., 120

50. "The Laura Ingraham Show—Donald Trump 'Proud' to Be a Birther," Laura Ingraham, YouTube, March 30, 2011, www.youtube.com/watch?v= WqaS9OC0TZs.

51. Hal Lindsey, *The Late, Great Planet Earth* (Grand Rapids, MI: Zondervan Publishing House, 1970), 97.

52. Michael Calderone, "Fox's Beck: Obama Is 'a Racist,'" Politico, July 28, 2009, www.politico.com/blogs/michaelcalderone/0709/Foxs_Beck_Obama_is_a _racist.html; Mark Leibovich, "Being Glenn Beck," *New York Times Magazine,* September 29, 2010, www.nytimes.com/2010/10/03/magazine/03beck-t.html.

53. Glenn Beck, "This Can't Be The Same Country I Grew Up In," Fox News, July 22, 2009, www.foxnews.com/story/this-cant-be-the-same-country -i-grew-up-in.

Notes

54. Tim Alberta, *American Carnage: On the Front Lines of the Republican Civil War and the Rise of President Trump* (New York: Harper, 2019), 190.

55. Henry K. Lee, "Alleged Gunman Says He Wanted 'a Revolution,'" *San Francisco Chronicle*, July 21, 2010, www.sfgate.com/crime/article/Alleged -gunman-says-he-wanted-a-revolution-3180744.php.

56. John Hamilton, "Progressive Hunter," Media Matters for America, October 4, 2010, www.mediamatters.org/alex-jones/progressive-hunter.

57. Kevin Sack and Alan Blinder, "Jurors Hear Dylann Roof Explain Shooting in Video: 'I Had to Do It,'" *New York Times*, December 9, 2016, www.nytimes .com/2016/12/09/us/dylann-roof-shooting-charleston-south-carolina -church-video.html.

58. Alexander Zaitchik, "Meet Alex Jones," *Rolling Stone*, March 17, 2011, www .rollingstone.com/culture/culture-news/meet-alex-jones-175845/.

59. Marlow Stern, "Erica Lafferty Lost Her Mother in Sandy Hook. Trump's Ties to Truther Alex Jones Disgust Her," Daily Beast, November 18, 2016, www.thedailybeast.com/erica-lafferty-lost-her-mother-in-sandy-hook -trumps-ties-to-truther-alex-jones-disgust-her.

60. "Shooting at Sandy Hook Elementary School: Report of the Office of the Child Advocate," Office of the Child Advocate, State of Connecticut, November 21, 2014, 100.

61. Angela Nagle, *Kill All Normies: The Online Culture Wars from Tumblr and 4chan to the Alt-Right and Trump* (Winchester, UK: Zero Books, 2017), 14.

62. Ibid., 26.

63. Tim Wu, *The Attention Merchants: The Epic Scramble to Get Inside Our Heads* (New York: Knopf, 2016), 298.

64. Shoshana Zuboff, *The Age of Surveillance Capitalism: The Fight for a Human Future at the New Frontier of Power* (New York: Public Affairs, 2019), 11.

65. Mike Isaac, "Facebook Said to Create Censorship Tool to Get Back into China," *New York Times*, November 22, 2016, www.nytimes.com/2016 /11/22/technology/facebook-censorship-tool-china.html.

66. Vindu Goel, "Facebook Tinkers with Users' Emotions in News Feed Experiment, Stirring Outcry," *New York Times*, June 29, 2014, www .nytimes.com/2014/06/30/technology/facebook-tinkers-with-users -emotions-in-news-feed-experiment-stirring-outcry.html.

67. "Exposing Russia's Effort to Sow Discord Online: The Internet Research Agency and Advertisements," Permanent Select Committee on Intelligence, February 16, 2018, https://intelligence.house.gov/social -media-content/.

Notes

68. Tom McCarthy, "How Russia Used Social Media to Divide Americans," *Guardian*, October 14, 2017, www.theguardian.com/us-news/2017/oct/14/russia-us-politics-social-media-facebook.

69. Stephanie M. Lee, "Mark Zuckerberg Says Fake News on Facebook Didn't Change the Election," Buzzfeed, November 10, 2016, www.buzzfeednews.com/article/stephaniemlee/zuckerberg-techonomy-fake-news-election#.ysK5A2arO.

70. Claire Allbright, "A Russian Facebook Group Organized a Protest in Texas. A Different Russian Page Launched the Counterprotest," *Texas Tribune*, November 1, 2017, www.texastribune.org/2017/11/01/russian-facebook-page-organized-protest-texas-different-russian-page-l/.

71. Mike Glenn, "A Houston Protest, Organized by Russian Trolls," *Houston Chronicle*, February 20, 2018, www.houstonchronicle.com/local/gray-matters/article/A-Houston-protest-organized-by-Russian-trolls-12625481.php.

72. Gabriel Gatehouse, "The Confusion Around Russian 'Meddling' Means They're Already Winning," *Guardian*, March 25, 2019, www.theguardian.com/commentisfree/2019/mar/25/russian-meddling-vladimir-putin-vladislav-surkov.

73. Russ Buettner and Susanne Craig, "Decade in the Red: Trump Tax Figures Show Over $1 Billion in Business Losses," *New York Times*, May 8, 2019, www.nytimes.com/interactive/2019/05/07/us/politics/donald-trump-taxes.html.

74. Clare O'Connor, "Fourth Time's a Charm: How Donald Trump Made Bankruptcy Work for Him," *Forbes*, April 29, 2011, www.forbes.com/sites/clareoconnor/2011/04/29/fourth-times-a-charm-how-donald-trump-made-bankruptcy-work-for-him/#d6030497ffa6.

75. Patrick Radden Keefe, "How Mark Burnett Resurrected Donald Trump as an Icon of American Success," *New Yorker*, December 27, 2018, www.newyorker.com/magazine/2019/01/07/how-mark-burnett-resurrected-donald-trump-as-an-icon-of-american-success.

76. Philip Bump, "Assessing a Clinton Argument That the Media Helped to Elect Trump," *Washington Post*, September 12, 2017, www.washingtonpost.com/news/politics/wp/2017/09/12/assessing-a-clinton-argument-that-the-media-helped-to-elect-trump/.

77. Jonathan Mahler, "CNN Had a Problem. Donald Trump Solved It," *New York Times Magazine*, April 4, 2017, abcnews.go.com/Politics/donald-trumps-surprisingly-honest-lessons-big-money-politics/story?id=32993736.

78. Yanan Wang, "Network Exec on 'Circus' of 2016 Race: 'It May Not Be Good for America, but It's Damn Good for CBS,'" *Washington Post*, March 2, 2016, www.washingtonpost.com/news/morning-mix/wp/2016/03/01/network

-exec-on-circus-of-2016-race-it-may-not-be-good-for-america-but-its
-damn-good-for-cbs/.

79. Sarah Begley, "Hillary Clinton Leads by 2.8 Million Final Popular Vote
Count," *Time*, December 2, 2016, time.com/4608555/hillary-clinton
-popular-vote-final/.

80. David A. Fahrenthold and Robert O'Harrow Jr., "Trump: A True Story,"
Washington Post, August 10, 2016, www.washingtonpost.com/graphics
/politics/2016-election/trump-lies/?utm_term=.b4939ebc6a91.

81. "Kellyanne Conway: Press Secretary Sean Spicer Gave 'Alternative Facts',"
Meet the Press, NBC News," NBC News, YouTube, January 22, 2017, www
.youtube.com/watch?v=VSrEEDQgFc8; "Rudy Giuliani: 'Truth Isn't Truth',"
Meet the Press, NBC News," NBC News, *YouTube*, August 19, 2018, www
.youtube.com/watch?v=CljsZ7lgbtw.

82. Steve Benen, "Trump Tells Supporters, 'What You're Seeing . . . Is Not
What's Happening," MSNBC, July 25, 2018, www.msnbc.com/rachel
-maddow-show/trump-tells-supporters-what-youre-seeing-not-whats
-happening.

EPILOGUE

1. "The Inaugural Address," WhiteHouse.gov, January 20, 2017, www
.whitehouse.gov/briefings-statements/the-inaugural-address/.

2. Christopher Ingraham, "Wealth Concentration to 'Levels Last Seen During
the Roaring Twenties,' According to New Research," *Washington Post*,
February 8, 2019, www.washingtonpost.com/us-policy/2019/02/08/wealth
-concentration-returning-levels-last-seen-during-roaring-twenties
-according-new-research/.

3. Catie Beck, Jackeline Pou, and Ben Kesslen, "Sallie Mae Execs Tan at Maui
Retreat While Student Debt Crisis Tops $1.6 Trillion," NBC News, October
17, 2019, www.nbcnews.com/news/us-news/sallie-mae-execs-tan-maui
-retreat-while-student-debt-crisis-n1063826.

4. Beth Macy, *Dopesick: Dealers, Doctors, and the Drug Company That Addicted
America* (New York: Little, Brown and Company, 2018), 5.

5. Tim Arango, Nicholas Bogel-Burroughs, and Katie Benner, "Minutes Before
El Paso Killing, Hate-Filled Manifesto Appears Online," *New York Times*,
August 3, 2019, www.nytimes.com/2019/08/03/us/patrick-crusius-el-paso
-shooter-manifesto.html.

INDEX

Index

Index

Index

Index

Index

Index

Index

Confederate States of America and, 68–69

Douglass on, 74–75

election of, 64

Emancipation Proclamation and, 71–72

emigration of freed slaves and, 72–73

myth surrounding, 84

reelection campaign of, 75

on secession, 69–70

on slavery, 70–71

Lindbergh, Charles, 143–144

Lindsey, Hal, 207–208, 241, 278

Linkletter, Art, 161

Lippard, George, 206–207

Lippmann, Walter, 128

"Little Boy," 157

Lloyd, H. D., 92

Locke, John, 10–11, 13, 26

Lodge, Henry Cabot, 96

Long Telegram, 159

Loose Change, 280–281

Lost Cause mythology, 111, 114–116

Loughner, Jared Lee, 280–281

Louisiana Purchase, 36

Luftwaffe, 143

Lumumba, Patrice, 172

lynchings, 78, 120–121, 131

Macdonald, Andrew, 245–246

Madison, James

The Federalist Papers and, 25–27

Philadelphia Convention and, 17, 19, 20–23

presidential election of 1800 and, 30–31

slavery and, 28–29, 59

Maine, USS, 95–96

Malaise speech (Carter), 204

Malenkov, Georgy, 169, 170

Manafort, Paul, 198

Mandate for Leadership: Policy Management in a Conservative Administration, 208

Manhattan Project, 155–156

manifest destiny, 47–49, 50–51, 99

Marbury v. Madison, 32

Marias River country, 39

market segmentation, 186, 190, 247

marriage and breeding restriction laws, 134

Marshall, John, 32

Marvin, William, 77

Marx, Karl, 223

Mason, George, 22, 24, 25

mass media. *See* media/mass media

mass shootings, 279–282, 297–298

Matrix, The, 253–255

Mayer, Jane, 275

McCain, John, 272

McCarthy, Joseph, 177, 179, 188

McGovern, George, 229–230

McKinley, William, 92, 98–99

McNamara, Robert, 183

McVeigh, Timothy, 245–246

media/mass media. *See also* journalism; social media platforms; television; *individual news outlets*

civil rights movement and, 181–182

influence of, 61

Spanish–American War and, 95

Vietnam War and, 182

Megiddo, 113

Mein Kampf (Hitler), 138

Mellon, Andrew W., 89

Mercer, John, 22

Mexican–American War, 53–55

Mexico, 51, 52–56

Michels, Robert, 137

Middle Ages, 48

Midnight Judges, 32

midterm elections of 1994, 239–240

Miles, Bob, 243

military-industrial complex, 168–170

Mills, C. Wright, 169

mind control experiments, 170–171

minority coalition building, 228

"Mission Accomplished" banner, 269

Missouri Compromise, 59

Mitchell, James, 73

Mobutu Sese Seko, 172

Mohammad Reza Pahlavi, Shah, 171, 217–218

Mohonk Conference, 82–85

Molotov, Vyacheslav, 157

monarchy of England, 9–11

Index

Index

Index

Index

Index

Index

surveillance capitalism, 283

Survivor, 287

Tabor, Damon, 259

Taft, William Howard, 109–110, 134

Taliban, 266

Taxi Driver, 196–197

Taylor, Frederick, 110

Taylor, Zachary, 52, 53

Tea Party, 274–277, 291

tech bubble, popping of, 253

tech giants, 282–284

technocracy, 185

Telecommunications Act (1996),
    250–251, 253

televangelism, 202, 215–216

television

    Nixon and, 188, 189, 192–193

    Reagan presidency and, 210

Television Code, 179

Tenet, George, 264

Texans for secession movement, 285–286

Thomas Road Baptist Church, 202

Thoreau, Henry David, 34, 35, 63

Three-Fifths Compromise, 23–24

Thurmond, Strom, 191

Thurston, John M., 96

Tilden, Samuel, 80–82

Tillman, Benjamin, 99

Tokyo bombing, 153, 167

Tokyo Electric Power, 225

Tomorrowland, 163

torture, 100–101, 170, 266

Traitor, The (Dixon), 114

transcendentalism, 34–35, 49

Transcontinental Railroad, 91

traveling shows, 54–55

Trevor, John, 148

trias politica, 21

Trinity, 155

Truman, Harry, 152, 154–156, 158, 165,
    170, 182, 262

Truman Doctrine, 158

Trump, Donald

    The Apprentice and, 287–288

    author's reflections on, 1–2, 3, 5–6

    birtherism and, 277–278

    election of, 286–287, 288–290

inauguration of, 293–294

Peale and, 203

presidency of, 290–291, 294–295

during Reagan's presidency, 214

Russian election interference and,
    285–286

truth, Trump's attacks on, 290

Tubman, Harriet, 62

Turner Diaries, The (Pierce/Macdonald),
    245–246

Two Treatises of Government (Locke), 10–11

Two-Party South, The (Lamis), 200

Uncle Tom's Cabin (Stowe), 113

Underground Railroad, 62

Union Pacific, 91

unions, 104–105, 107, 130, 235

United Daughters of the Confederacy, 116

United Fruit Company, 102–103, 171

United Muslims of America, 285–286

United Nations, 151–153

*United States Magazine and Democratic
    Review, The*, 50–51, 54

vagrancy laws, 78

Vanderbilt, Cornelius, 89

Veracruz, Siege of, 55

Versailles Treaty, 126, 138

Victor Emmanuel III, King, 138

Vietnam War, 182–184, 189–190, 212–213

Virginia Plan, 19

Virginia State Colony for Epileptics and
    Feebleminded, 133–134

Völkisch World History (Wirth), 147

voting rights, 76, 77, 108, 297

Wachowski sisters, 254

Waco, Texas, 242, 244, 247

Waite, Morrison, 86

Walden Pond, 35

Wallace, George, 181, 197

Walmart, 215

War of 1812, 42–44

War on Terror, 265–266

Warburg, Paul, 136

Washington, George

    Brown compared to, 63

    chair of, 24

353

Index

ABOUT THE AUTHOR

Jared Yates Sexton is the author of *The Man They Wanted Me to Be* and *The People Are Going to Rise Like the Waters Upon Your Shore.* His political writing has appeared in publications including *The New York Times, The New Republic, Newsweek,* Politico, and Salon.com. Sexton is also the author of three collections of fiction and is an associate professor of creative writing at Georgia Southern University.